The Guardian Year '99

Introduction by **the Rt Hon. Marjorie Mowlam, MP**
Edited by **Victor Keegan**

FOURTH ESTATE • *London*

First published in Great Britain in 1999 by
Fourth Estate Limited
6 Salem Road
London W2 4BU
www.4thestate.co.uk

10 9 8 7 6 5 4 3 2 1

A catalogue record for this book is available from
the British Library

ISBN 1-84115-231-5

Typeset by Rowland Phototypesetting Ltd,
Bury St Edmunds, Suffolk
Printed in Great Britain by The Bath Press Ltd, Bath

Contents

Wonderful world

War drums in Europe

Contents

Arts

Politics: arts of the possible

Contents

Crime and punishment

Media matters

Science and technology.com

Contents

Over there

So much to lose

Miscellany

Contents

Sporting moments

Passing through

. . . .

The Rt Hon. Marjorie Mowlam, MP
Introduction

I must confess to feeling a little wary when approached by Victor Keegan, the man charged with editing this volume. Not so much because he wanted me to write the Introduction, but more because I wasn't sure if I quite liked the very idea of the *Guardian Year*.

As a sort of once-yearly cuttings service, a pick-and-mix selection, I feared it might take me a while to read it, and perhaps even longer to get round to doing so. Happily, such fears were dispelled with an early cast through the manuscript. The *Year* was not to be a worthy slog of interest to a few political anoraks, but a collection of writing as rich and various as the paper itself. It is a welcome reprise of some of the best bits of the year, a second taste of some favourites. As such, it's equally good as a general introduction for any reader still unversed in the *Guardian*'s idiosyncrasies and innocent of its wiles.

There is a great deal here which entertains and intrigues: tales of ex-prisoners turned sculptors and of anxious parents dutifully shopping their own children to the police. If, like me, you don't always get through all the additional supplements each and every day of the year, it's amazing what you can miss.

You'll not be surprised unduly to learn that I tend to spend more time poring over the politics pages and op-ed columns than is either normal or healthy. Inevitably, this means neglecting other parts of the paper. I'll cite the science and technology chapter as evidence of a pleasure missed the first time around, with its heady combination of romance on the worldwide web ('Love bytes') and Alan Rusbridger's attempt to balance falling in love with the Internet with fears of becoming a computer nerd. Anyone who's had but the briefest of forays into the virtual world, and seen the remarkable ease with which information can be accessed, will share his excitement.

That said, I doubt that the on-line supplement will ever become my first port of call. That privilege is reserved for an old familiar. Perhaps this should have remained a secret, but Steve Bell keeps me sane. I think it's his robust combination of sharp eye and even sharper wit that I find so compelling. Although often irreverent to the point of offensiveness (and all the better for that), there is always a choice of comment and a laugh.

I certainly can't approve of Michael White's wishful thinking about two busloads of 1997 intake MPs going over a cliff in a botched Millbank-run photo opportunity, but it's a characteristically colourful image. For one who has spent so long observing Westminster, Michael remains remarkably human. All down to that Steve Bell character again, I suppose.

Michael is aided and abetted by, among others, the burrowing David Hencke, a former Journalist of the Year who sadly doesn't get a mention here. As I write, I know he will be chasing facts to stand up the latest conspiracy theory and checking if there's any substance to the hottest gossip.

Time now to clear up that myth about the *Guardian* and its reported unpopularity in Labour government circles. I think there's something of a case for protesting too much here – to be honest, it was just as bad when we were in opposition! On a serious note, however, there can be no complaint with fair criticism justly levelled. Nor can we question the importance of expressing, and reporting, differences in opinion, except when that involves wilfully getting the wrong end of the stick.

The *Guardian*, of course, maintains the highest standards of journalism. And when the *Guardian* does it well, it can be very good indeed. Not just on the campaigning side, where it breaks big stories and keeps with them as they run, such as Jonathan Aitken's libel action. The quality of the writing on international affairs is often second to none in its ability to move, to explain and to inform. Maggie O'Kane's powerful 'One family's story' opens the second chapter. The chilling story of the death of the Berisha children brings home to us, quite literally, the terrible brutality and devastation which has been repeated across Kosovo. It is a world of absences and separations, of desperate losses felt desperately. A world of people, in Jonathan Steele's words, 'disabled by fear'.

Over the years, the people of Northern Ireland have known that feeling all too well. Fittingly, coverage of Northern Ireland reflects the personal and the political. It is not confined simply to Westminster or Stormont, but probes the human cost of the Troubles with moving accounts of loss, and of courage, and of hope. These have an effect. They open eyes to the complexity of the situation, and open hearts to the suffering endured, mainly by the innocent, on all sides of the community.

Northern Ireland has a good range of media outlets of its own, with a strong hand of regional dailies and broadcasters. The past year has certainly generated enough headlines and deadlines to keep them busy around the clock, and they've worked tirelessly to keep the people of Northern Ireland interested and informed. Where fatigue and pessimism can set in all too easily, that's no small achievement. I'd like to take this opportunity to put on record my recognition of how much the press – particularly the *News Letter*, *Irish News* and *Belfast Telegraph* – have contributed to the growing confidence shared across communities in Northern Ireland.

They too have shown courage. Their sensitivity to their readers' fears and needs, and their understanding of the implications of peace, have given them an authoritative voice. It is a voice worth listening to, because it speaks in constructive terms in support of the cause of peace. In the case of the joint editorials run in the *Irish News* and the *News Letter*, that voice has been as one

– itself a powerful symbol of how Northern Ireland is changing, and wants change to continue.

So many people – some famous, others working away quietly – have contributed to creating the circumstances in which peace has the opportunity to flourish in Northern Ireland. And as the efforts towards a new future continue, so does the media continue to have a role in addressing the communities' interests, leading the debate and holding politicians to account.

So read on. Let *Guardian* writers address your interests, and hold them to account as well. I am sure you will find plenty here that informs, educates and moves; all of which goes to highlight the paper in its various strengths. What emerges is a snapshot of the *Guardian* which shows it to be, to borrow from Jonathan Glancey's homage to Barcelona, not just 'a book of bits' but 'an organism to be nurtured and treated as a whole'.

. . . .

Editor's Preface

I well remember my first experiences on the *Guardian* in Manchester in September 1963. On the second day I thought I was going to be fired – but by the end of a week I had had a light-fingered article printed on the front page which a visiting dignitary from the London office described as a 'cert for the *Bedside*'. After I had discreetly inquired what the *Bedside* was (the *Bedside Guardian* was the ancestor of the *Guardian Year*) I waited patiently and unobtrusively for my big moment.

It didn't happen. Not then, nor for well over a decade afterwards – an experience that injected into me not only some much-needed humility but also a sense of awe at the contents of the anthology that not even editing it can puncture. Yet the *Guardian* I joined, notwithstanding its international reputation for writing, was tiny in size. The edition of the paper on the day I joined was only 18 pages in total, including advertisements, one of them a full page for Jaguar cars. The front-page splash on the Labour Party conference in Scarborough was written by someone called Bernard Ingham (whatever happened to him?). These days the whole paper could be accommodated comfortably in the back half of our 'Thursday Society' section.

If it was difficult to get into the *Bedside* in those days – when the paper ran only one regular feature a day (the leading-page article), it is much more so by an order of magnitude today. The book has remained more or less the same size while the paper has grown exponentially. It would now take a major editorial effort even to fillet the contents of one Saturday issue into a book this size.

It was for these reasons that the abiding impression left with me is not what remains in the *Guardian Year*, but what was discarded – for reasons that could never be justified before a jury. I had, with the help of my scissors, set aside at least three times too many candidates for inclusion – not difficult in a year that included such dramatic events in Europe and the Middle East.

When I thought I had got it about right I received a telephone call on the day of the deadline that there were still far too many articles chasing too little space. So it was while faced with losing another 50,000 words that morning that I took the arbitrary and indefensible decision to cut nearly all of the articles above 3,000 words on the grounds that each one would save the literary life of three or four smaller gems. I don't expect many people to agree with this, especially those with articles on the cutting-room floor. But at least these days there is an alternative. Thanks to the wonders of digitalisation it is now possible for anyone to assemble their own *Guardian Year* from the archives. I have a suspicion that very few choices would be similar.

*   *   *

I would like to thank Danny John for his unflappable courtesy when I bombarded him with requests for pictures and Catherine Blyth at Fourth Estate and Mathew Clayton of our marketing department for their invaluable help in steering me through.

V.K.

Graham Turner

Charlie Hull, stonemason, and her statue of St Martin of Tours in St Martin's Church, Exning, Suffolk

Wonderful world

. . . .

31 December 1998

Ian Aitken

Warwards fastest

Until very recently it was a truth universally acknowledged that *Scoop*, Evelyn Waugh's great comic novel about the Abyssinian war, wasn't so much a satire on the British press as an all too accurate account of the foreign correspondent's game. Today is the fortieth anniversary of the day I learned that lesson personally.

I was then working for Lord Beaverbrook, on whom Waugh is alleged to have based his frightful Lord Copper. As New York correspondent for the *Daily Express* – a newspaper not vastly different from the *Daily Beast* – I could easily have been the model for Scoop's innocent hero, William Boot, except that the real one is still around in the person of Bill Deedes.

For reasons too Scoopish to explain, I was in Caracas at the end of my very first trip away from base. It had been a flop, and I needed a decent story to redeem myself. On the hotel newsstand I found the answer – a front-page report of a big battle at a place called Santa Clara, with thousands of casualties, which would finish off the Cuban civil war.

Until then I hadn't really known there was a war in Cuba, for in those pre-Castro times the news value of a Latin American war came only slightly ahead of the proverbial small earthquake in Peru. Moreover, I wasn't absolutely confident about where Cuba was, except that it was in the Caribbean. But I was desperate, so I cabled London to suggest that I drop in on this carnage on my way home.

This was, of course, long before satellite telephones, and we conducted most of our business by cable, resulting in a minor literary art form known as cablese. So my message probably read something like: 'Unipressed twentythousand dead cubawise stop suggest eye incall havana before rebasing regards ian.' With the inspired brevity characteristic of the then foreign editor, one Norman Smart, the reply read: 'Okay warwards fastest regards smart.' So warwards I went, and fastest.

My plane reached Havana late on 31 December 1958. Weary after a wild goose chase in the jungles of the Orinoco, I headed straight to the Hotel Nacional, ate a quick meal, and left everyone else to celebrate Hogmanay while I went to bed. When I awoke, it seemed that the revelries were still in progress, only louder.

Cars on the seafront outside my window were honking their horns and cheering people were waving flags. Bootishly, I reflected that Havana seemed even jollier than Glasgow at New Year. My breakfast arrived by an unseen hand while I was in the shower. Then I descended the stairs and summoned a taxi to visit the *Express*'s stringer. My driver, too, was in ebullient mood.

But not for long. As we weaved through the revellers, he suddenly slammed on the brakes, flung open the door, rolled into the gutter and yelled at me to follow him. Lying beside him in the gutter, I heard him explain above the hubbub that Cuba's hated dictator, Fulgencio Batista, had fled in the night, and that we had driven into the first shooting of the revolution. He then drew my attention to the little holes which were appearing in the boot above our heads.

It was, I confess, a glorious moment for an aspiring foreign correspondent, and my first experience of the idiotic sense of invulnerability most reporters feel in such circumstances. It was only later when I encountered my only rival on the story, a *Daily Mail* man, also from New York, that I realised the similarity to *Scoop*. He too was in Havana by mistake, having been sent on the same duff story – about a balloon as it happens – as the one that had taken me to the Orinoco. But unlike me, he had celebrated Hogmanay. As a result, he had been woken up by his bedside telephone to find an unknown woman lying beside him.

On the phone was the *Mail*'s foreign desk telling him to dump the balloon and cover the revolution. Proudly he boasted that his desk man never discovered that he hadn't known anything about the revolution – not even when the woman woke up in mid-phone call and started complaining.

We two had the first few days of the Castro story entirely to ourselves, since the airport closed and the phone lines stayed open. It was a foreign correspondent's dream, including a piece of pure Hollywood when a waiter brought me a white telephone on a silver salver so that I could take a congratulatory call from London while standing chest-deep in the hotel pool. But the final touch was pure *Scoop*: there had been no battle at Santa Clara, just a small skirmish – not many dead. •

. . . .

23 December 1998
Peter Preston
Parents: Learning to suck eggs

The Christmas card from my most fecund cousin has hand-written triumphalism below the seasons greetings: 'We now have 15 grandchildren.' A full rugby team already, and she's barely into her sixties. Mind you, she did have eight kids to begin with, seven of them beautiful girls: she toiled for her victory. And us? We only have three, no more points than a dropped goal. But then, most of our contemporaries haven't even got out of their own halves yet.

That is one thing about grandchildren. Where, a decade before, the prospect of their coming was the first, chill shiver of mortality, now they're desirable collectibles, the trophies of survival. And the other thing is that they make you feel useful – perhaps, actually be useful. This is more than mere assertion. Some researchers from the Centre for Family Studies at Newcastle University have just published an analysis of interviews with 60 families around Britain. They produced an irrefutable equation: more working mothers plus increasing longevity equals involved grandparents. 'All three generations talked about the fact that they provided a lot of practical help, advice, babysitting, DIY, decorating, housework, even letting the gas man in. The grandparents thought they played a more valuable role than their parents had.' But this (the Newcastle team add) is also responsibility without power. They found 'considerable negotiation' over the dividing line between 'support' and 'unwelcome interference'. They found many bitten grandparental tongues over 'marginal input' into crucial decisions. As the sainted Sheila Kitzinger so plangently observes: 'When we get older it's not only the muscles that seize up. We risk losing our mental agility and becoming narrow-minded and authoritarian.' Shurrup, grandpa, and pass him the chocolate biscuits.

The trouble with Sheila, as with most stuff in this rather barren field of counselling, is that the general too glibly becomes the banal. People are different, marriages are different, relationships are different – so hand me a few relevant specifics. When is a wise opinion, rooted in years of experience, just a load of old dogma? When is the rock of ages a pebble on the beach? I have lately (three grandchildren lately) discovered a few great changes in the world. The first, an earthquake of a difference, is disposable nappies. Once upon a time – our time – you switched the squares of terry-towelling before and after feeds, padding downstairs to the bucket of Milton through the night: the logistics of mess and exhaustion. Now one strip of space-age absorbent solves all for hours on end. The impact on sleep and stink and space for each other is life-altering.

Life has also altered almost everything else. The bibles and the gurus are different. Spock is that pointy-eared one from the *Star Trek* re-runs. You lay them on their backs in the cot, not their fronts. The thought of a sleep at set times (in the pram, in the garden) is bizarre, going on ridiculous. Voices, let alone hands, are never raised in anger. Strapping kids into car seats is a performance akin to taking off in a jumbo-jet. Food may or may not be eaten according to inclination. Injunctions may or may not be heeded. My patent remedy for nocturnal yowling – a teaspoonful of Jamaica rum and milk, with a little brown sugar – is regarded with fear and derision: probably rightly.

In short, I remember virtually nothing of relevance. My children born and reared – and the sum total of applicable knowledge for negotiation isn't marginal, but zero. I have no experience of dealing with (or through) nannies. The French au pair we once had left throwing stones at the kitchen window: the Iranian (pre-Ayatollah) au pair had to be taught to make toast. I don't recognise the storybooks or the pop records or the £100 electric toys in fuzzy purple. Nor is the context of child-rearing existence comparable.

I went off to work at the *Guardian* early in the morning and returned – 'Hi, honey! I'm home!' – too late at night. 6.30 p.m. sharp was bedtime (until they woke up). My wife, of gallant necessity, ran the day shift of clinics and school ferryings and shopping in a pre-supermarket world. But we'd finished with childbirth by the time we were 30. Now, on the actuarial calculations Barclays life insurance assessors make, the average woman is getting close to 30 before she has her first child. She's worked and she needs to keep on working. The 'opportunity cost' of taking time out to have two children is £250,000 gross. The mortgage has to be paid.

That's taught me three other things I didn't know. How grindingly tough it is to keep all the balls in the air at once: how lucky I was, in one way, to keep my daytime nose away from the action, an old man not a new one: and, conversely, what I missed as well. 'Quality time' when my daughter-in-law comes back from the office after six o'clock isn't two hours of passive child-watching: it is vibrant interaction, because every minute counts. Weekend quality time for my elder son - freed from what his two-year-old calls 'daddy's workhouse' – matters. Who wants to wreck it with snarls and slaps? The children, in their sunniness, seem to answer that question for themselves.

Being a grandparent (according to the hectoring Sheila) 'propels you, whether you like it or not, into an exciting future'. Agreed. The excitement of first steps and first words – with the prospect, this time, of being on hand when they happen. The excitement of feeling part of a family renewed. And the excitement of perspective. Did I really believe the old child-rearing books from the 1930s which used to litter my parents' house? Spock made them redundant, and they were gone. Now the lectures and prescriptions of the 1960s are gone too, and there are new gods to be worshipped.

My younger daughter, her baby three weeks old, has the full collection of oracles. But perspective, I think, puts them in their place. When she had that baby, in a Spanish hospital, the wonder was Sunday visiting. You couldn't get into a lift or into most of the flower-filled rooms for families – an explosion of families. They were there to show that, in need, they were there: echoes of an older society united by need, duty, love. My daughter's mother-in-law, who has lived most of her life in a remote Galician village, has her own take on breast-feeding: 'It is so convenient. You can get the cows in or the water from the well and feed your baby at the same time.'

And she's not funny, but the bearer of a greater truth. She comes from a society where life goes on and everything fits. She carries her love with her. Grandparents, in that society, aren't somehow apart: they belong and they have their roles. Maybe, tottering into the millennium (and down to Sainsbury's for an emergency pack of Pampers) our role isn't the demographic stuff of the millennium, but something much simpler. Maybe we're beginning to do again what we were always meant to do. ●

· ·

14 May 1999

John Cunningham
First of the summer wine

Michael Winner, who probably never drinks a wine under £100 a bottle, has never heard of it; students, who rarely pay more than £2.99 for plonk, reckon it's a bit beyond their means – and passé, anyway. But for the rest of us, Jacob's Creek is the label we've partied through the 1990s with.

So claims a survey of changes in the ways we live, earn and spend, compiled by the Institute of Management. The survey's really interesting findings concern the way our tastes have changed. As relatively nouveaux wine drinkers, we've put our collective faith in one brand per decade. In the 1970s it was Hirondelle, in the 1980s Piat d'Or and now the drink is Jacob's Creek.

Hirondelle is no longer produced. It has disappeared into the squiffy mists of time, along with flares and glam rock. It was an Italian white table wine masquerading under a French name. For supermarket customers – first-time wine drinkers whose dads still swore by Double Diamond – it was safe, but with a hint of sophistication. At £1.39 a bottle in 1979, it had the right economic bouquet, though a Good Food Guide survey that year rated it as no more than 'acceptable'.

Seduction, continental-style, beckoned in the 1980s. The French, the ads purred, 'adore Le Piat d'Or'. We swilled velvety glasses of the stuff, never doubting that the brand was equally popular in France, and unaware of laughter from across the untunnelled Channel at the way we had swallowed a wine the Frogs hardly bought.

Piat d'Or, both red and white, is still a big seller here, in its opulent-looking pot-shaped bottle with its oval gold label. However, its TV ads, where a posh, suspicious father is won over by his daughter's suitor when he turns up for dinner with a bottle of – surprise, surprise – Piat d'Or, now seem chokingly smug. Just the right bevvy for those entering the placid confines of middle age, you might think.

No wonder we turned to uncomplicated New World wines with relief in the 1990s. Many were from Australia. In stores and supermarkets, Jacob's Creek, with its brand name in clear, large letters, had the effect of anglicising and making friendly such confusing foreign terms as Chardonnay, Shiraz-Cabernet, Riesling, Grenache-Shiraz.

Wine writers attribute the success of Jacob's Creek to its accessibility – you didn't have to be a buff to know where this tipple was coming from. They might perhaps add democracy – in that JC is free of all the Old World cant associated with European wine – and taste. When the first exports arrived in the 1980s, Jacob's Creek had a lower acidity than other New World wines. It was fruity, and didn't need to be sweetened up for the British palate, unlike Piat d'Or.

In the 1990s, it's been lightened a little, in line with perceived trends. Judith Candy, Tesco's product development manager for wines, says: 'It used to be a bit fuller, a more oaky blend; now it's more citrusy.' It's also moved, she says, from the 'experimental' fringe, bought by customers willing to try something new, to the mainstream. 'It's now much more mass market than you'd think.' Jacob's Creek became successful by an unclassical route. Kim Tidy of First Quench (owners of Threshers and Victoria Wine) recalls that it reached the top position by word of mouth: 'The timing of its arrival was spot on in the mid-1980s, with Castlemaine XXXX, Fosters, *Neighbours* and *Crocodile Dundee*. It was fashionable, not naff, to be associated with Australian products.' Tidy thinks the brand might not now be so dominant as it once was; maybe that's why its first UK TV ad campaign has just been launched. But it doesn't detract from JC's success as wine of the decade, and if you suspected that success was based more on smart marketing than smart wine growing, you wouldn't be wholly wrong.

There is indeed a Jacob's Creek in South Australia. It was there in 1847 that Johann Gramp, a settler from Bavaria, planted his first vine cuttings. Jacob's Creek is a stream in the Barossa Valley, an hour's drive from Adelaide. It was unknown to tourists until the popularity of the brand led to the first wine pilgrims visiting in the 1990s.

The marketing suits must be glad the names weren't the other way round. If it had been Johann Jacob's vineyard at Gramp Creek, they might have come up with 'Don't get cramps, drink Gramps', instead of the current slogan, 'Australia's top drop', which, on reflection, sounds hardly more inspired.

Jacob's Creek jumped from map to label only in 1976, when owner Orlando Wyndham (not a person, but the biggest wine and spirits group in Australia) decided to name a Shiraz-Cabernet-Malbec after the site of Johann's original vineyard. Orlando Wyndham and its UK importer, Caxton Tower, know much more about their customers than their customers know about them. They know that if you drink their drinks, you're probably either a 'confident wanderer' in a supermarket or a 'reassurance buyer' who puts his or her faith in the brand. What we Brits want most is consistency, says Christian Porta, managing director of Caxton Tower: 'The quality is improving all the time. The customer will never be disappointed.' The suits from Jacob's Creek are steering us away from both the old French snobbery of vintages and *appellation contrôlée*, and the new snobbery of American wines. And they're trying not to let their Chardonnays or Shirazes become fashion accessories for those living cool lives. 'We don't want to get into lifestyle, to say that if you're young and beautiful you should drink our brand,' says Porta. Other drinks that have played the sophistication card have run into trouble.

So, in the new TV commercial the images are of a wholesome Australia where the popularity of the brand has metamorphosed from a drop into a ripple into a wave. We will keep lapping it up. ●

· ·

21 April 1999

Libby Brooks
Love me, love my job

Cupid may appear in any variety of exciting guises but never before, one suspects, sandwiched between pension contributions and healthcare schemes. Until now, with the news that City firms are considering incorporating dating agency subscriptions into their employee benefits packages.

Inevitably Stateside in origin and one short step from happy pills in the water filter, the concept may seem comic, but it speaks to a society in which work has become more like home and home more like work. Chronic casualisation, an increasing reliance on technology and the slow emasculation of the trade union movement have created a labour force riven with insecurity and stress, working long and antisocial hours. Loyalty must be garnered where it can. Having robbed the overworked employee of health, fitness and the time in which to conduct a fulfilling private life, how better to minimise the damage than to sell these things back to him or her as perks? And given that a happy employee is a productive employee, why not encourage single workers to put in the hours by matchmaking?

Janetta Hamilton-Brown, managing director of London-based dating agencies Only Lunch and Virginia Charles, is pioneering the new scheme. She believes an increasing onus on staff welfare has encouraged firms to take a more proactive stance. In the US, she points out, as well as the more typical family-friendly policies – flexitime, crèche facilities, etc. – larger companies offer on-site gyms, outings, counselling and birthday cakes. One company even offered 15-minute desk massages in a month when it was laying off staff.

Sam, 41 and single, has personal experience of the rise in importance of work in the US. Head of a surgical unit at a major New York hospital, he believes his workaholic lifestyle has cost him a committed relationship. 'I start work at 7 a.m. and usually finish at 7 p.m.,' he says. 'The minute I leave the hospital, my beeper starts to go off. If I am on a date and am called to supervise surgery, I have to leave the woman in the restaurant and race off. There are only so many times you can do that to someone.'

As a specialist, he points out, he must work, publish and travel to build and sustain his reputation. 'A relationship takes time and effort,' he says, 'and I don't have the time. I am getting depressed about the situation and thinking seriously about cutting back on work, but if I do I will suffer professionally. I love my work, but the price I have paid is in my personal life. I should be married with kids by now and I am not even close.'

Like Sam, most of Hamilton-Brown's clients are professionals, with obvious common denominators: antisocial hours, ambition and high expectations for relationships that conflate into that well-worn 'single, successful and falling apart' tagline so beloved of Ally McBeal. 'As you climb the career ladder, what you are looking for in a partner becomes very different from when you were 20 and the only requirement was looking good in a pair of Levis,' Hamilton-Brown explains. 'Women especially are more demanding. We are all looking for someone to share our lives with, but we want someone who can understand the pressures of a career.'

So far, so middle class. But overwork is a universal canker. One third of workers now put in a 48-plus-hour week, with the number of women working 50 hours or more having doubled in the past 10 years. One in five non-shift workers now rises before 5 a.m. to add extra hours to their day, one in six employees works in the evenings and 1.2 million people in this country have two jobs.

Professor Cary Cooper, BUPA Professor of Organisational Psychology and Health at UMIST, argues that our quality of life has been severely affected by this Americanisation of the British economy and the ensuing culture of visibility rather than productivity. According to recent research carried out by Cooper, 77 per cent of employees believe the long-hours culture adversely affects their social life. For those who are single, he asks: 'How are they supposed to meet potential partners?'

Paula Bernstein, 25, is publicity manager for a television company and says it is easier to spend time with work colleagues than with non-work friends: 'The vast majority of new people I meet are either at the office, at meetings or at after-work drinks, and because of the work connection there is a real reticence – certainly you wouldn't have a one-night stand with any of them. It's true that women of my generation are increasingly happy about being single – but it's a shame when work becomes your dreams.'

She argues that as the work environment becomes more social and comfortable, it becomes even harder to prevent it encroaching on one's private life: 'Look at the layout of a modern office. You live at your desk. I have my vitamin pills there, my photographs around me. It is more my environment than my bedroom is. You take up the fringe benefits, join the company gym, you are encouraged to become a corporate person. When I left university, I was determined I didn't want a job that became my life. But you have no option. It's impossible to do both.'

Meanwhile, for those in relationships, the impact of work can be no less severe: 72 per cent of the employees Cooper surveyed believe it adversely affects their relationship with their partner. 'If you work long hours, you don't spend enough time at home, which causes conflicts at home, which means you spend more time at work,' he points out. 'Work can become an avoidance activity.'

Rachel Blomfield, 35, resumed her job in personnel management after six months' maternity leave. 'When I get home,' she says, 'I have such a short time with my daughter, it's really intense. And by the time she's gone to bed, I'm exhausted. But then I force myself to stay awake, so that I can kid myself I'm putting some effort into my relationship. It's a struggle not just to stay at work. I can really see the temptation.' While a consuming focus on work may be exciting and energising, it can also be difficult to relinquish. 'When you have kids, it is even harder to give up work because by that time work has become your life. Since having a baby, I have gone through a slow, painful letting go of ambition.'

In her 1997 book *The Time Bind*, American researcher Arlie Hochschild argued that these demands translated into a reversal of the way we view work. While home had become the status-free forum for frantic timetabling of quality time, and unequal sharing of household tasks between working partners, work had become a place of sanctuary and refuge. She discovered that although 88 per cent of America's top firms offered family-friendly policies, fewer than 5 per cent of staff were taking advantage of them. Many of Hochschild's interviewees told her the office was simply a more interesting place to be, offering 'a natural theatre in which one could follow the progress of jealousies, sexual attractions, simmering angers. Home, on the other hand, offered fewer actors on an increasingly cramped stage.' Emotional identification with our working environment may leave us more inept in our private lives, she adds. 'Cooperating with people, learning how not to take things personally and accepting authority are all skills we learn at home, practise at the office and apply as adults at home again. But relations at home also take commitment, sacrifice and authenticity. Being at home is more than a matter of applying skills and too much office time can lead one to lose touch with that.'

It is difficult to relax back into non-work relationships when private time is brief, Rachel Blomfield adds. 'Human relationships are not goal-oriented; they require you to be relaxed. But when your head is full of tasks, it becomes easier to interact with someone from work who is on the same wavelength as you, and much harder to connect with someone from outside.'

One further explanation is that today's much trumpeted hyper-flexibility at work has yet to translate into freedom for employees. Author and social commentator Melissa Benn voiced her doubts about so-called family-friendly policies in an essay for this paper last year. 'The issue of modern working parents,' she concluded, 'is, essentially, how to relegate the place of work in our lives.' Which is surely the issue for any employee, parent or not. It is time to reclaim the psychological space that work has taken up within our lives. This is not simply a question of economics, but of a culture that leaves us with no choice but to fight to reclaim our private lives. ●

8 March 1999

David Ward

Where there's brass, lads, there's pluck

This story is best read while listening to a soulful cornet solo and drinking Tetley's bitter in the rain. It is a reminder that northern values such as honour and responsibility remain strong at a time of millennial doubt.

The Black Dyke Band, the Vienna Philharmonic of British brass ensembles, has turned down a chance to sample the glitz and fizz of the Oscar ceremonies next week in order to honour a prearranged engagement in Bournemouth.

Nice as the pearl of the sun-kissed Dorset coast may be, it lacks the exotic allure of Los Angeles. So the missed transatlantic trip has prompted pangs of regret among Black Dyke's 28 virtuosi.

'I feel disappointed that we are not going, to be honest,' said cornet player Matthew Baker as the band headed south in the rain yesterday from its base in the West Yorkshire village of Queensbury for a concert at Warwick University. 'I'd love to be going to the Oscars. But the fact that we have a concert booked and that all the tickets have been sold means we have to stick by what we originally planned to do.'

Eight members of the band, founded in 1855 and garlanded with success ever since, accompanied Peter Gabriel in a song on the soundtrack for the film *Babe: Pig in the City*. The number has now been nominated for an Oscar.

'The ceremony's producer came on and said they wanted the whole band over there,' said Geoffrey Whiteley, Black Dyke's administrator. 'We thought about it long and hard and tried to work out how we could do it. But we had committed ourselves to the concert in Bournemouth, which has already sold 1,700 tickets and which should raise £10,000 for a local heart charity. On the following day we are doing a master class for youngsters and mature players in the area. It was all booked a long time ago, so the only thing we could do was turn down the Oscars invitation.' He added: 'The producer pointed out that more than a billion people were likely to see the Oscars ceremony on television and he thought we would have gone for the greater audience. But our motto says: "Act justly and fear nothing." We would dearly love to have gone. But we felt we had committed ourselves to these people in Bournemouth. So the moral thing to do was to honour the engagement.'

The decision was greeted with incredulity by media moguls unable to understand how anyone could turn down the Californian West Coast for the English South Coast. But Bournemouth is delighted. 'It just shows how professional they are,' said Tony Hardman, manager of the Winter Gardens. 'They are true Yorkshiremen who are honouring their commitment.'

Mr Baker, a southerner who moved north to play with the band, was stoical. 'It was very exciting to be asked,' he said, seeking consolation as the bus sped down the M1. •

15 February 1999
David McKie
Marginal feats

Ought one to write in books? This is a different question, please note, from, Should one write books?, to which the answer, when 10,000 of the creatures are now published each year, is, in 95 cases out of 100, Probably not.

No, the issue this morning is tougher than that. Ought one to write, in the margins of books published by other people, comments of praise ('a brilliant exposition of Heidegger's thinking!') or of blame ('shows no understanding at all of Alf Ramsey's modus vivendi')? An academic who's been editing the marginalia of Coleridge thinks we should be encouraged to do so, Coleridge's being so lively and brilliant.

But this contradicts the rule drummed into me in my youth by a wonderful history teacher: that the only thing you should always write in a book is your name, and the date of purchase, and also the place. I cannot recommend this practice too strongly. It reminds you, what seems like centuries later, not just how long a book has been part of your life but how you came by it first. This book of Macaulay's prose and poetry, for example: bought in York in March 1988 for 50p. Was 50p ever better spent? And why was it only then that I started to dote on Macaulay? Or this, on the press in Ireland, bought for me by my wife 'on the quayside at Dublin'; yes, I remember that day. I like to find the names of previous owners in second-hand books. What sort of man, for instance, was Bernard Mountain, of the Old House, Dorking, who in August 1922 inscribed his name in such a scholarly hand in my copy of Arnold's *Essays in Criticism*? I enjoy dedications too. 'Stephen: a handbook, perhaps? Dad', someone has written at the front of *Our Master's Voices*, a study of political speech-making by Max Atkinson. Who was Stephen? Is he now on the Labour benches, perhaps? And why did he sell on the book which Dad had so thoughtfully given him?

The dictionary in the *Guardian*'s features department at the end of the 1960s bore the poignant inscription: 'To Jean, from Auntie Muriel, in the hope that this dreadful war will soon be over.' The *Guardian* was so strapped in those days that it couldn't afford a new one.

It is when a reader begins to scribble a running commentary on the proceedings that accusations arise of vandalism or worse. Here, for instance, is a book called *The Revolution in Statecraft: Informal Penetration*, by Andrew M. Scott of the University of North Carolina, which I picked up on Saturday. Its previous owner clearly began by thinking quite well of Andrew M. Scott, festooning the pages with ticks and vigorous side-lining. But soon disillusion set in. By page 35 he's becoming sarcastic, and by page 59 the author's pro-American sentiments are provoking retaliation. 'Shows which side you are on!' he snarls, pressing grimly on the page.

One certainly shouldn't do this to library books, though even in an institution as hallowed as the London Library some readers do; and sometimes you're secretly glad they have done so. A kindly hand has altered an author's reference to the introduction of life peerages from 1962 to 1958, thus saving subsequent generations from error. Another begins to dispute, in a courteous way, some of an author's wilder contentions on the merits of poets laureate.

The book has become interactive, which we all hope to be nowadays. With one's own books, the practice, though still best avoided, is more defensible. True, re-reading such note-bespattered books can be galling. Was I really so crass at 18? Why on earth did I have it in quite so fiercely for S. T. Bindoff, author of *Tudor England*? And yet I am glad of these juvenile scribblings. Once a book is heavily marked it cannot be sold. Most second-hand bookshops prefer their books clean; and even with those that don't, can one really allow such embarrassing commentary to pass into other hands when one's name is indelibly marked on the title-page? Rule number one with books is never to get rid of anything. There's a kind of vengeful law which ensures you will need it later.

Next week I shall search high and low for a book in which the old Republican Willie Hamilton, MP for West Fife, analyses the circumstances to which various stately people owe their peerages, which have more to do, as I remember, with dirty deals and general political usefulness than conspicuous services to the state. I owned this book once. If only I'd written 'attaboy' and 'so perish all privilege' lavishly though its margins, I would have it still.

Though, on the other hand, if no one disposed of books, there might not be second-hand bookshops at all; and my 50p on a cold afternoon in York would never have bought me Macaulay. My thanks to whoever got rid of it. I only wish you had written your name on the title-page. ●

· ·

9 March 1999

Gary Younge
Bad vibes

Not for the first time, the spirit of the US Declaration of Independence and the rule of the American Constitution are at loggerheads. The founding fathers said everyone had the right to the 'pursuit of happiness'. Now the state of Alabama has told women they have no 'fundamental, constitutional right to an orgasm'.

A recently passed law, designed to save the deeply religious and highly conservative South from the perils of sexual obscenity, now has the airwaves, bar-rooms and beauty parlours of small-town Dixie humming with talk about vibrators, the plight of Southern womanhood and the right to privacy.

The law, which was passed last year, forbids the selling or distributing of 'any obscene material or any device designed or marketed as useful primarily for the stimulation of human genital organs' and those who flout it face a year in jail and a $10,000 fine. In short, selling things that turn people on could result in the salesperson being turned in. The law is being challenged and the issue is now sitting before a federal judge, who has to decide whether to throw the case out or allow it to proceed to a higher court.

For women, arguing the case for using a vibrator in the buckle of the Bible belt is not always easy. If mythology counts for anything, Southern women are not supposed to enjoy sex at all. The idea that they are not only enjoying it but might be supplementing it with some assistance from the local electricity board is more than most of their menfolk can bear.

'It doesn't surprise me that we would have some problems in the South,' says Sherri Williams, one of the plaintiffs in the vibrator case, who owns two stores selling, among other things, 'marital aids' in Huntsville as well as an Internet mail-order business. 'Attitudes to women and sex there are pretty backward,' she adds.

Popular iconography has reserved two main positions for Southern womanhood. For black women there was the oversized Mamie, best known from the knee down in *Tom and Jerry* and from the bosom up in *Gone With the Wind*. For whites there was the Southern belle: precious, dainty and emotionally forceful in a manner that none has personified more faithfully than Scarlett O'Hara at the beginning of *Gone With the Wind*.

Since most black women worked in the fields and most Southern whites were poor, these images bore little relation to reality. But the myths had other, far more potent uses. White Southern women were, if we believe the bellicose, to die for. When Confederate forces went into battle in 1861 it was, their leaders said, for their women as much as it was for slavery. A century later, when the segregationists fought against civil rights, one of the main reasons given was to protect their women from the attentions of black suitors.

From the vertiginous and virtuous heights of these pedestals, white Southern men clearly hoped their wives and daughters would not then see them having sex with their female slaves. Also from this vantage point they could neither see nor be seen by male slaves, whose virility plantation owners first invented and then feared.

In one of the most authoritative books on Confederate culture, *The Mind of the South*, W. J. Cash wrote: 'The shield-bearing Athena gleaming whitely in the clouds, the standard for its rallying, the mystic symbol of its nationality in the face of the foe . . . merely to mention her was to send strong men into tears – or shouts.' When the civil war came it was time for a new construct. White men went off to fight, leaving their women to run the plantations. The Southern belle turned into the Steel Magnolia – a hybrid of the dainty and the doughty.

But with the war an ancient memory and legal segregation abolished, the South has in many respects become more like the rest of America – a place where gender and racial inequalities persist but women have become increasingly assertive and independent. Female employment, divorce rates and family sizes are converging towards the national norm, although as the poorest region in the country it still lags behind the average.

A handful are even getting on. The first woman to make a serious bid for the presidency may well be Elizabeth Dole, born and raised in North Carolina; the nation's highest-paid entertainer is Mississippi-born Oprah Winfrey; its latest pop sensation, Leann Rimes, is also from Mississippi. But Southern law has evidently taken time to catch up. Alabama's lawyers say there is no fundamental right 'to purchase a product to use in pursuit of having an orgasm'.

'This is really a case about the power of the legislature to prohibit the sale and manufacture of products it deems harmful,' says state Assistant Attorney General Courtney Travers. If women want sex toys, the authorities point out, they can go to neighbouring Tennessee, buy them where it is legal and then bring back the contraband. Tennessee, the plaintiffs point out, is a long way to travel for an orgasm.

It says something about Alabama, whose motto is 'We dare to defend our rights', that the law was introduced before November's elections because politicians thought denying people a means of attaining sexual pleasure would be a vote catcher. It went in as part of a much larger bill aimed at shutting down strip clubs.

'It's quite common around election time for something like this to go through without anyone really noticing it,' says Martin Mcaffrey of the Alabama American Civil Liberties Union. In this case, however, the women decided to challenge the state before the state got to them.

In a nation founded by puritans, the South is still a region administered, for the most part, by some of the most religious zealots. One of the state's key defence points is that two other Southern states, Texas and Georgia, have a similar law and have not been found to be violating the Constitution.

Alabama's law was signed by the former governor, Fob James, who once threatened to call out the National Guard to keep the Ten Commandments on a courtroom wall. Just outside Montgomery, the state capital, a billboard barks: 'Go to Church or the devil will get you.' Alabama is not the only state in the country to encode such strict sex laws – although most are concentrated in the South. Oral sex between married, consenting heterosexual adults is illegal in 15 of the 50 US states. Adultery is still a crime in 24 of them.

In Alabama it is presumably OK to have sex with a donkey (there is no law against bestiality there) but not to engage in oral sex with your husband (they definitely have a law against that). Mcaffery says the legislators had to insist that the sex-toy law applied only to the stimulation of human genitalia because if it hadn't then cattle breeders would also have been flouting the law.

In this extremely patriarchal patch of America, where modernity often clashes with cultural views of yore, most regard the law not as a moral crusade but as a rather ridiculous joke. On one radio talk show a woman asked Montgomery mayor Emory Folmar whether he supported her right to buy a vibrator. Folmar said he had no objection so long as they were not publicly displayed. As soon as the woman was off the air he told listeners: 'If she wants a vibrator she ought to just go and sit on a washing machine.' ●

21 January 1999
Matthew Fort
The great caviare crisis

I t's enough to wring your withers. You are not, I repeat not, allowed to eat any more Russian caviare. Well, bang goes the daily dose of the black stuff. It's going to mean major changes to the Fort family diet, I can tell you.

All right, all right, you may think that caviare is something of a minority interest. But someone's eating the stuff. According to John Stas of caviare house W. G. White, we import seven tonnes or so a year, and the diet of such diverse folk as Michael Winner, Will Self, Peter Mandelson, Lord Lloyd Webber and Joan Collins could take a battering if the World Wide Fund for Nature has its way.

This democratic body wants the catering industry to go easy on caviare consumption because all but one of the 25 varieties of sturgeon are threatened with extinction as a result of uncontrolled fishing, poaching and pollution. Actually, the situation is a bit more complicated than that.

To start with, anyone wanting to export caviare to Europe needs to get a licence from CITES (the Convention on Trade in Endangered Species) first. And anyone wanting to import the stuff needs a parallel licence too. On top of that, there have been a few seismic shifts in the caviare industry in the last couple of decades.

Once upon a time, in the USSR, the caviare industry was tightly controlled by the Ministry of Fisheries. At that time, the Iranian caviare industry was in chaos: there was the small matter of the revolution; the consumption of caviare was banned under the Koran; and, in any case, most of the sturgeon were in the Russian part of the Caspian Sea. But then the USSR fell to pieces and various bodies – mostly Ministry of Fisheries officials who had joined forces with the Russian mafia and the newly independent countries round the Caspian Sea – squabbled over what had been the caviare industry. So dealing in Russian caviare has become a very dodgy business indeed.

At the same time, the Iranian caviare industry pulled itself together. In spite of their revolutionary ideals, the Iranians have woken up to the fact that caviare is their second largest foreign exchange earner. The new pragmatism was aided, believe it or not, by the late Ayatollah Khomeini, one of whose last acts was to approve the consumption of caviare by Muslims.

The Iranians now have a well-organised industry, with hatcheries and restocking programmes, and the flow of their caviar is controlled through 10 agencies and all is tickety-boo. The Russian caviare industry, on the other hand, is in a right mess. Supplies are irregular. Quality control is up the creek. There's no monitoring of fishing. Fraud is rife and loads of stuff that's sold as Russian caviare isn't any such thing.

But what about Chinese caviare, I hear you call. What indeed. The sturgeon fishing stations on the Amur river in far eastern China were built by the Bechtel Corporation – with investment from the Sunshine Corporation of America and Russian expertise – at the height of the Cold War, when, in theory, the Russians weren't talking to the Americans and the Chinese weren't talking to the Russians and the Americans weren't talking to anybody. Sadly, it seems that the Chinese are not exporting any caviare at present.

That, I think, only leaves me with French caviare, although I have heard rumours of both Italian and Turkish varieties. Once there was a thriving caviare industry based on the Gironde, but the war put paid to it. Now Alan Jones, a bright-eyed Brit, is reviving the sturgeon farming business and will be supplying three tonnes to the French restaurant trade next year.

So there you are. A hundred grammes of top-dog Iranian Beluga (incidentally, the different kinds of caviare are named after the species of sturgeon from which they are stripped – Beluga, Sevruga and Oscietra) will set you back around £150. But if you think that all this has nothing to do with the real world, just remember there's some poor sod bobbing around in a boat in the chop of the Caspian Sea for whom caviare is a meal ticket. ●

26 July 1999
Simon Hattenstone
Meet Britain's most notorious chef

Marco Pierre White asks me to wait in the garden for a minute. He flicks a finger and I walk on obediently. You don't argue with White. I'm not sure whether it's the stillness of his brown eyes, the bulk, or the authoritarian hush of his voice. White was the youngest chef to be awarded a Michelin star and the first British chef to win three stars, which is as good as it gets. Twelve years ago, he opened his first restaurant, and now he owns so many that he can't remember them until he starts counting on his fingers – The Oak Room, Titanic, Quo Vadis, The Criterion, The Mirabelle, where we are today, and . . . He gets to eight and stops. So many trendy, expensive, sexy restaurants, and he still cooks five nights a week at The Oak Room. He must love his work to keep at it so relentlessly? No, he says, he's not sure that love is the right word. 'I have created a world in which I feel comfortable. I have made myself prime minister of my own world.'

White wears a chef's tunic topped off with a blazer. There is something Jacobean, macabre about him. Almost devastatingly handsome, almost Ken Dodd. He talks the posh accentless English of the new establishment, the self-made, reinvented classes. There is no hint of his Yorkshire roots except for the flat 'o' of 'Nothing'. White was in the news last week. He put two millennium parties up for auction at Sotheby's and hoped they would fetch £90,000 each (£640 a head at the 140-seater Mirabelle, according to reports; a mere £450 at the Criterion). Both parties failed to meet their reserve price, and the newspapers giggled at his presumption.

White is always in the news. Last month he was starring in a row with former Quo Vadis partner Damien Hirst when the artist's paintings and dead animals were removed from the restaurant and replaced with the chef's substitute art works. Hirst accused White of copying, White said who's calling who a copycat. A few months before that he made the headlines pleading mercy for the burglar who stole £20,000 worth of goodies from his flat and then apologised.

White introduces me to a little Japanese man called Mr Ishi. Ah, Mr Ishi, he's the guy I read about in the *Daily Mirror* – the man you hired as your own personal postman to deliver missives and bouquets across the country? White laughs his dirty, urbane laugh. Things are rarely how they appear in newspapers, he says. 'Mr Ishi is my personal assistant. He does everything for me.'

It's funny how the media creates you, White says. But didn't he create himself – all that petulant talent, those tantrums as he kicked out undesirables from the restaurant, terrified his staff, shed two wives and slid from partner to partner. 'I'm a very different monster to what I was 10 years ago,' White says. But still a monster? 'Oh yes. I think we're all monsters really.' What kind of monster is he these days? Well, he says, in his twenties he wouldn't let go, wouldn't trust anyone. He had to do everything himself, his blood pressure shot up, and in the end he lost control. 'I made a tremendous amount of mistakes in my twenties. I just behaved badly in many ways.' But the new White has learned to delegate, to trust, to lay off. What changed him? He talks about the security of his present family – his partner Mati and their two sons (he also has a daughter from his first marriage). And he talks in much greater detail about the insecurities of his childhood family in Leeds: how his mother died when he was six, how his father was riddled with cancer by the time he was 10 but somehow held on for another 20 years, how he was dyslexic and still hasn't got to grips with words. White was unconfident with children his own age, and felt he could never please his father, who was also a chef. He says he thought he could only come to terms with his childhood if he learned to understand the mother he barely knew. So over the past few years he has begun to trace her life, flesh out the skeleton of his memories, discover what kind of woman she was, whether she could really live up to his dreams.

White floats between the fears of childhood and the certainty of today. He says now, at 37, he feels in control. Control, strength and weakness are favourite words. 'Weak people let you down.' 'Always appoint strong people.' 'A strong man should always marry a strong woman, weak people should marry each other.' 'Self-control is true power.' If you shut your eyes you could be chatting with a master eugenicist. White expands on his philosophy. Though staff must be strong they must remain loyal. 'They must give loyalty, not breed loyalty.' What's the difference? 'Those who breed loyalty, demand it for themselves, and will end up betraying you.'

Having risen from his council house in Leeds to become a multi-millionaire, does White consider himself, as many others do, a poster boy for Thatcherism? He nods his head, and says he supposes that's right, though in his heart he feels like a socialist. 'But I think you need to be a successful capitalist to generate wealth and do good.' White looks above my head. 'Isn't it wonderful the way that wood pigeon blends in with the lavender? It's been a nice morning, hasn't it?'

Lady Thatcher visited one of his restaurants recently, and they were sitting side by side, talking to each othr. He shared his creed about giving and breeding loyalty with her. 'She repeated it out to herself and said: "You know you are right." It was my little dig at her cabinet because, in the end, they put the knife in, didn't they? But she was a very impressive woman, the most impressive person I've met in my life.

'Do you think Blair is losing popularity?' he asks. 'His hair is all over the place, he's a mess, he isn't in control.' White compares the Prime Minister unfavourably with the chairmen of the great PLCs. 'They never look tired . . . Blair is a weak man,' he says dismissively. White says he has reinvented himself time and again, that you have to if you want to remain successful. Every five years, he sets new targets. At 35, he decided he would give his business roots, make the future secure for his family. In the *Sunday Times* list of Britain's wealthiest he is ranked 471st, worth £50 million.

Is he upset that the millennium parties failed to meet their reserve prices? No, he says, his directors sort that stuff out for him, he didn't know what the asking prices were, and anyway, £600 a head is outrageous. 'The future of restaurants is to provide affordable glamour.' He says a fair price for the millennium night out is £250–£350. White exercises a wonderful gangsterly control of his voice. When he lowers his voice you know he wants to be taken seriously, when you can barely hear him the menace is staring you in the face. I ask him whether his own paintings are still hanging in Quo Vadis, and what the spat with Damien Hirst was all about. White suddenly turns the tape recorder off. He doesn't ask or prepare me for it. Flick, and we're off the record. He says he feels betrayed, cheated, and is talking in such elliptical riddles I feel dizzy. He flicks the tape recorder back on. 'Anyone who tries to damage my life or my family, or take away security from my family, I will fight to the end. It's my nature. What Damien tried to do to me, I will fight to the bitter end. That's not a threat, that's just me being honest.'

So what did he do? It's a messy row. White claims that he ordered the withdrawal of Hirst's art works from Quo Vadis, while Hirst claimed that he withdrew them himself. Hirst also claimed that White aped his paintings, while White counters that, actually, Hirst copied one of his. Boys! White has often scrapped in the public eye, and I feel as if I've walked on to the set of a Mafia sit-com. 'At the end of the day he will pay his price. He made me look like a fool. That's fine. Let's play the game then. You position yourself, and I'll position myself, and let the battle commence. I know who'll win.'

White seems relieved to have it off his chest, and returns to the simple life – good friends, loyal workers, classic French cuisine, family. He talks tenderly about two brothers who are gardeners in Leeds, asks where I am from, and runs through a list of people I may known from Manchester. You will stay for lunch won't you? No, I say, I must return to the office to write you up. Before I know it, I'm being manoeuvred into a seat, and a napkin is spread on my lap. Mati arrives with a friend who spends an hour telling a joke, constantly distracted by her own stream of consciousness. She mentions a girlfriend who reminds her of White. ('But she's not as talented as me,' he says) and a former boyfriend who also reminds her of him ('You must miss him dreadfully,' he says.) White wolfs down his liver, mash and wine, leans back, and sucks lavishly on a cigar. 'Would you like one? Champagne maybe? Brandy? Is 1900 OK for you?' A waiter takes away his glass, which has the faintest stain of wine stuck to the bottom. 'Excuse me,' says White tersely, 'I've not finished yet.' Mati's friend interrupts her joke yet again to talk about another former boyfriend, so buttoned up, so unlike White who just lets it all out. 'Yes,' says Mati. 'You just reduce people to a quivering wreck, MARCO.' He cuddles her and she smiles. Does he reduce her to a quivering wreck. 'Oh yes, like with the green trousers today.' 'Well, you know how much I like my green trousers.'

I say I'm going to the loo, and White offers to keep me company. 'You know, when I realised I liked you?' he says. 'When I realised you could look me in the eye. A lot of people find that difficult. I am a strong man.' White is almost as famous for his compliments as for his arrogance. He says that when he finally managed to piece his mother's life together he was so proud of her. 'She was the type of person who would check the chimney before putting a fire on to make sure a bird hadn't fallen in.' He holds out his hands as wide as they'll go, and I can't help thinking of Citizen Kane strutting round Xanadu. 'Every man should leave a monument to their mother,' he says. 'This is my monument to my mother . . . We've had a nice time, haven't we?'

I feel I should despise this man for his monstrous narcissism and Nietzschean aspirations. But yes, we have had a nice time, you have been good company, this is a fantastic monument to mummy. Maybe I'm drunk. Maybe he has seduced me. Maybe, worst of all, I'm tickled that he thinks I'm strong enough to play with his supermen and superwomen. Help! ●

. . . .

27 February 1999
Tom Bussmann
Zeitgeist

Hoots

The *Wall Street Journal* reports an unholy row brewing in the world of competitive bagpiping. Gore-Tex or nylon bags are replacing traditional sheepskin – and, what's worse, seem to be superior. Breathable Gore-Tex allows vapour through the walls of the bag, thus avoiding the problem of 'piper's drool sloshing about the bottom'. Last year, first prize at the World Bagpiping Championship in Glasgow went to the Victoria (Australia) Police Pipe Band, which uses a patented moisture-control system based on cat litter. Trad bags require a special Scottish moisturiser, which smells of petrol and 'looks like mucus', which the hills are alive with the sound of.

The name of the game

Ahoy there, *Sea River Mediterranean*! A lovely name, redolent of fresh water and clean air, and befitting a fine, freshly painted supertanker plying her trade in the Firth of Forth. And bon voyage with your cargo of 11,000 gallons of crude North Sea oil. Shame you're barred from Prince William Sound, but then they remember you as plain old *Exxon Valdez*. A pathetic subterfuge, about as daft as renaming infamous Windscale Nuclear Power Station something bucolic like, say, Sellafield.

Going nuts

Airlines faced with plunging profits have limited options. They can't cut fuel, landing fees or rudimentary maintenance. And, after grinding down staff costs, what's left is peanuts. Precisely. Per-passenger spending on domestic US in-flight food has dropped by a third since 1991. Now it's an average $3.03, which might just buy you an M&S sandwich. Profitable Southwest prides itself on a per-passenger spend of 20 cents. There may be a cost. Nutritionists suggest that 'lack of food' plus nicotine withdrawal and dehydration (not helped by economies in air-conditioning) may lead to 'unpleasant behaviour'.

Hold your hearses

As previously Zeitgeisted, 454 doctors in the Venice region are under investigation for 'providing treatment' to 15,000 long-dead patients. They stand accused of continuing to claim an annual allowance of 70,000 lire (£26) per patient. Many also charged for prescriptions, or for making home visits. Some patients had died more than 15 years ago. Giuseppe Greco, spokesman for the Italian doctors' association, was quick to spring to his members' defence: 'A doctor does not necessarily know when his patient is dead.'

Porkies go walkies

A herd of abandoned Vietnamese pot-bellied pigs was pursued through Essex woodland by RSPCA inspector Chris Bacon. This gift to journalism was greeted with predictable lack of restraint, the *Daily Mail* thoughtfully speculating that the remaining pigs would be caught 'when hunger makes them rasher'.

Laughing to the bank

The recession in Japan is beginning to bite. In an effort to boost trade, Tokyo store owners are paying for their surly staff to take smiling lessons. At a 'Smile Amenity School', they are told to bite on a chopstick. The 'smile expert'

Yoshihiko Kadokawa orders them to 'lift the edge of the mouth higher than the edge of the stick, hold your cheeks and count to three'. No way of knowing if this works, but it's a fair bet that Yoshihiko Kadokawa is smiling. •

. . . .

19 December 1998

Alexander Chancellor
Side by side

As Christmas approaches, the spirit of peace and goodwill prevails in Hammersmith. The next-door neighbours with whom we had a flaming row earlier this year after they'd cut down the old sycamore tree straddling the fence between their garden and ours have moved away to the country, probably to escape their own 'neighbours from hell'.

But down there in Monahan Avenue, Purley, that suburb of the London suburb of Croydon, a great feud between neighbours carries on. And what neighbours they are: Sir Bernard Ingham, Margaret Thatcher's former press secretary, and the builder Barry Cripps. Relentless, litigious, unforgiving! They have been fighting for 10 years now, and will doubtless be fighting for another ten. For, unlike us wimps here in Hammersmith, these two men are not the kind of people who give up. They will carry on until one or the other is the victor – and then they will carry on until the loser has got his revenge. They are like Sicilians, and the feud could well continue for generations.

There is already some evidence to support this prediction – in letters from Sir Bernard to his solicitor – published this week in the *Daily Mail* and written between 1994 and 1995, after Mr Cripps had won retrospective planning permission for a roof extension to which Sir Bernard had objected. He wrote at one point: 'Cripps's son, aged about eight, appeared beside their garage with another boy. Cripps's son began to cackle at me and to pull faces, including sticking his tongue out.' The boy was only eight, but already fully committed to his father's cause.

But the biggest danger for Sir Bernard, it seems to me, is that his reputation as a larger-than-life character could well be in jeopardy. Nobody denies that he remains outspoken and aggressive and often given to colourful language, but Mr Cripps appears to be even more outrageous. He not only has three Mercedes cars with personalised number plates, but seemingly one or two other vehicles, and a caravan as well.

And Mr Cripps, gloating over his planning permission victory, was quite magnificent. He sprayed V for victory on eight of his windows overlooking Sir Bernard's bungalow, cackled at him whenever he saw him and finally left him a bottle of champagne with a card that read: 'God be with you in your time of sorrow.' •

....

31 October 1998
Ian Mayes
Expletives. And excess

Perhaps I should preface this column with a warning that it contains words which will offend some readers, although the difficulty is that the column is written in response to readers already offended. In the past year the *Guardian* has used more four-letter words than any other 'quality' newspaper on earth.

Not to beat about the bush, there have been more than 400 pieces in the *Guardian* since 10 October last year in which the words fuck or fucking appeared at least once (even more, no doubt, in the couple of days since I wrote this) – and that is eliminating any references to the play *Shopping and Fucking*. In the same period there were 28 references to cunt in the *Guardian*. Our nearest rival was the *Independent*, almost 100 items behind in its use of fuck or fucking and offering only nine pieces in which the word cunt occurred (*The Times* and the *Telegraph*, by comparison, are expletive-free zones).

When both words were included in the Oxford dictionaries for the first time, in the supplement of 1972, the definitions of fuck were preceded by this note: 'For centuries, and still by the great majority, regarded as a taboo word; until recent times not often recorded in print but frequent in coarse speech.' The argument of a steady stream of our readers is that since then the printed language has coarsened too, with the *Guardian* bearing some of the responsibility.

Why, a reader inquires of the editor, do you permit your journalists to spatter your pages with vulgarities and obscenities? Why do you think such gross language (examples provided) is appropriate in a supposedly 'quality' newspaper? Can you not see that its deployment contributes to the coarsening of English life and civility?

Another reader – who notes in passing that women writers now seem prone to what he calls the F word (something that the compilers of the Oxford dictionaries agree could be a factor in its increasing prevalence) – accused us of being 'as responsible as anyone for the proliferation of swearing'. One of the most persuasive objections ran as follows: 'If you were with a group of friends and you knew that just one of the party was very puritanical about bad language, wouldn't you moderate your language out of consideration for this person?'

The figures I've given do not, by the way, include words in which asterisks were used, as in the *Guardian Weekend*'s interview with Robbie Williams last Saturday, when cunt appeared as c***, but twat (a synonym) was spelt out. Initially I told the reader who remarked on this that it was just another example of the *Guardian*'s inconsistency. On further reflection, I think it may indicate someone's perception of the differing strength of the taboo applied to the two words. Asterisks, I think, should probably be abandoned altogether. The same correspondent argues: 'Every reader merely substitutes the correct letters and the offensiveness of the sentence remains intact. It seems coy to suppose otherwise and insert the asterisks.'

So we come to the point where the presence of the words is either justified by the context or not. Frequently it isn't. To give one example which raised objections: a property column in our 'Space' supplement, published with some southern editions, suggested that East Sheen was sometimes confused with the East Cheam of Tony Hancock fame, prompting the author of the piece to remark: 'Fucking droll.' Why?

Many staff journalists seem to object to the gratuitous use of swearwords in print. One of the younger generation of editors on the paper put it like this: 'I think it's a privilege to work on a paper which has the liberal values and readership to permit publication of the strongest of swearwords, a privilege that we should guard by not abusing it. I believe we should use swearwords only when absolutely necessary to the facts of a piece, or to portray a character in an article. The stronger the swearword the harder we ought to think about it, and there's almost never a case in which we need to use a swearword outside of direct quotes.'

The editor says this is pretty much the approach that he expects to find and the one he would like to see prevail. He makes the point that the language used in the *Guardian* generally probably reflects (more than it influences) changing use in society at large, and certainly does this better than papers which simply ban the words. Nevertheless, he expects individual editors and writers to exercise judgement and restraint. He accepts that swearwords do upset some readers, and that it is something that has, as he put it, 'slipped'. He has promised to put a note for the guidance of *Guardian* journalists into News-wir, our electronic notice board, calling for things to be tightened up a bit. ●

. . . .

12 May 1999
Leader
Elegy for the pram

T he pushchair and the buggy have won. The last great manufacturer of British perambulators, Silver Cross, of Guiseley, Leeds, may have to go out of business.

The pram was the chariot of the upper-class baby, which the middle classes adopted at more modest expense. Your ideal pram, pushed by a nursemaid, made daily excursions to some favoured place like Kensington Gardens, where it encountered others similarly propelled. While their charges snoozed and crooned, the nursemaids compared them, never failing also to note how their own prams compared with those of their rivals in the ease of their progress, the gleam of the paintwork, the size of the shining wheels.

But all that belongs to an age which has gone. Middle-class mothers, denied the space of Kensington Gardens, found prams were too hard to manoeuvre up and down pavements, too prone to collide with people and other prams, too bulky for public transport. When the buggy appeared in the middle 1960s, pram-makers quaked, scenting extinction. Now Silver Cross must close unless a buyer is found.

Yet perhaps some entrepreneur will be tempted. Consider the tram. Thirty years ago, municipalities were ripping up tracks, declaring them done for. Today we have rediscovered the tram. It is back on the streets of Manchester and Sheffield, and will soon return to the streets of Croydon, not least for its environmental merits. A similar case can be made for the pram, which raises its passengers high above the fumy exhausts which puff into their faces when buggies transport them close to the ground. Sociologists too may debate the security children lost when they started to travel gazing forwards into the world rather than backwards into the adoring faces of those who pushed them. If trams, as Richard Hoggart wrote, were the gondolas of the people, prams were the gondolas of fortunate under-fives. ●

30 November 1998

Alex Brummer
Day trip to the death camps

Trussed up in a blue anorak against the wind and belting rain, framed against the grey sky, Rabbi Barry Marcus clambered on to the ruins of the crematorium, lifted the sacred ram's horn to his lips and sounded the plaintive cries handed down the generations since the days of Joshua. Then there was a moment of deathly silence. For a few brief seconds, standing at my side, I could visualise my grandfather Sandor, his long red beard swaying in the wind, wearing his long dark Sabbath coat, emaciated from illness and hunger, smiling.

Both he and my grandmother Fanny died in the killing fields of Auschwitz, and I never met them. Neither have I ever seen a photograph of them. In the haste in which they were marched down the hill of their home town of Tiszaujlak, in what was then Hungary, in June 1944, the family snaps seem to have been lost. But over the decades, listening to the reminiscences of my two aunts, uncle and cousin – who all, miraculously, survived Auschwitz – his image has become imprinted in my psyche. Being so close to the spot where he and my grandmother perished brought him back for a few precious and mystical moments.

The journey to Auschwitz-Birkenau seemed like a natural progression from a journey I made 18 months earlier, with my father, Michael, and cousin Shindy, an Auschwitz survivor, to their birthplace in the Transcarpathian region. This time I travelled with a friend, Dr Peter Feldschreiber, who lost all of his grandparents in this place of dread. It had seemed to me that the act of visiting the site where so many atrocities had been wrought on my family would have been too much for my father and Shindy. It was Shindy's enterprise, after all, that had helped to keep my two aunts, Rosie and Sussie, alive, despite the best efforts of Josef Mengele and his Nazi doctors.

Our escort on this most challenging of day trips was Marcus, a young South African-born rabbi who dreams every young British Jew will visit, see, smell and better understand the sheer scale of the industrial methods of slaughter perfected by the Nazis. Marcus's exploration of the system of more than 40 separate concentration camps in southern Poland began in 1995, when he joined the March of the Living, the annual pilgrimage of 5,000 young people to the camps, the delegations from each country carrying their national flag. On the solemn walk from Auschwitz to Birkenau, Marcus was disappointed to find that the smallest group of all was from Britain: even the tiny Jewish communities of Greece and Chile were better represented. 'It was as if British Jews didn't want to know,' Marcus said. So he began organising visits, and the day trip seemed to be the right format. 'No one wants to spend more time here than you have to.'

Every moment of the stormy autumn day was made to count and connect. At Luton Airport, a small room was set aside for a morning prayer service. The men put on their black and white prayer shawls and *tefillin*, the carefully crafted black boxes filled with prayers and joined by leather straps. At that moment it seemed routine, but a few hours later, after crossing the railway tracks which had carried the 1.3 million condemned people into Auschwitz, it would become more meaningful. There, in the pictures on the walls and behind the glass in the barracks, were the prayer shawls and *tefillin* of the dead. Stripped from the bodies and removed from the suitcases, they were now hanging from clotheslines, looking right at you, like ghosts with their arms outstretched.

The atmosphere on the flight was strained and tense. The entertainment consisted of video footage about the fate of European Jewry. The conversation was conducted in whispers. Jennifer, who sat to my left, lives in Edgware, is married with adult children. She was there for her mother, a death-camp survivor, who had told her: 'When I was about 10 years old, I heard my parents talking about the camps. We should really try to find out if anyone is left there.' She had come alone to try to understand what happened, to say prayers for those never heard of again.

On my right was a well-known theatrical impresario; one of Anglo-Jewry's success stories. He had come to bear witness, to heed the words of Elie Wiesel: 'Never shall I forget these things, even if I am condemned to life as long as God himself. Never.'

The coach ride from Cracow Airport to Auschwitz takes an hour. We set off in bright sunshine, speeding through cultivated fields that could be Hampshire, past white-painted houses with bright orange roofs. Our Polish guide spoke of the statistics, the trains, the transports, the separations and deaths in a matter-of-fact way that made them seem almost inconsequential. By the time we crossed the railway tracks and saw the most chilling station name that there can be anywhere – 'Oswiecim' – the sky had darkened, with winds swirling around the coach and the rain pelting down incessantly. The horror of what faced us became real: there was a dull ache in the pit of my stomach.

We were inside the concentration camp almost before we realised it. This is not some remote, hidden-away facility, it is surrounded by industrial structures and army bases. There are shops and petrol stations, whose architecture mimics that of Auschwitz 1 itself. It is a death camp in suburbia, and the smell of burning corpses, which more than five decades later still permeates the crematoria, must have once been suffocating. The mask of ignorance – pierced by Claude Lanzmann in his movie *Shoah* – is instantly pulled away. Almost before we knew what was happening we were passing beneath the iron sign that reads 'Arbeit Macht Frei' (Work Brings Freedom).

There is nothing immediately alarming about Auschwitz 1. Superficially – without the icy wind, and the rain that had turned the tracks to mud – the reconstructed barracks, surrounded by grass verges and lined with trees, could be mistaken for a pleasant housing estate. Like the buildings, the Polish guide's interpretation of events was bland, filled with Polish and Catholic heroes as if the Jews who 'mostly' perished here were a sideshow. But at Block 4, there was a quiet, terrible reality. In a stark room, where the smell of chemical preservative took one by surprise, human hair is piled up like a mountain. Shaven from Jews as they were led to gas chambers, much of the hair is grey now, turned so by time and poor conservation. But I searched for a trace of red or colour, as one looks for some reminder that one's family was here.

So it was as we passed all of these ordinary, terrifying exhibits: enough eyeglass frames to equip a small nation; the enamelled pots, pans and jugs which were part of the victims' chattels; and leather suitcases each carefully marked with names, dates and towns. The party vainly looked for a familiar name among the hundreds of suitcases: Judith Gella Cohen, Marie Kafka, Tausik Raphaelia. It was an impossible search, as was surveying the thousands of photos of early victims lining walls for a few among the million or more who perished, but it didn't stop us looking.

Our guide was asked if anyone had ever spotted a FAMILY member. 'Yes,' she replied definitively. 'Yes, they have.' She then revealed that since she began working in this place, six years ago, she had discovered that one of her uncles – with Jewish blood – had died here.

The most bizarre exhibit of all was a room filled with artificial limbs, trusses, surgical supports and medical devices torn from the disabled before they were bundled into the gas chambers. The limbs blended into one another like the shapeless bodies on the old newsreel footage of the clearing-up operation.

Out in the bitter cold, we sheltered from the weather beneath a ledge of Block 10. This was a gruesome spot. Our guide, on auto-pilot, talked of the sterilisation experiments that went on behind us. My mind flashed back to the whispers of my childhood: visiting my Auntie Sussie in Hemel Hempstead after she had given birth to a tiny baby kept alive only by the skills of modern medicine. Mengele and his henchmen had experimented on my father's sisters, who were barely out of puberty. Yet Mengele failed and, having survived and moved to suburban Britain, they were with difficulty able to conceive.

The physiological scars may have healed, but the psychological impact has cascaded down the generations. Adjacent to Block 10, where the windows were blocked out, is the 'Wall of Death', where thousands of prisoners, having been tried by Gestapo kangaroo courts, were summarily shot and their bodies dragged away on carts to the permanently smouldering funeral pyres.

Adjacent to the wall and surrounding barbed-wire stands is the now empty Carmelite monastery and the field of crosses which have caused such serious offence to the Jewish communities. There, Marcus's temper rose. He pointed out that until 1992, when President Chaim Herzog of Israel visited the camps, there was 'not one small Jewish monument' in a place which has been filled and surrounded by Christian imagery. It was a potent message for us to carry as we climbed down into the cool of the only gas chamber not destroyed by the SS as Russian troops approached. Standing under the grates in the ceiling, where the Cyclon B had been showered upon naked Jewish bodies, the tears flowed. A faint smell of burning, from the preserved crematorium next door, intensified the effect.

After Auschwitz 1, our coach made the short journey to Birkenau, a site as different from the prettified layout of the other camp as it is possible to be. The entrance, along the railway tracks, was used in the opening scene from Spielberg's film *Schindler's List*. But what's on the other side is more frightening.

As far as the eye can see are the rough wooden barracks and chimneys of the Nazi death factory, which catches the breath because of its vastness. Inside the barracks, the roughly hewn wooden bunks, which held five or six souls, remain intact. In the centre of the room, crude, unfinished concrete latrines, with drains running through the barracks, catch the eye. More than 1,000 people in each barrack, each with a life expectancy – if they survived the selection – of six months. Grass now grows around the buildings, but at the entrances, where our feet sank into the mud and ashes, one could almost smell the faeces and urine which would run down the pitted tracks.

We walked for a mile or so down the side of the railway that brought the cattle trucks of Jews, gypsies and political dissidents from every corner of occupied Europe. Journeys of 2,000 kilometres or more, without water or food, journeys on which the corpses would outnumber the living. I recalled Shindy describing her departure from Hungary: the Jews begged for water through the cattle truck openings, and were offered salt. At the end of the track, Marcus stood atop the blown-up debris of Crematorium 2, in which up to 1,000 people a day were incinerated, and delivered his sermon.

'Many times I have visited this hellhole,' he declared, 'but never on a more appropriate day than this. Not just because of the stormy weather, but because 54 years ago today, Crematorium 4 was bombed by Jewish prisoners, who had smuggled in explosives from outside.' This, Marcus pointed out, was the most important rebellion at Birkenau, a source of hope for all the other inmates, which resulted in the saving of Jews who could not be burned in time.

Looking down at the group he had brought to Poland, the rabbi pointed out that we, ordinary citizens of Europe, were no different from those who were brought here. Yet we would have filled only one-fifth of one barrack block.

We opened the prayer book, brought from London. The rabbi, in best cantorial tradition, recited the memorial prayer for victims of the Holocaust: 'O God who art full of compassion, grant a perfect rest in thy divine presence to all the souls of our holy and pure brethren whose blood was spilt by the murderers in Auschwitz, Majdanek, Treblinka and other extermination camps in Europe; who were killed, burned and buried alive for the sanctification of thy Name.'

Then came the tragic roll-call, the names of the people in our families who had perished: my grandparents Sandor and Fanny; my uncles Daniel and Ference, who fell in work camps in the forest after they were taken from their families at the outbreak of war. The prayer, recited with quiet dignity among the assembled company – men and women together – somehow sanctified the ground and reclaimed for it a Jewish heritage. Sheltering against the wind, I found a crevice in the rocks and quietly lit a single memorial light. The whole pilgrimage, I realised, was worth it for this moment of remembrance – remembrance of my grandparents and of the six million who suffered with them. ●

Time . . . is . . . clearly . . . on . . . our . . . side

War drums in Europe

. . . .

17 June 1999

Maggie O'Kane

One family's story

Zoran Petkovic left in a hurry. The floor is scattered with stale bread rolls, the budgie's cage is empty. In the front garden a black and white football lies among pink rose bushes. Lying on the mustard velvet sofa is a photocopy of a newspaper article that details the terms of the Serbian withdrawal. They were to be out of Kosovo by last week, but Zoran Petkovic wasn't waiting that long.

He is 42, and the town of Suva Reka knew him well. They knew him as the man who drank beer outside the Boss Hotel with the owner, his friend Misko Nisavic. He was a Serb who was friendly with the Albanians of Kosovo, even as relations deteriorated between the two ethnic groups.

His father was a wine importer and well off, but Zoran had trouble holding down a job. He was sacked from the Schweppes factory in the town when he was 17 – nobody knew why. He got a job as a bus driver in Austria and then with the Lasta bus company in Belgrade, but he got sacked from there as well. He drifted through two marriages and then moved back to the family's large three-storey house. When he divorced his third wife, his father threw him out.

Things improved for Zoran. He gave up the driving and used his Serbian connections to run a small, corrupt business. Nothing too serious: false papers for cars imported from Germany, illegal work permits. He charged too much, but he had the connections and welcomed everyone who needed some done, especially the Kosovars, who were having more and more trouble getting papers from the Serb-controlled local authorities. He was Suva Reka's Mr Fixit.

Last week there was a lot of fixing to be done in Suva Reka. The town is as dead as the large rust-coloured Alsatian lying on the main road with its belly slit open. The homes of the ethnic Albanians who once came to Zoran are black, burned and empty. At the far end of this town of 20,000 people, behind the row of hawthorn bushes, are the mounds that mark the graves of Albanians killed in the past three months. They do not tell the whole story – the trucks that disappeared into the distance, the blood streaming from the hinges on the doors, or the field that has a suspiciously fresh rubbish dump spread evenly as manure over a mound that nature did not make.

In the days before the Nato air strikes Zoran still did a little bus-driving, and every Sunday morning he did the weekly run to Prague, picking up his bus outside the Berisha house.

The Berishas were the best-known and among the richest Kosovars in town. Zoran knew them, but there was not much mixing. The grandfather had been the headmaster at the secondary school before he retired. Among his four sons there was an economist, an engineer and a businessman. Bujar was the business-man. He rented out office space and cars, and when the Organisation for Security and Cooperation in Europe (OSCE) wanted to billet a couple of their men there as observers, he offered the cheaper rate, undercutting the Boss Hotel. It was business and Bujar did not even think about it. But it made dangerous men angry.

The OSCE moved its offices from the Boss Hotel to Berisha's house and Zoran's friends lost their hard-currency guests. But then, as talk of air strikes began, the three OSCE men, two Germans and one American, were rapidly pulled out.

Things started happening fast in Suva Reka. Local Serbs got into uniform to fight for their homeland. Zoran, the weekend bus driver with too much time on his hands, became a soldier. A man with not only a mission but a Kalashnikov. Islam Yashari, a policeman, knew Zoran all his life: 'I don't know what happened to him. He was just a guy who didn't like work too much, then when the war started he changed. He wanted to be somebody.'

Then came the night when the Nato bombs first fell. By then the OSCE men were far away. 'I wished they could take us with them,' said Vjollca Berisha. 'I don't know why they didn't tell us. They left and said everything will be all right. Milosevic will sign and the OSCE will be back.' That was 22 March, two days before the bombing started.

Vjollca Berisha was crying gently in a sunny garden. Of the 26 Berishas gathered in the large three-storey house that had taken the OSCE's business, 13 of them children, only three are still alive – Vjollca, her son, Gramos, aged 10, and her sister, Shyreta.

It was midday on 26 March. 'Bujar,' the five masked men called from outside. 'Bujar, come on out. Where are your Americans now? You want Nato? We'll give you Nato.'

Bujar stepped out and saw Zoran and Misko Nisavic, the owner of the Boss Hotel. The Berishas watched from inside. Bujar smiled at Zoran, the man who came to pick up the bus from outside their house. Zoran smiled back. The men lifted their Kalashnikovs. Bujar did not have time to step off the porch.

The Berishas were then split up. Men were shot first and then Lily, the wife, who was seven months pregnant. The other Berisha women fled screaming, carrying their children in their arms. They ran through the smashed shopping centres looted by paramilitaries the night the bombing started. They ran past the Beni Tours travel shop, past the Drina restaurant with the places still set for breakfast – and into a coffee shop. No one knows why they all ran there to hide.

Last week, almost three months later, there is blood everywhere. Blood on the fake Doric pillars, blood on the radiators, bloodstains from whoever was hiding behind the cappuccino maker. The lilac tablecloths are strewn across the a floor. On the coffee bar the bread baskets have been prepared for lunch that never happened, and in the fridge are the dozen eggs that have been there for a month and a tub of Belgrade yoghurt. On the pavement outside are the spent cartridges of 72 rounds of ammunition from a Kalashnikov.

'It's so hard to see children,' says Vjollca. 'You can't imagine the sound of the scream when a child dies. They fired at us through the door. There were two of them. I saw a little boy without a head. There was blood everywhere. The little babies were dead. Ismet, who was three, was crying, "Mummy, I want water." And they shot him in the face. Eron, the baby, was 10 months and he was crying, so they shot him. I saw my daughter. We were looking at each other across the bodies and she moved her lips as though she was trying to say something to me. I held my son in my arms and I saw my sister holding her baby in her arms. Her baby was dead, but she kept holding her.'

In the sunny garden there is silence. Relatives listen as Vjollca, a woman who has been hiding like a wounded animal in the hills, tells them for the first time what happened in the coffee bar. She is very composed until you ask her to list the names and ages of the children.

She had three children: her daughters, Daphina and Drilon, and a son, Gramos. Now she has only a son. Her sister, Shyreta, had four children: Majoinda, Erorinda, Altin and Redon, aged 16, 14, 10 and two. They are all dead.

Majoinda had called to her mother: 'Mummy, what are we going to do?'

'Don't worry. We will survive,' Shyhrete said, and then they threw a hand grenade in on top of Majoinda.

'I saw Altin look across the room at his mother and then he made a noise like "Ooof" and he died,' Vjollca says.

When the men came back, Vjollca buried her face in the bodies around her. Only Shyreta dared to look up. 'Shyreta told me that the man who lifted the Kalashnikov to finish them off was Zoran Petkovic.'

She escaped by pretending to be dead when the bodies of her children and family were piled in the back of a civilian truck. 'They dragged me out of the café by one leg and threw me into the truck on top of my dead mother. My son was lying on top of me. I heard the sound of a child calling for help from deep under the bodies, but I couldn't help him. I couldn't see anything. I was covered in bodies, but I heard that they were cleaning the blood from the outside of the truck. A crowd of Serbian civilians were gathered around the truck. I looked over and I saw Flore, who was dead, but she looked so nice. Then they started to drive very, very fast. Shyreta spoke and she said: "Are you alive? We have to jump." I saw that Shyreta still had Redon, her baby in her arms. He was dead, but she couldn't let him go. Shyreta said: "I'm going to jump, and if I die it is OK because I am already a dead woman." Then she put down her baby and jumped. I said to my boy we must jump and he said: "No, please, Mummy. I'm afraid."'

They jumped and the woman, who had bullet wounds in her body, said that somehow she found the strength to run with her only surviving son. She hasn't seen a doctor since March. Her body is still full of bullets, but she was afraid to leave the house where a Serbian family helped her to hide. She is still in Kosovo and last week she was reunited with her family as the German Nato troops took over southern Kosovo.

Shyreta got to Albania – a woman who lost her husband and all her children. She spent five weeks trying to get across the border on a convoy and told a friend: 'I am dead inside. I am staying alive only to bear witness to what has happened.' She has been moved first to Switzerland and then to Italy under the protection of the War Crimes Tribunal in The Hague and is staying at a secret location.

Last week, when the *Guardian* spoke to a brother of the family, Besha Berisha, in Switzerland, he said Shyreta's last words to him were: 'Even if I die, please find Zoran Petkovic, because he is responsible for everything. It was him who gave us this present.'

They say in Suva Reka that Zoran has gone to Belgrade. Maybe, some day, he will be found driving a bus in the homeland that gave a drifter a mission in his shabby life. ●

. . . .

24 March 1999

Jonathan Steele
Disabled by fear

I t is a strange thing to see a man shaking with fear. What I always thought was a metaphor, a little bit of literary exaggeration, was actually happening in front of me. A middle-aged father, a person of authority, was flapping like a sail in a high wind. His arms were moving from side to side, his legs wobbling. His ashen face had started to twitch.

With four other reporters, I was standing just below a railway embankment in Kosovo's Drenica region in the village of Bajince. A few men and boys stood talking to us. Others were sprawled along the 12-foot slope. The boldest were on their bellies, peering gingerly over the top of the embankment. Every few minutes they would shout as they saw the puff of smoke from a tank which was firing across the fertile farming country from a distance of about two miles. We braced as a whistling sound passed over us, then a thud and a whoosh of brown earth.

What caused our friend to shake was an impact that seemed nearer than the others, though still at least 100 feet away. As the minutes elapsed and no new shell landed, the man's shaking gradually subsided. He was disabled by fear.

The war in Kosovo has gone on for over a year, but you would be hard put to it to find any fighting. What was happening in Bajince yesterday was just another all-too-familiar one-sided Serb offensive with no sense of strategy and certainly no awareness of the rules of war. None of the men and boys by the embankment was armed. They were as much civilians as the terrified people on the carts and tractors who began to emerge from the high-walled compounds to escape the shelling.

Whole families sat on mattresses in overladen carts – the stuff of video footage on television screens across Europe – and puttered into the unknown. As we sheltered below the railway track, the wheel came off one cart. Its load lurched ominously. A woman with five blond children ran to shelter beside us while the men tried to fix the wheel in direct line of fire from the tank. 'We don't know where we're going. Wherever we can find a place, I suppose,' she said. They had spent the previous four days in nearby Glogovac and only came home three hours before the shelling resumed. 'Are you going to help us?' she asked, before accusing us as though we were Nato officials. 'You've been delaying and delaying for weeks. Do it fast. We have nowhere to go.'

Sitting on the embankment, Halim Dvorani said he no longer had a view of Nato. 'Sometimes they say yes, sometimes they say no.' He shrugged. The tanks that were shelling us were doing it from his garden, he said. He and his friends had fled three days ago.

Scenes similar to the one we saw in Bajince can be repeated all over Drenica, as families travel up and down as randomly as the tanks. In the last four days more than 25,000 people have fled their homes. Some have made sinister, hard-to-verify allegations that refugees were stopped by the Serbs and the men taken away. A few have talked of men in black masks executing people. But what we saw is more typical. It is not combat, nor even an offensive. It is shoddy, sporadic and pointless terror. The pro-independence guerrillas of the Kosovo Liberation Army are as helpless as the families they are allegedly trying to protect. Most of them, after all, are just farmers in second-hand uniforms. In the village of Likovc, the KLA's headquarters for the Drenica region, armed men were standing around uselessly. Dirt-spattered cars roared around the backroads with no visible purpose except reconnaissance to make sure which way to retreat. Smoke was rising from half a dozen houses just south of Srbica, where the Serbs have a large base. The thud of shells punched through the crisp spring air.

The village is already a ruin. The high school has no roof and few interior walls. The shops are smashed, the houses destroyed. Likovc was annihilated by the last Serb onslaught in August, as indeed were most of the villages being targeted yesterday. Hitting them makes no strategic sense. The people flee, then return when they can. This is not ethnic cleansing, since no Serbs take their place. It is simply a policy of fried and refried earth.

When the shelling of Bajince paused, we drove back to the asphalt road in Glogovac. In the town hundreds of people were milling around, most displaced from nearby villages. Mothers with babies queued outside a clinic, waiting for a medical delivery from the International Committee for the Red Cross. Half a mile up the main road north, we were forced to slow down by a line of plastic drinks crates filled with stones placed across the road. Beyond it we saw four tanks in a muddy yard. The men at the barricade who waved us to stop were not from the Yugoslav army. They had badges saying 'Police'.

They seemed relaxed and confident. Had there been any 'terrorist attacks', we asked. 'Yes,' said an officer, as two of the tanks moved up the road. 'There was some automatic fire and a grenade.' Why tank shelling was the appropriate response for a police force to make even if his claim was true we decided not to ask. ●

. . . .

3 April 1999

John Hooper

In the heart of Europe, a lost tribe fights for a loaf of bread

It was like a scene from Africa, not from Europe. But this was Europe in early spring and it was cold and it was raining. More than 20,000 ethnic Albanian refugees from Kosovo were by yesterday massed on the Macedonian border at Blace near the railway line on which they were deported by the Serbs. As you draw closer to the frontier checkpoint across the road, you realise that the vast, dark expanse in the valley below is made up of humanity.

There is movement. There is faintly discernible murmur, punctuated by the cries of children and the screams of babies. There are lights here and there from fires the refugees have lit, and a pall of smoke that hangs over the vast crowd. Among them are heavily pregnant women, mothers with babies, old men and women – all sitting in a field. Some were entering their fourth night in the open.

Increasingly desperate Macedonian officials pleaded with the West for help yesterday, warning that they were losing the fight to cope with the surging numbers of refugees flowing across the border.

By yesterday the Kosovans had been offered no shelter, no sanitation and seemingly precious little food. The only provisions I saw taken down from the road that snakes through the pass were half a dozen crates of bread and some bottles of mineral water.

When ambulance drivers tried to distribute bread, refugees scrambled for it, punching each other, and 10 or 20 people fought over a single piece. When loaves were thrown into the crowd from a cart pulled by a tractor, everyone raised their hands to catch them in a scene resembling mass prayer. And when the first small camp hospital opened, a steady stream of stretchers headed for it. Many patients arrived unconscious. Yet the only person I saw evacuated came out of the crowd on a stretcher, his arm dangling limp from under a blanket.

'I am a doctor. There are many doctors here. We can help but we need at least medicine,' said Arta, a woman in her mid-thirties.

Yannis Behrakis

Kosovar refugees fight over a loaf of bread distributed by Macedonian Red Cross ambulance workers

A 17-year-old boy called Arden said: 'We are young. We can last here for days. But there are too many children and old people here. Unless the Red Cross does something, they are going to die.'

There is growing anger here that the West has been sufficiently concerned for the Kosovan Albanians to go to war with Slobodan Milosevic, and yet the humanitarian aid to arrive has been woefully inadequate. In an emotional statement, deputy foreign minister Boris Trajanov said that only 300 tents had been sent from abroad so far. 'Our neighbouring countries – let alone Europe – have lost their sense of responsibility to accept even one refugee.'

In Albania, where 90,000 refugees were by yesterday camped along the northern border, similarly desperate notes were sounded. The Albanian government issued what it called a 'strong SOS' to the world. 'We hope that the international community will not leave Albania alone at this moment,' the information minister Musa Ulqini said. He added that the amount of international aid was far outweighed by the scale of the problem. 'The situation is becoming more and more dramatic and it requires urgent intervention.'

Nato now puts the number of ethnic Albanians forced to flee their homes in Kosovo in the past year at 634,000 – a third of the province's population. Thirty thousand of them have been expelled from the capital, Pristina, in the past 24 hours alone.

Jamie Shea, the Nato spokesman, said that at the Macedonian border there was a queue stretching back six miles, with 25,000 people in it waiting to cross the frontier. 'Many of them have died in that queue and others have had to cross a minefield in order to get there,' he said.

It is not just the international community that has been slow off the mark. The sole visible contribution from the Macedonian authorities has so far been to allow people to enter at a painfully sluggish rate. Apart from that, there was a detachment of riot police to hold back the multitude, and some soldiers posted at intervals around the shifting perimeter whose job it was to turn back reporters.

When I climbed down from the road into the meadows that fall away to the valley floor to talk to the people who were spread across them, I was turned back at gunpoint by a Macedonian soldier.

'The first thing that strikes you is – if you'll pardon the expression – the smell of shit,' said a Macedonian woman. She recounted how an old man held up a loaf of bread to her and said: 'This is what I have to feed a family of eight with.'

While the Kosovans wait for bread, others are profiting. An ethnic Albanian employed by a UN aid agency said that at the village of General Jankovic, on the other side of the border, Serbian paramilitaries were extorting money from the more prosperous refugees who were waiting to enter Macedonia by car. 'They go from car to car. They ask for not less than 500DM. Nobody knows what will happen if they don't give it to them.' ●

. . . .

25 March 1999

Leader
Defeating Milosevic

As the bombers go in, for the first time in the long evolution of the Balkan crisis the outside powers are directly confronting the author of that crisis. Always before the Serbian leader has distanced himself from the tragic situations which he has played such a large part in creating. Notoriously, he has presented himself as the man who can arrange a solution, and it has been a strategy that has worked, again and again. But this unnatural partnership came to an end at Rambouillet, when it became clear that Slobodan Milosevic would not hand Kosovo over to Western protectors, in spite of both serious threats and serious inducements. The Western countries, on their side, could not accept that Milosevic should keep Kosovo, given that his only way to do so is by violent methods. Now, with the bombing, the break is, or should be, total.

Milosevic's fall from power cannot be a formal aim of the Nato operation, which must properly confine itself to the attempt to limit suffering in Kosovo. Yet it is also true that if the objective of limiting that suffering is to be attained, then the broad aim must be a general settlement in former Yugoslavia, and such a settlement is hard now to envisage if Milosevic is still in power. The story that began in Kosovo 10 years ago, when Slobodan Milosevic began his career as a master manipulator of ethnic and national feeling in the former Yugoslavia, must be brought to an end. Because of the bombing, Kosovars are fleeing danger in the countryside only to meet equal, or worse, danger in the towns. While it is true that the Kosovo Albanians were already under attack before Nato took its decision to bomb, it is obviously possible that Nato strikes could make it immediately worse for them than it would otherwise have been. But the balance of risk depends crucially on our estimate of the Serbia over which Milosevic presides. Is it a society likely to fight ferociously and effectively for Kosovo? The indications are that Serbia, while lacking any real sense of self-criticism and feeling it is unfair that it is the butt of everybody's anger, is not in the sort of shape that would enable it to fight a hard war.

Young conscripts do not wish to go to Kosovo, and, when sent, desert in considerable numbers. Many regular officers are doubtful both about Milosevic's policies and about their capacity to carry them out. The most prominent of such officers, General Momcilo Perisic, was sacked by Milosevic last year precisely because he maintained that it was not the job of the armed forces to oppress the population. The special interior ministry troops, who are not part of the army, are better paid and enjoy perquisites such as looting.

But the morale of Serb forces in Kosovo depends on their military edge over the Kosovo Liberation Army and the helpless nature of the population at large. Once they have to face punishing attack from the air, that morale may suffer enormously. It is worth remembering that the capacity of the Bosnian Serb forces, who included regular elements from Serbia, was vastly overestimated by many Western military analysts. They warned the Croats that an attack on Krajina would be bloodily repulsed. In the event the Croats beat the Bosnian Serb forces in three days and suffered virtually no casualties. Certainly Kosovo is not Bosnia; the forces there are stronger, and it would be foolish to count on a swift collapse. Equally, it is permissible to hope that the Serb forces will turn out to be less formidable in reality than they look on paper.

Even if that is the case, we ought still to be making preparations now, discreet but serious, for the use of ground troops. Their entry into Kosovo too might not be such a dangerous business as the pessimists contend. Throughout the Yugoslav wars of succession, it has been a persistent Western mistake to overestimate Serbian strength and to argue that Milosevic was a man with whom we had to do business. While accepting that Nato is taking serious risks, we ought also to bear in mind that Milosevic is a man whose time has passed and that Serbia is a weak society, in large part because of his foolish and criminal leadership. ●

. . . .

15 June 1999

John Hooper
Near anarchy

L ounging beneath a spreading medlar tree, bowls of fruit in front of him and three of the Kosovo Liberation Army's guerrillas behind, Rexha Ekrem – 'Commander Drini' – bristled when asked how he would react to a particular 'command' from Nato.

'When you say that someone is commanding someone else to do something, it does not sound so good to the other person,' he said.

Just hours earlier, uniformed KLA soldiers had made their first appearance on the streets of Prizren, apparently in defiance of what Nato claimed was an understanding with the guerrillas that they would remain in their positions until Serb forces had fully withdrawn.

Their arrival added another explosive ingredient to the cocktail that has made this the most tense of towns. Prizren has descended into near anarchy, barely two days into Nato's arrival here.

At least two people have died as German soldiers have struggled to assert their authority over angry ethnic Albanians, frightened ethnic Serbs, drunken and armed Yugoslav irregulars, and now an encroaching guerrilla army which thinks it, not Nato, should have responsibility for maintaining law and order.

Commander Drini, a member of the KLA's general headquarters, its top military body, himself noted that there were 17 Serb paramilitaries holed up in a block of flats just 400 yards from where we were sitting in the garden of a private house. 'They have said they will burn down the block before they leave,' he said. Earlier in the day, there had been a gunfight between ethnic Serbs and Albanians in the city. While he was speaking, wildly jubilant locals were letting off bursts of semi-automatic gunfire into the air.

German soldiers were checking out firing positions in the Theranda Hotel, where many of the foreign correspondents are based, after reports that snipers had been spotted on the hill opposite the hotel. A crowd outside the hotel was meanwhile celebrating what, in effect, was the ethnic self-cleansing of Prizren. Earlier, in a convoy of more than 300 cars, virtually the whole of its Serb population had fled, terrified of reprisals by the KLA once their own troops and police had withdrawn.

The independent Serb news agency Beta, quoting eyewitnesses, said six KLA gunmen intercepted a column of Serbs leaving the village of Kojlovica, three miles north of Pristina, yesterday evening and shot dead two brothers and another man. In Pristina, it said, a Serb employee of Radio Pristina was shot dead in front of his home and three other Serbs were abducted.

The perceived need to protect Yugoslavia's latest tide of refugees goes some way to explaining the checkpoints still manned by Serb regular and irregular forces on roads leading round and out of the city. By tonight this town is supposed to be fully under Nato control, but yesterday it certainly did not look like it.

Yesterday morning, a brief journey through the suburbs from north to west took me past three such controls, though none of the Serbs manning the checkpoints tried to stop the vehicle in which I was travelling. Your chances of being detained, however, are entirely random.

'The situation is very tense. There are a lot of armed Serbs in a very aggressive state of mind. They have, after all, lost,' said Lieutenant-Commander Hans-Christian Klasing of the German contingent in K-For.

Among the checkpoints set up by paramilitaries was one on the route back to the Albanian border and the Kukes area, where some 125,000 refugees are waiting to return to their homes. At the frontier crossing of Morina itself, the KLA was reported to have entirely taken control, presenting another direct challenge to Nato.

'We do not have the capability to patrol the roads and there are a lot of regular and irregular units still around,' said Lieutenant-Commander Klasing. 'We cannot guarantee security.'

The initially modest German contingent yesterday grew to 2,000 men. It ought soon to be in a position to extend its grip beyond the city, especially since the deadline for the Serb withdrawal runs out at midnight tonight. But the appearance of the KLA means that Nato is faced with a new variant on the perilous theme of competing military units.

The first KLA checkpoints appeared in Prizren early yesterday afternoon. Eight guerrillas, some in camouflage fatigues, others wearing the KLA's distinctive, all-black battle dress, were stopping vehicles in a street near Commander Drini's new HQ. He claimed yesterday: 'We control the main part of the city and we are in contact with K-For. We agreed that we will not [cause any] incident with the Serb forces who are now in town and in a very short time will be out.'

That undertaking, by itself, will be welcome to Nato. But the commander signalled that the KLA would begin immediately to play the role it has long seen for itself — as the main security force of the new Kosovo. He said the KLA intended to deal with 'criminals, people who want to make a profit [from the disorders]'. And he said the guerrillas had already made 12 arrests elsewhere in Kosovo. 'There are no police . . . so the main forces that will do that are the KLA,' Commander Drini said. The guerrillas would not try to control the arterial roads of the city, he said, but only 'the suburbs — the places where international forces will not pass every day'.

He said his men had begun to take up positions in Prizren at 5 a.m. yesterday, but their first appearance in uniform had been when a car full of guerrillas turned up as a long convoy of Serb forces was leaving the city in the morning.

It was immediately besieged by members of a crowd that had been stoning and cursing the departing paramilitaries.

It had the paradoxical effect of defusing a potentially very ugly situation. German soldiers were having difficulty holding back the enraged onlookers. Most were grouped around a car which the night before had been used in an apparent suicide grenade attack on the Theranda Hotel. One man was shot dead and another fatally wounded in the attempt. All morning, the car had remained outside the hotel, its tyres shot out, the dead man inside, and two lines of blood running from the sill to the base of the passenger door. In the furious confusion, the car was buffeted and the boot flew open to reveal a heavy machine gun that was pounced on by members of the crowd before the Germans could intervene.

Earlier, as Prizren's civilian population fled, onlookers had chanted 'thieves, thieves'. Ethnic Albanians have reported extensive looting by Serbs in the dying days of the conflict. Twice, men who said they had seen their cars among those being driven from the city, tried to burst through the lines of German soldiers.

'I don't think [the Serbs] can live here any more. My neighbour next door was brought up with me,' Prizren householder Sedat Sheqagi said. 'We speak the same language – Turkish. But he's gone too.' ●

· ·

27 March 1999

Martin Woollacott
The Serbs don't appreciate the force against them

When war knocks at the door, the most understandable question of all is 'Why?' But it can also be one of the most obtuse. Why bomb us, say the citizens of Belgrade, in their minds seemingly not even a fleeting vision of the serial battering of Sarajevo, the destruction of Vukovar, or the torching of villages in Kosovo. No good saying Milosevic keeps such images off the television screen. He does, yet any Serb who cares to find out knows the horrors for which Serbs have been responsible these last eight years.

The question the people of Belgrade might better ask, since almost everybody else in former Yugoslavia has suffered far more than they, is '*Why not* us?' In fact, they are still more or less inviolate. The bombing of Serbia is being orchestrated with painstaking care to avoid the civilian casualties which Serb forces, when they were waging war in Croatia and Bosnia, quite deliberately inflicted. As for Belgrade, its residents have more to worry about from burglars than from Nato aircraft. In no way can the Nato campaign be likened to the bloody pounding of towns and cities by Serb forces in the past.

This is a waltz by comparison. Of course, there could be accidents and there could also soon come a time when Serbian soldiers in Kosovo will be systematically struck from the air. Then, young men who cannot be blamed for the terrible mess which Milosevic has made, will be killed and their deaths will be as tragic as any in the history of Balkan wars. But, even if this comes to pass, it will be a discriminate use of force that can be defended precisely because it is discriminate.

Critics of the bombing whose understanding of air power is stuck at the Second World War or Vietnam do not grasp that it can be used in new, less lethal, ways. Whether these ways prove effective or not, it is obvious that neither Goering or Harris is in charge of the air attack on Serbia. To say, as the critics do, that bombing will strengthen Milosevic is to misunderstand the issue. That the Serbs do not grasp, for example, the efforts now made to limit Serb casualties is part of the general problem of consciousness in that country. In their addled scheme, they are always the victims, never the victimisers. They have done vicious things, but do not seem to realise that it is they who have done them.

An individual might reasonably feel, given that Serbia is a dictatorship, that he or she has little direct responsibility. It is another matter to feel, as a majority of Serbs apparently do, that there is nothing for which to *be* responsible, that they were innocently going about their business when, suddenly, without cause or provocation, 15 nations suddenly attacked them. To pander to the false consciousness of many Serbs by avoiding anything that might reinforce that consciousness would be absurd. Instead, one ought to extend to Serbs the courtesy of believing that they can *think* and ought in time to be able to puzzle out how they have brought themselves to the point where Kosovo Albanians can no longer accept any political association with them.

If the 'Why?' of the Serbs deserves a dusty answer, that is also true for another kind of 'Why?' raised in Western countries. The same tendency to absolve themselves displayed by the Serbs is also shown by people in those nations. It is a peculiar characteristic of democratic societies to create situations which governments are unable to address through logical policies, and then to rage against the resulting illogicality as though it arose solely from the stupidity of their leaders.

So it is with the wearily circular argument over ground troops for Kosovo. Of course it would be better if there were already in existence an adequate force of soldiers ready to move into Kosovo and able to deal with the Serbian resistance they might meet. Indeed, had such a force existed, Milosevic might never have embarked on the latest aggression in Kosovo, and we might not now be bombing. But one of the reasons the soldiers are not there is that Western electorates would have punished any politician who tried to put forces there, or at least the politicians believe they would have been so punished. It is certain that the American electorate would have punished Clinton, and thus prevented him from making the more limited military commitment which he has been able to offer and without which there would have been no Nato action at all. The West's dismal routine for these things is that in order to achieve the policies that would have prevented disaster we first must have the disaster.

The disaster in this case is the intensification of attacks on Kosovo Albanians that may now be taking place. It is not certain that air action will fail to inhibit these attacks, but it might well fail to do so. There would then be difficult choices. One would be to create that invasion force, justifying it to Western publics by the slaughter going on, and use it when ready. A lesser but still hard option would be to set up a safe zone for hundreds of thousands of refugees and try to manage the inevitable cross-border guerrilla conflict. The most risky choice is already hovering in the background, which is to scale down our demands on Milosevic to a mere halt of his operations in Kosovo, in return for which the bombing would be suspended. In theory, the threat of its resumption could then be used as a lever to manoeuvre him into, first, withdrawals and then acceptance of a Nato force.

In practice, resuming a bombing campaign is much harder than starting one. The Russians and other friends of Serbia would instantly jump in to declare that it was all over and Milosevic would probably be smart enough to act with special restraint while avoiding real concessions. We might once again find ourselves colluding with him, as we have done so often before. That would be to sell out Kosovo in order to 'save' it.

Richard Holbrooke said of Bosnia in a memorandum to candidate Clinton in 1992: 'Doing nothing now risks a far greater and more costly involvement later' – a sentiment equally valid for Kosovo. Much later, Holbrooke was to declare: 'Give us bombs for peace.' It is an Orwellian juxtaposition. Yet the answer to 'Why?' is 'Because', and the 'Because' of Kosovo today includes all the prevarications, wrong decisions and wilful refusals to face the facts, over the years, of Western policy making in the Balkans. This is that more costly involvement which could have been avoided, and that is why the mistakes which led to it should not be repeated. ●

8 April 1999
Letters
Artists against the war

US foreign policy can be defined as follows: 'Kiss my arse or I'll kick your head in.' Milosevic refused to kiss America's arse so Clinton is kicking in the head of the Serbian people (not Milosevic himself) with catastrophic consequences for the Kosovans. Nato's action is ill thought out, ill considered, misjudged, miscalculated, disastrous. It is also totally illegal and probably represents the last nail in the coffin of the UN. The justification for the action –

'humanitarian considerations' – is clearly a very bad joke. It also demonstrates a profound hypocrisy on the part of the US and UK. Sanctions on Iraq – led by those countries – have killed nearly 1 million Iraqi children. That's genocide for you – in no uncertain terms.

Milosevic is undoubtedly ruthless and savage. So is Clinton. Clinton continues the vicious Reagan/Bush tradition with no trouble at all. But he combines that tradition with a shy grin and a beguiling Southern drawl. He can really be so sweet on television. Blair is the one who kisses Clinton's arse fervently and dreams that he is Mrs Thatcher. The level of intelligence employed in this whole enterprise is pathetic if not infantile. The US is now a highly dangerous force, totally out of control.

Harold Pinter ●

16 April 1999
Jonathan Steele
The victims' tales

The survivors of the air attack on Wednesday which turned their expulsion from Kosovo into a scene of carnage were agreed on one damning conclusion yesterday: the pilot of the plane which bombed their convoy must have seen that it was full of civilians.

Interviews with shocked and traumatised Kosovans, as they huddled in tents in a newly erected camp in the relative safety of Albania, told a terrible but consistent story. 'There was only one plane but it came down three times. On the first two runs the bombs dropped at the side of the road but the third one hit our tractor and the trailer. It was uncovered and loaded with people. My father was killed,' said Nexhde Cela, a dark-haired 15-year-old. He had a bloody scar on his right cheek.

As the finger of suspicion pointed increasingly towards a Nato pilot, the only crumb of comfort for the alliance was the deportees' unwillingness to blame it. None of the deportees said the aircraft, which made three low-level passes over their convoy of tractors, cars and exhausted pedestrians, was a Nato plane.

Those who were ready to hazard a guess as to its identity said it was Serb. But none had solid evidence or claimed to have seen any markings which could have proved the plane's provenance. They could not recognise the aircraft type. The only basis for their claims that the plane was Serb was inference.

'It was flying very low, which Nato planes don't do. It couldn't have been Nato because it struck right at the convoy,' said Mihrije Dervishi, a middle-aged woman from Kastriod, a village in the Drenica region of central Kosovo. She did not want to think the unthinkable. 'I saw bodies without heads and others without legs, about seven or eight people at least. We did not want to stop but carried on towards the border.'

Nexhde Cela, the 15-year-old who saw his father blown to pieces, was making a brave attempt to remain calm as we spoke to him. As Italian medics treated scores of people for shock and minor wounds nearby, he stood outside a tent describing the tragedy quietly. But 10 minutes later we found him slumped on a tent floor, weeping beside his mother and grandmother. His mother had bandages on both hands. She parted his thick hair to show blood on his scalp.

A few feet away an elderly woman cradled a child in her lap. He was moaning and shrieking uncontrollably. He was terrified. His father had been blasted away in front of his eyes. The man, Ferhat Bajrami, from the village of Batusha, had been driving the second of the two tractors that bore the brunt. His widow, Xhevrike, was sobbing and her five other fatherless children sobbed with her. 'We thought of jumping out of the tractor and hiding when the plane came over. But there was no time,' she said, as she breast-fed her youngest child.

Wandering forlornly between the rows of tents, Sadik Rama, 84, had blood-stains on his coat and sweater. The explosion had pierced his eardrums. Like the Bajrami family, he had been riding on the second trailer. 'The plane bombed three times. It hit the orchards by the road the first two times. The third time it hit our tractor and trailer,' he said.

The tractor in front took the worst hit, sending an unknown number of people to their deaths. He could find no survivors from that trailer in the camp yesterday. Witnesses said Serb forces arrived shortly after the bombing and took the dead and severely injured away.

'Three died on our tractor, the driver, his sister and another man,' said Mr Rama. His account matched those of the other survivors on the second tractor. Apparently including some of the casualties from the first tractor, he added: 'Altogether I saw at least five dead, but I can't really describe it. I felt I was going out of my mind.'

Xhyle Hasani, a woman from Klodernica, was on a tractor behind those that were hit. As she passed the scene of the atrocity, she remembers hearing someone who had lost both legs screaming: 'Mother, don't leave me here.'

The attack happened as the convoy of several thousand people crossed a railway bridge near Landovica, about eight miles north of Prizren. The convoy included people from nearby villages in west Kosovo, as well as hundreds from the Drenica region who had been forced out of their homes at gunpoint in the now well-established pattern of ethnic cleansing by Serbs.

Two 18-year-old girls from Drenica provided one detail which might help Nato to explain the atrocity. Tanks and armoured personnel carriers escorted the convoy at front and back, they said. Luljeta Hasani and her friend, Shemsije Smakaj, said they also saw tanks hidden in destroyed houses along the road. 'Right after the attack, Serb soldiers came up and told us: "Look what Nato has done to you",' Luljeta recalled.

Hasan Hyseni, a middle-aged man, also said he had seen tanks hidden in houses shortly before the attack. A Nato plane had been trying to hit them, he recounted. Shortly afterwards the convoy was bombed by a plane which he insisted was Serb. But his version did not match the account of the vast majority of witnesses, who remembered seeing only one plane. ●

The engagement of Prince Edward and Sophie Rhys Jones

Arts

....

21 May 1999
Peter Bradshaw
King of the Hill

I t's here. Finally, *Notting Hill* is here.

Apart from *The Phantom Menace*, no other film has been so intensively promoted in advance. Sometimes it has seemed as if, with all the trailers, the press and the hype, it is possible to experience *Notting Hill* in its totality before seeing it. Perhaps we could have a 'live cam' website showing thousands of journalists writing articles about whether the real Notting Hill is different. I myself have written one of these, in which I was ungracious enough to note that the main difference is there are no black people in the celluloid *Notting Hill*, a film which is a teeny bit smug and snobbish about this frightfully smart bit of west London, while excluding the cosmopolitan and multiracial history on which its bohemian reputation is founded.

This makes it a more pallid movie than it might have been, but it would be snobbery of a different sort not to acknowledge the truth about *Notting Hill*: it is a thoroughly enjoyable, well-crafted, funny film – a buoyant romantic comedy about Hugh Grant, the diffident, floppy-haired bookshop owner, who, one day, accidentally bumps into the movie star, Julia Roberts, and begins an unlikely love affair.

Julia Roberts is really very good, better than she has ever been. Her credentials as a famous beauty are presented at the top of the show, in a collage sequence of premiere attendances and photo-ops set to Elvis Costello's ecstatic version of Charles Aznavour's 'She'; and she performs with a humanity and humour quite absent from, say, the gruesome *My Best Friend's Wedding*.

Despite the rumoured on-set *froideur* between Julia and Hugh, on screen they establish a workable chemistry from the outset, and the climactic scene in which Roberts declares her love for Hugh, begging him to think of her as 'just a girl', is carried off with affecting charm.

Julia makes Hugh look . . . well . . . not wooden exactly, because he is a natural comic performer of intelligence and style (qualities perhaps best on show in John Duigan's *Sirens*), but his emotional reticence is bound to be outshone by the glossy sheen of Julia, hogging the limelight with her sassiness and tears and generally glittering with celebrity *effect*.

I am thrilled that Hugh is still wearing glasses in this film. In *Four Weddings*, he was sporting a clunky, heavy-framed pair which he must have had since prep school – the sort of specs that look as though they really ought to be repaired with Sellotape. Now he wears discreet, grown-up spectacles with faintly oval frames – a pair he needs in order to watch Julia on telly or at the cinema, a pair he panics over not being able to find on his way out of the house. No one has ever used glasses to convey lovable vulnerability more convincingly than Hugh Grant. Am I the only person to have noticed the most heartbreaking detail of his police ID photo after the Divine Brown débâcle: those very same glasses, hooked miserably in the collar of his T-shirt because there was nowhere else to put them?

But whatever Hugh and Julia have in the film, they owe to Richard Curtis, who has given the lie to the Hollywood adage about the actress so stupid she went to bed with the writer. He is a writer who, remarkably, and almost uniquely, is at the very top of the status food-chain in his films. Perhaps only Nora Ephron has comparable clout. His success shows there is no law that says commercial movies have to be revamped and script-doctored by a committee of dunces so whatever flavour they once had is cooked out of them. Mr Curtis is unashamedly a writer with a strong, personal style and, by virtue of diligent crafting under the editorial eye of his wife, Emma Freud, produces witty, literate scripts with proper gags, including one about Pandora's Box which got a big laugh from me, and for which I suggest at least a couple of dozen Hail Marys.

Notting Hill might seem like a formulaic reworking of an old theme – the sexy culture clash of innocence and experience, with a Yank and a Brit, was what Curtis gave us in *Four Weddings* and, further back, before he'd got the nationality and sex roles right, in *The Tall Guy*. But so what? Curtis has sitcom training: it is his instinct to produce successive episodes of a situation replete with comic possibilities.

I don't have a problem with that. *Notting Hill* is a likeable, seductive film which also boasts a strong supporting cast, including Richard Bonneville, Gina McKee, James Dreyfus and Tim McInnerny, and an outrageous scene-stealer from Rhys (*Twin Town*) Ifans as the 'masturbating Welshman' sharing Hugh's house.

Notting Hill is funny. And I liked it. ●

. . . .

19 May 1999

Martin Kettle
Gimme a C please, PM

Back in his soldiering days, Israel's newly elected prime minister, Ehud Barak, had an unusual way of calming his nerves after one of those daring military missions of which so much has been written in recent days; he would sit down at home and play Beethoven on his piano.

Somehow, it is a deeply reassuring image. A prime minister who can play Beethoven is surely a prime minister to rely on. After all, it is hard to imagine Binyamin Netanyahu playing 'The Moonlight Sonata'.

Music in a political leader has long been recognised as a good sign of other achievements. 'If the King loves music,' said the Chinese writer Meng-Tzu more than 2,000 years ago, 'there is little wrong in the land.' If Israel's new leader can dash off a sonata to soothe his mind, then surely great things are possible in the peace process.

Not all political leaders would agree with this optimistic view. Lenin, who took a strict line about more things than just Beethoven sonatas, once said: 'I know nothing more beautiful than the Appassionata. I could hear it every day.' Every time he heard it, Lenin told Maxim Gorky, he was moved with wonder at what human beings could accomplish. 'But I cannot listen to music often, it affects my nerves,' Lenin continued impatiently. 'I want to say amiable stupidities and stroke the heads of the people who can create such beauty in a filthy hell.' Perhaps Lenin should have stuck to Beethoven too.

With 10 years of serious study on his instrument to rely on, the new Israeli leader is apparently an accomplished pianist. Though he remains a private man in many things, Barak can sometimes be persuaded to play in public. When he does so, they say, he is very good indeed. Even concert standard.

This makes him one of a select band of world leaders with a more than passing musical talent. Tony Blair, ex-lead vocalist of the Ugly Rumours, is the first British prime minister to bring his electric guitar into Downing Street, though he has not chosen to play it in public. Bill Clinton has kept his sax zipped up in recent years too, but he still blows wild in private sometimes. And Clinton is good enough for a recording to have been made of a session he once played on a visit with Vaclav Havel to a Prague bar. Maybe someone will now write some sax, piano and guitar arrangements for the Three Leaders. If the trio needs a drummer, then they could perhaps persuade Tipper Gore, the wife of Clinton's vice-president, to resume her one-time sideline career as drummer in an all-girl rock band called the Wildcats.

As usual, Shakespeare had it right. 'The man that hath no music in himself, nor is not mov'd with concord of sweet sounds, is fit for treasons, stratagems and spoils,' the Bard says in *The Merchant of Venice*. And then he adds: 'Let no such man be trusted.'

'Music was by far the best escape from my work,' recalled the veteran Labour politician Lord Healey yesterday. The former chancellor, who was more than a little mistrusted by some in his day, regularly stroked the ivories in what was something of a golden age for political pianists.

Those musical contemporaries included Edward Heath, who was an organ scholar at Oxford in the 1930s and who had his Steinway installed in Downing Street when he won the 1970 general election. Heath was by far the most talented and trained musician to rise to the premiership, and he regularly entertained musicians such as Mstislav Rostropovich at No. 10 during his four-year tenure.

The Heath–Healey years were also the years of Germany's most musical leader of modern times, the former chancellor Helmut Schmidt. An organist like Heath,

Schmidt was an excellent pianist. Shortly after he left office, he became the only world leader of the modern era to make a recording, playing the third piano in a commercial recording of Mozart's triple piano concerto.

Heath made recordings of Elgar as a conductor, and liked to play Bach. Bach's preludes and fugues were also Lord Healey's favourite way of putting a sterling crisis or a difficult meeting of the Labour national executive out of his mind, he says.

Lord Healey has often told interviewers that it is important for a political leader to have what he calls a 'hinterland', and music has recurrently provided just such an escape from the pressures of political life. Apart from Heath and Blair, few British prime ministers have been amateur musicians. Neither John Major nor Margaret Thatcher ever learned an instrument. Jim Callaghan could at least sing in tune but one must go back to Balfour, probably the nicest prime minister before Blair, to find another British leader with a taste for music.

Likewise in the United States. Before Clinton brought the saxophone to the White House, the American presidency could boast few amateur musicians. Perhaps the oddest exception was Richard Nixon, who liked to play the piano a little, and even played briefly at his daughter Julie's White House wedding.

Possibly the best musician to occupy the White House was Harry Truman. He could play the piano well, and would often entertain visitors during his presidency. Chopin and Mozart were his favourites, but he also liked to play waltzes and American songs.

Few leaders have managed to combine leadership and music to such a degree as Frederick the Great of Prussia. In addition to waging war throughout Europe and bringing his emerging state into the heart of European politics, 'Old Fritz' was a talented flautist who used to play every evening after dinner and composed several pieces for his instrument, including flute concertos which are often played to this day.

Though some politicians turn to music, very few musicians have made the journey in the opposite direction. The great exception was the Polish pianist Ignace Jan Paderewski, who was a professor of piano at the Warsaw Conservatory by the age of 18 and who enjoyed a fabulous international career as a concert virtuoso starting in the 1880s. During the First World War, Paderewski emerged as the focus of Polish national aspirations. At the Versailles conference of 1919, he led the delegation which successfully secured the rebirth of his nation, and became premier and foreign minister of the new Polish republic. Though he remained in power for only 10 months, Paderewski has a genuine claim to be regarded as the father of twentieth-century Poland.

Ehud Barak is no Paderewski, nor is Lord Healey. But the former Labour chancellor maintains that music is the best of the arts for a modern statesman and political leader to cultivate. 'It is the most effective way of getting clear of the world of events,' he says. 'I felt that it put my mind in order.' ●

9 March 1999
Dan Glaister
Stanley's finished

On Saturday afternoon, just 12 hours before he died, Stanley Kubrick was his usual, expansive self. Sitting in his famously private home in Hertfordshire, surrounded by all the trappings of the nerd, Kubrick was engaged in a surprisingly mundane activity: the workaholic director was glued to the television, watching the Ireland–England rugby match.

Proving that he could engage in more than one activity at a time, Kubrick was also on the telephone to an old friend and colleague. While the two were supposed to be discussing the poster design for his latest film, *Eyes Wide Shut*, Kubrick was providing a running commentary on the match, obsessing on the England scrum-half Kieran Bracken.

'I kept saying: "Stanley, will you go away? I'm trying to watch the rugby too."' Julian Senior, the grandly titled senior vice-president of European advertising and publicity at Warner Bros, the studio behind *Eyes Wide Shut* and every other Kubrick film for the last 19 years, was trying to make the most of his weekend.

Kubrick, however, was having none of it. 'Stanley did not understand what weekends were,' says Senior. 'His work was his life. He was excited about the release of the film. He wanted to talk about the publicity schedule. It was the same voice we'd known for the last 20 years – young, vibrant. He'd had flu a couple of weeks ago but apart from that there was no hint of illness. He said: "Let's think about what we're going to do. Get me a list of the top four or five magazines and the best writers. We'll do a few interviews."'

Kubrick had finished an 80-second trailer for the film, to be shown tomorrow before an audience of 3,000 polyester suits at ShoWest, the forum for American exhibitors. But it is not just the polyester suits who are excited at the prospect. With speculation about the film at fever pitch before the director's death, the rumour mill has gone into overdrive since he died in his sleep at 4 o'clock on Sunday morning.

With a 15-month shoot, and over two and a half years since the project got under way, *Eyes Wide Shut* had become one of the longest-ever film productions. The question 'Will he ever finish it?' had moved from humour to anxiety. On his death, the fans were sent into a state of panic, clogging up Internet chat lines with speculation about what the studio might do to the master's film. With Kubrick reportedly having a clause written into his contract that a film could be released only when he said so and only in the final version he submitted, there were fears that *Eyes Wide Shut* would never be shown on a public screen.

Like *A Clockwork Orange*, which Kubrick withdrew from exhibition in the UK following the outcry over its effects on an impressionable youth and an even more impressionable establishment, it seemed that an unfinished *Eyes Wide Shut* might never be released. After all, could anyone imagine the ultimate perfectionist allowing anyone else to finish his film, even from the grave?

There have been several Kubrick projects over the years that have not seen the light of day, including an Eastern European project and the rumoured – everything was rumour with Kubrick – film before *Eyes Wide Shut*, titled *AI*, shorthand for 'artificial intelligence'. Film-makers have an unhappy habit of dying mid-production, and many have left treatments behind which have been shot by their successors. Seen the new Kurasawa movie? Not yet, it is only just going into production. A year after the Japanese director died, his director of photography is shooting a script left behind by the master. And the habit of bringing in a director to finish someone else's work – usually because of a falling-out with a studio or a star – led to Kubrick's decision to leave Hollywood and settle in England. Brought in to take over from director Anthony Mann on *Spartacus*, Kubrick was convinced by his experiences with star and producer Kirk Douglas that the only way to play the Hollywood game was on his own terms.

But for once the paranoia surrounding Kubrick was misplaced. 'The film that will be released is Stanley's film,' says Senior. 'The film is over, the trailer is done, he was working on the poster artwork. We'd even talked about which stills to use for the publicity.' Then Senior, with his smooth, comforting Bob Monkhouse voice, chooses a strange turn of phrase: 'Stanley finished with his life less than a week after he finished with his movie. If you'd stood back and written it, people would have laughed.'

The polyester suits behind the American movie industry will not be the first to see the finished film. That privilege came on Tuesday last week, to an audience of just four. In the screening room at Warner's New York headquarters on Fifth Avenue were the company's two co-chairmen, Terry Semel and Robert Daley, and the film's two co-stars, Tom Cruise and Nicole Kidman. None of them, it is safe to say, was wearing a polyester suit.

The screening was an emotional affair. It was held in New York to suit the stars. Cruise was in New York with his wife before flying to Australia to begin work on the sequel to *Mission: Impossible*. Kidman was nursing a sore throat, the product of her Broadway run in David Hare's *The Blue Room*, which transferred from London earlier this year.

'Nicole and Tom were both weeping,' says a source at the company. 'Nicole kept saying, "He was like a father figure to me."'

The film, the sole print to date, was taken by a member of Warner's staff from Kubrick's home near London to New York and then flown back the same day. As ever with Kubrick, secrecy was everything. Before and during filming, Warner's executives were reportedly shown the script in a London hotel. Kubrick would not allow them to take the screenplay, which was amended every day by Kubrick, out of the room. It even seems unlikely that co-writer Frederic Raphael knows too much about the final shape of the film.

But now, with a July release fixed for the US and the rest of the world pencilled in, starting with the UK in late August, tongues are looser about the film. The 70-year-old director reportedly called it his best film, and Warner's – or at least the two people at Warner's to have seen the film – say they are delighted with the finished result. Loosely based on the 1926 short novel *Dream Story* by Arthur Schnitzler, the German writer whose version of *La Ronde* provided the basis for Hare's *The Blue Room*, *Eyes Wide Shut* is the story of two sexual psychologists whose work crosses over into their personal lives. According to Kubrick, in a rare comment about the film: 'It explores the sexual ambivalence of a happy marriage and tries to equate the importance of sexual dreams and might-have-beens with reality.'

The film moves the action from Vienna to present-day New York. Shot at Pinewood and laboriously reconstructed locations around England, it goes from a masked ball featuring hundreds of extras to a smaller masked orgy. Cruise's character is called Bill. Other than that, and some of the details of the location shooting, little is known.

'The couple's fantasies intersect and interact with their real lives,' says Senior, who has seen 'most of the film. Possibly that's the thread that connects it to his other films. Stanley had this thing about trying to control the uncontrollable. HAL, the computer in *2001*, is supposed to deliver total control but becomes uncontrollable; the aversion therapy in *A Clockwork Orange* produces a quite different result to that which was intended; in *Full Metal Jacket*, the soldiers being turned into killing machines for the Vietnam War turn in upon themselves.' And now we have Cruise and Kidman playing a Manhattan couple charged with helping other people through their sexual dysfunction who find their dreams seeping into their reality – again, the theory cannot cope with the reality.

If the subject matter sounds difficult – and films about sexual dysfunction have a habit of bombing commercially – Warner's is confident about the prospects for *Eyes Wide Shut*. 'It will have enormous appeal,' says Senior. 'Hollywood's favourite couple in a movie about sexual obsession and jealousy. One of the things I was due to talk with him about on Sunday was the Venice Film Festival. They'd already approached us and if somebody says we want to open the festival with Stanley Kubrick's film as a tribute, it would be churlish to turn them down.'

And the rumours that there is still work to be done on the film? Kubrick would almost certainly have continued to tinker. He was known to attend cinemas screening his films to check that the projection and sound levels were right. Perfectionist? As one collaborator said: 'There's nothing wrong with being a perfectionist.' Tom Cruise, however, might disagree, and reportedly asserted his influence as a star during the filming of *Eyes Wide Shut*, telling the director that he probably had enough to work with when asked to do his fiftieth take walking through a door. Kubrick ended up with a million feet of film, which he has managed to edit down to two hours 21 minutes, the same length as *2001*.

Following the New York screening, work will continue as normal, preparing the film for certification in the US, and then dubbing it for foreign territories, a process Kubrick would normally have worked on himself together with a translator. 'Now the movie comes back, Stanley goes through the normal routine he always does,' says Senior. 'Does? Did . . . did – the word is what Stanley did.' •

. . . .

21 January 1999

Derek Malcolm
Best of the West

I was tempted to tuck away half a dozen Westerns inside my 100 best movies, as I believe that almost everything the American cinema has to say has been said within this genre. And if I allowed my heart to rule my head, there would be half a dozen Howard Hawks movies in there too.

Westerns seem to best express the myths of American history and the often noble, sometimes absurd, fantasies Americans have about themselves. As for Hawks, he was a master of this and most other genres – an intuitive director whose extraordinary subtleties could make even a piece of pure entertainment like *Bringing Up Baby* into a blazing classic.

Combine my love of Westerns and my admiration for Hawks and you have *Rio Bravo*, a great film and the most personal one he ever made.

I have to tell you, with some shame, that when the film arrived in Britain in 1959, the *Guardian*'s review (not mine) read as follows: 'Rio Bravo is a typical Western of this age of the long-winded, large screen. It lasts for 140 minutes and it contains enough inventiveness to make do for about half that time. It is, in fact, a soporific blockbuster. John Wayne leads its cast.' Thus we disposed of a piece of flawless story-telling, admirable in its basic simplicity and outward lack of guile, and of a great and selfless performance from Wayne, who helped Dean Martin give the best portrait of his career.

Hawks always said that he made *Rio Bravo* as a riposte to *High Noon*, in which Gary Cooper's sheriff went 'running around the town like a chicken with his head off asking for help'. That wasn't his idea of a Western hero. To him, it was politically incorrect and morally reprehensible.

Sheriff Wayne in *Rio Bravo* needs as much help as Cooper when he imprisons a murderer and gunmen lay siege to the jail. But he gets it by being his flawed, sometimes comic but fundamentally decent and honourable self. This makes even the drunken deputy (Martin) stand up and fight, and the odd partnership it engenders teaches the sheriff to temper his own insistence on independence. Beside the sheriff and the drunk are Ricky Nelson's young gun, Angie Dickinson's

Arts

lady gambler, with whom Wayne constantly spars, and Walter Brennan's toothless veteran.

In all this, *Rio Bravo* is a deeply traditional Western. The way it is worked out, however, is anything but that. It's a long film with a pretty slim plot and lots of comic diversions, like Wayne modelling a pair of bloomers for Dickinson, who tells him: 'Those things have possibilities, sheriff. But not on you.' So firmly is the whole thing based on character, however, that you come out of it feeling you've seen something special about humanity in general. It's a feel-good movie that for once rings true, even as you admit a certain strand of orthodoxy, even cliché, that is seen in Westerns time and time again. It's also quite exciting, because, although you know things will probably turn out OK, Hawks never lets you be quite sure of it. Someone's going to have to die.

Watching the film, you won't see any great vistas like John Ford's Monument Valley or backdrops like Budd Boetticher's Lonesome Pine nestling in the Alabama Hills. This is just a scrubby little township with a seedy hotel, a saloon, a jail and nothing whatsoever to commend it, bar the characters who live there.

If Ford had made the picture, it wouldn't have been possible to avoid a larger cast and more of an idea of the community at large. If Anthony Mann, another great master of the Western, had done it, there would have been more directorial philosophising and the psychology would have been less basic. What we get from Hawks is austerity, rigour and intensity.

Of course, there are a dozen different ways to make Westerns, and Hawks's way in *Rio Bravo* lacks the epic nature of *Red River*, the greater flamboyance (and Mitchum) of *El Dorado* and the sheer if nonsensical fun of *Hatari!*. But it's a better film than any of them because of its concentration and the deep feelings that Hawks clearly poured into it.

They say he modelled the Wayne character on himself – but if so, it was surely unconsciously. What he did do was allow a great script by Jules Furthman and Leigh Brackett to flow as naturally as possible, while burnishing it with bits and pieces of extemporising, right down to what the actors wore, like Martin's soiled sweatshirt and dirty old hat.

When Hawks showed Jack Warner the film, Warner said: 'We hired Dean Martin. When's he going to be in this picture?' Hawks replied: 'He's the funny-looking guy in the old hat.' 'Holy smoke,' said Warner. 'Is that Dean Martin?' It was, and in a way it was his picture. ●

58 The Guardian Year '99

9 February 1999

Tony Harrison
Laureate's block

for Queen Elizabeth

I'm appalled to see newspapers use my name
as 'widely tipped' for a job I'd never seek.
Swans come in Domestic, Mute, and Tame
and no swan-upper's going to nick my beak.

I'm particularly vexed that it occurred
in those same Guardian *pages where I'd written*
on the abdication of King Charles III
in the hope of a republic in Great Britain.

I wrote the above last night but what comes next
I wrote the day that Ted Hughes, sadly, died
and to exit from the lists I've faxed the text
for inclusion in the Guardian *[op.ed side?]:*

No doubt inspired by the lunchtime news
the salesman, passing volumes by myself,
was selecting all the second-hand Ted Hughes
to move to the window from the poetry shelf.

A poet's death fills other poets with dread,
timor mortis like Dunbar's, and of the fate
of being remaindered, and not ever read,
but this bookshop window's got *Crow* laid in state,

with front cover showing now not just the spine.
At least they get your books out on display.
I'm doubting that they'll bother much with mine,
as I buy an old 4 volume Thomas Gray.

It was in this Stratford bookshop that I heard
Ted died, and needed my lover, stuck on stage
as Queen Elizabeth in *Richard III*,
to help me not to brood I'm near Ted's age.

While she ran the gauntlet of gut-curdling guile,
child murder, mayhem, lust for monarchy,
I walked by the swollen Avon for a while.
The plastic bag with Gray in banged my knee

The swans' feet were slapping on deep towpath mud.
They wouldn't venture on the Avon out of fear
of the overflowing river in full flood
and getting their necks wrung dragged into the weir.

While my lover had to do two *Richard III*s
I went to bed and read from front to back
all those four vols of Gray and found these words:
the saponaceous qualities of sack

in a letter that I think's worth perusal
especially by unversed journalists
who speculate which poet after Hughes'll
get a post Gray wouldn't credit still exists.

Though I could, because I've practised, paraphrase
in his *Elegy*'s quatrains if I so chose,
the following remarks of Thomas Gray's.
I'll quote them as he wrote them in plain prose:

Though I very well know the bland emollient saponaceous qualities of sack and silver, yet if any great man would say to me 'I make you rat-catcher to his Majesty, with a salary of £300 a year and two butts of the best Malaga; and though it has been usual to catch a mouse or two, for form's sake, in public once a year, yet to you, sir, we shall not stand upon these things' I cannot say I should jump at it, nay, if they would drop the very name of the office, and call me Sinecure to the King's Majesty, I should still feel a little awkward, and think everybody I saw smelt a rat about me . . . The office itself has always humbled the professor hitherto (even in an age when kings were somebody), if he were a poor writer by making him more conspicuous, and if he were a good one by setting him at war with the little fry of his own profession, for there are poets little enough to envy even a poet laureat.

That's Gray 2 centuries and more ago
with sentiments I find quite close to my mine
And anyone who knew my work would know
which words of Thomas Gray I'd underline.

And the new rat-catcher to our present Queen,
who must have palace rodents sleek and fat,

though he/she washes after catches and keeps clean,
still sports retainer's raiment rank with rat.

There should be no successor to Ted Hughes.
'The saponaceous qualities of sack'
are purest poison if paid poets lose
their freedom as PM's or monarch's hack.

Nor should Prince Charles succeed our present queen
and spare us some toad's ode on coronation.
I'd like all suchlike odes there've ever been,
binned by a truly democratic nation.

Are there poets who are monarchists who'll try?
They might well get a Garter for their guts.
You'll never hear me heave an envious sigh.
I'd sooner be a free man with no butts,

free not to have to puff some prince's wedding,
free to say up yours to Tony Blair,
to write an ode on Charles I's beheading
and regret the restoration of his heir,

(I'd hoped last week that would-be royal hacks
that self-promoting sycophantic flock
would whet their talents on the headsman's axe
but it seems like a bad case of laureate's block –

30th January 1649
though it's hard to use the date for self-promotion
the anniversary's gone by with not a line
from toadies like Di-deifying Motion.)

free to write what I think should be written
free to scatter scorn on Number 10,
free to blast and bollock Blairite Britain,
[and alliterate outrageously like then!]

free to write exactly as I choose
and heed both Thomas Gray's and Milton's ghost.
It's not for Laureate poems we'll miss Ted Hughes
nor any past pretender to the post.

And free, once Richard's off and Richmond's on
the battered throne with hacked crown on his head
and widowed women wan and woebegone,
when my unpainted queen's back in our bed,

to kiss my dedication, hot with scenes
of regal wrath, rage, wrangle, kiss away,
as we kiss equals and do not kiss queens,
the bitter taste of Shakespeare's bloody play.

A poet's death fills other poets with dread,
a king's death kings, but under my duvet
is Queen Elizabeth, and off our bed
slide these quatrains and all of Thomas Gray. •

8 June 1999
Michael Ellison
Poet in a prize position

Paul Muldoon has been having a good time of it lately. His two-week-old son, Asher, is thriving; he has been granted one of the highest honours in the English literary firmament; and no one has made him the target of a stream of invective. Not bad going for a poet.

What's more, he didn't really need to make any great effort to secure the position of Professor of Poetry at Oxford. He wasn't even sure that he wanted the job. After all, Muldoon has it made already. The attraction of another academic title is limited when you are the Howard G. B. Clark Professor in Humanities at Ivy League Princeton University, New Jersey.

He has been described as attracting more imitators than any poet since Auden and has won prizes and accolades in Ireland, the United Kingdom and America – as well as having written plays for the stage and television and edited and translated poetry collections.

In short, he has more honours than you could wave a bag of shite at. Ah, yes – while Andrew Motion was being abused in such terms for having the temerity to accept his appointment as Poet Laureate, the cultural agent provocateur Tom Paulin was making it his business to see to it that his friend Muldoon won the other big job, the finally uncontested Oxford seat.

'There are aspects of the Oxford thing that I'm not too keen on,' says 47-year-old Muldoon, closing his eyes below a wild thatch that looks like it has not seen a brush since he was Seamus Heaney's student at Queen's University, Belfast. 'One was the very thing that was avoided – the "Muldoon is a bag of shite" tendency. Historically there's been a bit of a slagging match that has nothing to do with the quality of the people involved. People like a bit of a dogfight – not that I'm above it. This time I guess no one else was up to the hassle, though that didn't stop people from running in the past.'

Perhaps it's partly because the glittering prizes have always sought him out that Muldoon is able to regard them with a healthy disinterest. 'Do you really believe that people care very much about who the Poet Laureate is? The answer is no.'

Actually, there is at least one person who cares about the job of Poet Laureate – Paul Muldoon. As president of the Poetry Society he cared enough to suggest that the title should be awarded for a limited period rather than for life. The idea was taken up and Andrew Motion is there for 10 years. The American laureate is in position for three years and Muldoon believes that a short stint helps to maintain energy and enthusiasm.

'Ted Hughes was a great poet laureate and he was constantly derided for what he wrote. When Andrew got the job, somebody called me up and asked for a quote. I said: "He'll do a fine job." And the guy said: "You're the first one to say so." Actually, Andrew will be great. The people who say these things wouldn't even want the job, but if you're going to say them then it shouldn't be done anonymously. You've got to back it up.' He does not buy the line that bickering over prizes stimulates interest in art. 'It would be nice to think that people would go out and read Andrew Motion now, but I've serious doubts as to whether that will happen. Maybe a few will do it.'

I had the dubious pleasure once of marvelling at the poet Michael Horovitz, the late Allen Ginsberg at his side, discussing the intimacy of poetry and the relationship between the reader and the page. Then he had to blow it by suggesting that if only there were a weekly television programme called *Pick of the Poets*, modelled on *Top of the Pops*, poets would be every bit as popular as rock stars.

Muldoon has a more fundamental approach to the poetry problem. 'Poetry is something that happened to you at school – when some jerk of a teacher said you had to learn a poem and kicked your head in if you didn't. They say: "Eliot is a great poet but you wouldn't know that because you're just a moron. See this line? You might think you know what it means but you don't, you need me to show you."'

But he is optimistic about the form and believes that poetry is healthy, diverse and less dominated than before by a narrow consensus about big names. Muldoon, a man who laughs easily and has an endless curiosity, must deliver 15 lectures a year at Oxford over the next five years in return for an annual fee of £4,695. Clearly, he is concerned that his lectures should be something special.

'Filling football stadiums is not the norm for poets. It's not the norm for football. It is the norm for the Rolling Stones. Young people want to be rock stars and, let's face it, who wouldn't want to be a rock star? I've got a guitar in my basement; I'd love to be a rock star. My wife thinks I'm crazy. Why do you and I know all about Keith Richards but almost nothing about Keith Douglas [a soldier-poet who died in the Second World War]? The answer is that we've had such a great time listening to the Rolling Stones. The combination of words and music gets us. The grammar of a documentary movie [Muldoon is a former BBC Northern Ireland radio and TV producer] is very sophisticated. We know we are not seeing everything that was recorded and that it may not have been shot in that order. We understand the genre. When we look at *Spinal Tap*, the rock parody, we understand its allusiveness, what irony is. The thought of a poem having any impact is something we don't generally think very much about. Part of the problem is exposure, and sympathetic exposure.'

Muldoon could go on like this for ever. Let's say instead that you might have just read a preview of his first lecture as Professor of Poetry. •

13 February 1999

Michael Billington

Putting the screws on a prison opera

Brecht, you feel, would have loved it: *The Threepenny Opera*, with its vision of the bourgeoisie and criminals as mirror-images of each other, being performed by a mixture of professional singers and inmates in one of Her Majesty's prisons. What he might not have loved quite so much was the sudden industrial action that led to the cancellation of three of Pimlico Opera's five scheduled performances.

Pimlico have already staged *Sweeney Todd* in Wormwood Scrubs and *Guys and Dolls* in Wandsworth with great success. Wasfi Kani, their founder and outstanding musical director of this production, explains what happened: 'Six days before we were due to open, the local branch of the Prison Officers' Association withdrew its support. They refused to put in the time needed to escort visitors on and off the premises before the evening roll-call at 8.45. The inmates in the show, who had put in five weeks of hard rehearsal, were devastated. Many of them are in disgrace with their families. They had invited them to see the show partly to prove something about themselves and their creative potential. Pimlico Opera will also lose £10,000 in cancelled bookings.'

No one disputes that prison officers have a tough job. Graham Clark, ex-governor of Wandsworth Prison, also argues that many officers do a fantastic job in aiding recreational activities. But curtailing a production of a Brecht—

Weill musical is hardly likely to aid the association's dispute with the Home Office over pay and conditions.

One inside observer also alleges there is more to the dispute than meets the eye. The prison officers are predominantly white; many of the inmates in the production are black. 'The officers,' says one observer, 'simply didn't want it to succeed.'

But the work will go on. Sir Stephen Tumim, former Chief Inspector of Prisons and patron of Pimlico, says: 'I saw the show on Thursday with the governor of Winchester prison, who is keen on the idea of repeating it there. I also believe that if we are serious about rehabilitation, then theatre is much the best way to do it. It requires highly disciplined teamwork both front and back stage and it is something which prisoners can pursue on their release. It is the best of all the arts for this situation.'

Sir Stephen's point was proved by Emma Jenkins's production, which I saw with a small, invited audience in Downview, a medium-security training prison just outside Sutton where many of the 343 inmates are being held for drug-related offences. Despite being played in an echoing sports hall with shaky acoustics, the production itself had enormous brio. Professional actors and singers played many of the lead roles: outstandingly so in the case of David Antrobus's dapper, bowler-hatted Macheath and Arabella Nathan's wily Polly Peachum in baby-doll dress. But two inmates, Trevor Toussaint as the Narrator and Ricky Fearon as the Chief of Police, matched the pros in sheer force of personality. And other inmates were excellent as Peachum's army of beggars – one of them brandishing a sign saying 'Victim of police brutality' – and as the corrupt rozzers and members of Macheath's weapon-wielding gang.

The Brechtian ironies multiplied. Here were we, a small, invited middle-class audience, watching real-life offenders performing a parodic opera telling us that bourgeois and criminal values are interchangeable. The anthems were also rousingly sung, not least the one sardonically informing us 'What keeps a man alive is his capacity to steal and cheat.' But Brecht's ironic cynicism was, in a strange way, offset by the show's ensemble vigour. I came out of Downview moved by the event and seeing the force of Sir Stephen Tumim's argument: that theatre is a perfect way of instilling the idea that, in society at large, we are all dependent on each other. ●

16 January 1999

Lyn Gardner
The heart in the closet

t was about 11.15 on a brisk winter's morning just before Christmas that I thought I had a rare but unmistakable sighting of Tom Stoppard's heart. Stoppard's heart – or rather its absence in his work – has made him something of the Tin Man of British theatre. A playful dramatic exhibitionist, Stoppard has dazzled with his hallucinogenic trips on words and dizzying mix of acrobatic philosophy and philosophical gymnastics ever since he first burst on the scene with his play *Rosencrantz and Guildenstern are Dead* in 1966. But the plays have seldom had much connection with human emotions. For all their undoubted firework brilliance, there has been a certain lack.

John Osborne once spoke of his own plays as 'lessons in feeling'. Stoppard's might more accurately be described as lessons in thinking. You feel it is Stoppard himself speaking when one of the characters in Arcadia cries: 'It's wanting to know that makes us matter; otherwise we are going out the way we came in.'

Clever Tom – or Tomas Straussler, as he was called when he was born in Czechoslovakia 61 years ago – has always been very good at doing joined-up thinking. Over the past 30 years, playgoers have often found that, along with their ticket for the afternoon matinée, they have also bought a crash course in subjects as diverse as quantum mechanics, Marxist theory, landscape gardening, journalistic ethics, espionage, chaos theory and moral philosophy. But, as they stagger exhausted from the theatre three hours later, they are unlikely to be much the wiser about the conditions of the human heart. If plays reflect what it is like to be human, what do *The Real Inspector Hound* or *Travesties* – two of Stoppard's most glitteringly brilliant early plays – tell us about our own hearts, or about their writer's heart? Almost nothing.

As Stoppard himself has cheerfully admitted, he is not much interested in writing about people. No, it is ideas that fire Tom's foolery – that exquisite blend of seriousness and custard pies that is as uniquely Stoppardian as the menacing pause is Pinteresque. His plays are driven by concept, not character. He leaves it to the actors to provide a heart and soul and history for his characters. Which is not to say that he hasn't been happy to plunder history for ready-made characters: Shakespeare, Housman, James Joyce, Lenin, Tristan Tzara. Nobody is safe, not even fictional characters. Rosencrantz and Guildenstern had quite happily hung around as footnotes to dramatic history for 350 years before Stoppard came along.

Like all the very best playwrights, including Shakespeare, Stoppard is a magpie and a master thief. The only person he resolutely refuses to borrow from is himself. While most playwrights, at least in their early work, draw strongly

upon their own lives, Stoppard has made his a no-go area. This is the more odd
– and self-denying – considering he had a very dramatic early life, touched by
the great tragedies of the century.

'The events of my life are not in my work. I simply don't use my life. *The
Real Thing* was about a playwright, but the playwright was not me. My opinions
may filter through, but never my life.' He makes a small concession: 'As an
epigraph – and this doesn't interest me in the slightest – I can detect that, over
the years and the plays, there has been the loss of one skin or another, the
shedding of layers of protection.'

Why doesn't it interest you?

'It's an aspect of literary criticism in which I have no interest. The relationship
of a writer's life and work doesn't interest me.' He pauses. 'Do I really mean
that?' he wonders. As well he might. The new film for which he wrote the
screenplay, *Shakespeare in Love*, is precisely and entirely about the relationship
between the playwright's life and his work.

So there's nothing to be gained from knowing about your own life?

'I lack whatever it is that would make me self-analytical. I don't like reading
about my work. People send me books about my work – and I'll read anything,
even a sauce bottle – but that is the only kind of literature that I really can't
bear to read. I can't bring myself to open them. My lack of interest turns into
a positive.'

When he was younger, Stoppard was fond of describing himself as 'a bounced
Czech'. In his famous 1977 *New Yorker* profile of Stoppard, Ken Tynan argued
that the essential thing to remember about Stoppard is that he is an émigré.
Stoppard coolly bats this away ('Ken was a romantic about that – it fed into
his character'). He is equally dismissive, perhaps unjustifiably, of theories suggesting that the brilliance of his language, like that of Nabokov, Conrad and
Ionesco, derives from his being born into one language but writing in another.

Stoppard was born the second son of Eugene and Martha Straussler in Zlin,
Czechoslovakia, in July 1937. His father worked as a doctor for the Bata shoe
factory, a company that in 1938, fearing imminent invasion by Hitler, shipped
out to Singapore those employees who were Jews or had Jewish connections.

'My mother always made out that we were sent to Singapore because of the
Jewish grandparent, but we were Jewish by race. My mother didn't consider
herself Jewish, she wasn't a religious woman. I recently got hold of the employment records for the factory at Zlin from the 1930s and she'd put herself down
as a Catholic. Since the fall of Communism, I've started to meet people whose
existence I knew nothing about. A few years ago I was at a PEN conference,
and when I got back to my hotel in Prague there was a young man who had
been waiting for me for four hours. He was the son of one of my mother's
cousins. I discovered that my mother had two siblings I had known nothing
about and that one of them had died in a concentration camp.'

Singapore was supposed to be a safe haven. But in 1942 it fell to the Japanese. Stoppard, his elder brother, Peter, and his mother escaped to India. The boys' father had to stay behind with the rest of the men. For almost 60 years his fate has remained a mystery. But recently Stoppard was sent an article written by an elderly Bata employee who survived Singapore; he told how the men were put on a Japanese prison boat that was sunk. Along with many others, Stoppard's father survived to be put on a smaller vessel, which was also shot up. 'He died at sea, that's all I know.'

In India, Stoppard and his brother attended an English-speaking convent and, when their mother married Major Kenneth Stoppard, the boys accompanied the newlyweds to Britain in 1946. 'Very early on, I found a very satisfying affinity with all things English – the language, the landscape and the architecture,' says Stoppard, who received a typical minor English public-school education and who embraced all things English, including a new name, the eminently English Tom Stoppard. It is at this point – like Stoppard, but for different reasons – that I think Tynan was wrong when he decided that the key to Tom Stoppard is his being an émigré, an exile. Émigrés must come from somewhere else. Exile suggests a longing for something, a sense of loss for something known. But Stoppard has no sense of loss for Czechoslovakia. In fact, he has no sense of it at all. Not even a glimmer.

More curiously, although the family presumably spoke Czech for the first year or so of Stoppard's life, and a mixture of Czech and English in Singapore for four years thereafter, Stoppard says he can't remember a time when he spoke any language other than English. He has never had any desire to relearn his mother tongue.

Perhaps even more tellingly, he says he has never had any curiosity about his past. But surely he must have done as a child? Surely he must, at the very least, have wondered about what happened to his father? After all, he wasn't a baby when the family fled Singapore for India. He was five.

'No, I didn't wonder. I wasn't curious.'

Why not?

'I wasn't interested,' he says. 'When my mother came to England in 1946 with us and her new husband, she simply turned her back on the past. One of the reasons she buried the traces was that my stepfather wasn't sympathetic. She was a conforming woman and she deferred to his preference.'

Suddenly, I have this mental image of the Stoppard family all taking tea and being terribly English and diffident and nice with each other and just not mentioning it.

Stoppard's stepfather and mother are now both dead; his mother – whom he describes as 'delightful but highly nervous' – died just over two years ago. Since her death, Stoppard and his brother have begun to find out more about their past. As the playwright will almost certainly point out if you try to imply that it was his early life that moulded him, the same set of circumstances turned his brother into a successful and happy accountant.

'Even now that I've started to find out about my past, I'm ashamed to say that I have very little interest,' says Stoppard. 'The fact that my past is largely missing from my consciousness is something that doesn't bother me.'

Why?

'Maybe I'm the last person to know why I'm not bothered, but I'm undisturbed by not knowing.'

Are your children interested?

'Yes, they are. So are my half-sister and brother. They are all much more interested than I am. Maybe I'm undisturbed by the past because I jumped the rails. The rails I'm on only began in 1946. They don't disappear into the mist.'

The lack of curiosity or – that killer word – interest in his early childhood or in his close relations killed in the war suggests an objectivity, a lack of feeling, that chimes well with the supposedly cerebral, uninvolving nature of his plays. But things are never that straightforward.

Back to that cold, pre-Christmas morning in a Soho movie preview theatre, where I was faced with incontrovertible evidence that Stoppard has a beating, squelchy heart. The evidence? A shamelessly enjoyable romantic comedy called *Shakespeare in Love*. Already nominated for six Golden Globe awards and widely expected to win a clutch of Oscars, *Shakespeare in Love* is a great, lush, witty piece of froth about the young William Shakespeare (played by Joseph Fiennes, Ralph's younger, warmer brother), who cures his bad case of writer's block by falling in love with Gwyneth Paltrow's Lady Viola Lesseps, an aristocrat about to be married off against her will to Colin Firth's vile Lord Wessex. Eager to catch Shakespeare's eye, the stage-struck Viola dresses as a boy to secure a part in his latest, but as yet unfinished epic, *Romeo and Ethel, the Pirate's Daughter*.

Immensely Stoppardian in its wit and melding of fact with the fantastical, but completely un-Stoppard-like in its blissful romance, the screenplay betrays an utter conviction in the power of love to change people's lives – and literary history. As the course of true love fails to run smooth, the comedy *Romeo and Ethel* transmutes into the great tragedy of *Romeo and Juliet*. *Shakespeare in Love* is not a product of the imagination of a writer who is unnerved by emotion. It is absolutely awash with the stuff.

Of course, *Shakespeare in Love* is Stoppard in holiday mood. The ideas for the serious business of writing plays have always come painfully slowly to Stoppard, and he fills in the pauses, sometimes pauses of several years, with movie scripts and radio plays. 'I wouldn't write any films if I had enough plays in me. I don't suffer from writer's block like Shakespeare in the film. I have a different sort of problem, which is finding something to write about. I finished *The Invention of Love* 18 months ago, and I am only just beginning to get a sense of the next one. If I was more puritan I'd simply wait it out and maybe shorten the intervening period between plays. But I get fidgety after about two weeks if I haven't got a job.'

Shakespeare in Love stands out from the Stoppard oeuvre too because it is full of sex, or at least kissing. But then, it is not all Stoppard's own work. The original idea and script came from the American screenwriter Marc Norman and it was snapped up more than five years ago by Universal as a potential Julia Roberts vehicle. That came to nothing, and eventually the script fell into the hands of Stoppard, who had a connection with the studio.

The final screenplay bears Stoppard's inimitable signature, but its curious gestation means that he is able to distance himself from it. When we meet after the screening, he has his alibi in place, ready to demolish any theories that the film is evidence of the new, emotionally naked Tom Stoppard, the Stoppard who was just visible flashing his heart above the emotional parapet in his two most recent plays, *Arcadia* and *The Invention of Love*.

'Don't let me put you off, my objections are a mere detail,' he murmurs with an old-world, very English courtesy that is so completely disarming that I immediately begin to feel suspicious. He points out that he inherited the script of *Shakespeare in Love*. 'Actually, I felt rather sheepish about taking on another person's work. But Marc Norman was very amiable about it. He has grown up in the movie business, he understands its pragmatism.'

Well, if he has provided only the flesh and not the emotional bones of *Shakespeare in Love*, Stoppard can hardly hide behind the same excuse for *The Invention of Love*, a play in which A. E. Housman's passion for his heterosexual friend Moses Jackson is sublimated into a love of classical scholarship. Inevitably, it turns out that I'm completely wrong about that too.

'Love is only an illusion in *The Invention of Love*,' he says gently. 'I decided to write about Housman long before I knew anything about his personal life. What I was interested in was the idea of two people in one – the Latin scholar and the poet, the classical and the romantic. It says a lot for my ignorance that I was rather hoping that Housman would turn out to be hopelessly in love with an older woman.'

Even the illusion of love presupposes that there can be a reality of love. The truth is, although Stoppard may not write about the real world or real people, a good many real people like his plays very much. And, over the years, several of them have suggested that the emotional blankness that characterises Stoppard's plays was actually a bit of an illusion itself. There were some who detected in *Jumpers* the quiet pain of a marriage in the final throes of disintegration. Plenty, despite Stoppard's vehement denials, believed that *The Real Thing* in 1982, about a writer whose marriage is failing, must have some autobiographical basis and that the playwright was speaking for himself when one of the characters declared: 'I think that love might be the only area that might be private to a writer.' (It was a play that came back to haunt Stoppard several years later when he split from his second wife, Miriam, and was hounded by the tabloids over reports of a relationship with the actress Felicity Kendal, who had appeared in the original production of *The Real Thing*.) Like almost everyone else who saw it, I wept at the tragic fate of Thomasina, the eighteenth-century mathematical prodigy in *Arcadia* – Stoppard's most satisfying play to date – even as I was appalled by the heartlessness of a playwright who could quite so easily sacrifice her to the laws of thermodynamics (she burns to death). I am also quite ready to believe – despite those many poor souls who depart at the interval because they had not appreciated that a classical education is every bit as essential as a Visa card when buying tickets for *The Invention of Love* – that large numbers of critics and the general public have found the play enormously affecting. I begin to think Stoppard's objections are not entirely convincing, 'a mere detail' as he politely describes them. Why would a playwright want to disclaim an emotional content to his work anyway? Perhaps because of the same puritanism that makes him see film-making as a self-indulgence.

'I know films aren't really what I should be doing, but I do love them.' There's been *Brazil*, *The Russia House*, *Empire of the Sun* and *Billy Bathgate*. 'I've enjoyed working with the people. It is a curious paradox that, as a collective noun and idea, there is something alarming and corrupting about Hollywood, but the reality is that, generally, you only work with one person at a time. It is a very exciting medium to work in because it continues to be controllable, or adjustable at any rate. There is almost no cut-off point. Long after the actors have departed, you can work on what they were doing. Orson Welles was right when he said that film-making was the biggest and best train set a boy could ever desire.'

Stoppard himself has made a brief foray behind the camera, directing his own script of *Rosencrantz and Guildenstern are Dead* in 1990. It won him the Lion d'Or at the Venice Film Festival, only the second British film to win the award – in a neat piece of symmetry, it was Olivier's 1948 *Hamlet* that was the first. Stoppard is typically self-deprecating about his effort. 'It was OK, but I remember after a few days of shooting the producer came up to me and said: "The camera isn't moving very much." It was at that point that I realised that it wasn't moving at all. I was doing seaside photography. Thanks to my cameraman and cinematographer, it was all right in the end, but only because I had the sense not to pretend that I knew how to do something that I couldn't do.'

Although he has expressed an interest in directing his own work again, for the time being he is more likely to stick to the holiday job of writing screenplays. 'When you read one by someone who is really good, you realise that thinking cinematically is a qualitatively different way of writing. My screenplays are epic, picaresque stage plays. The scenes are more numerous and much shorter, but telling the story by moving the camera is something I don't think about. There are other ways in which it is the opposite of writing for the theatre. In the movies, nothing in the text is sacred. You have to accept as the premise of your involvement that you are there to serve the true author of the piece, which is not you. In the theatre, playwrights are placed in the position that does them great honour and that flatters them.'

Few have been more honoured than Stoppard, who in 1997 became the first playwright since Terence Rattigan to be knighted. Since he became an overnight success at the age of 29, as the National Theatre's then youngest-ever playwright, Stoppard has attracted admiration and envy in equal amounts. Sometimes, the respect can be grudging – he is almost certainly the model for the fictional characters of Tim Stripling in Clive James's novel *Brilliant Creatures* and Miles Whittier, the stinking-rich, much-fêted playwright in Peter Nichols's play *A Piece of My Mind*.

Stoppard often seems to collude with other people's idea of him as a playwright who is too clever for his own good. For a man so at pains to avoid cheap emotion, he has an almost reckless affinity with the cheap joke or aphorism. It may have been witty, but it was almost certainly not wise of the young Stoppard, when asked of *Rosencrantz and Guildenstern* 'What's it all about?' to reply: 'It's about to make me very rich.'

Is there an eternal struggle going on between Stoppard the serious writer and Stoppard the prankster, the person the *New York Times* once called 'the theatre's intellectual P. T. Barnum'?

'Writers don't have a game plan. We don't write to make us look this way or that. But, for better or worse, you are what you write. And you write what you enjoy. It comes out as some sort of an expression of yourself. In my case, there are two balls rattling around – one is frivolous and the other is serious.'

Stoppard may write like an Oxbridge wit, but he hasn't got any A-levels, let alone a degree. He left school at 17 and started as a cub reporter on a Bristol local paper. 'If I had a regret about not going to university, it is that I feel that I am out on a bluff most of the time. On the evidence of my plays, people believe me to be far more erudite than I am. The truth is that in a limited but significant sense the plays are an extension of my journalism in another form. If I am writing about philosophy, or physics, or Housman, I go into a long period of investigation. On one level, I just report back on my findings and use only what I need. Once the play is finished, I drop the whole thing and move on to the next thing. Of course, I choose subjects that appeal to me, and the appeal survives the finishing of the play in question.'

Quite how far the appeal extends can be gathered from the fact that he has only just cancelled his subscription to the journal *Philosophy*. *Jumpers* was completed in 1972.

Stoppard counters the charge that his plays are flashily erudite by saying: 'When somebody looks at a play and says "Too clever by half", that person is saying something that is true for him or her. Isn't it true of art – in fact, a way of defining art itself – that there is a correspondence between art and being human? And that the variety of responses to art reflects the variety of humanness, of ways of being human? To personalise this, there have been one or two people who have written to me to say that *The Invention of Love* is the best play of the century. I also know there are those who leave halfway through. A great mass of people occupy a position between those extremes. The variety of response isn't something to query. On the contrary, it is that which tells us we are dealing with a piece of art. That's what art is. It is the nature of the beast. That's why it is not a science.'

But is art alone enough? During the 1960s and 1970s, and even the 1980s, while many other playwrights were struggling to make political statements, Stoppard was juggling with abstracts.

'Your premise,' argues Stoppard, 'is that an artist would naturally respond to the political situation around him, and I don't accept that. I write plays, I work in the theatre, I think I have as much right – and no more than anyone else – to have an opinion. Something in me resists the idea that I should be taking an interest. I simply don't. When a local issue happens, I'm always surprised that everyone around me immediately knows what they think. I don't know what to think. Years ago, *Omnibus* did a programme about me called *Tom Stoppard Doesn't Know*. Twenty-five years later, I haven't changed. I still don't know.'

But he knew enough of what he thought to become an early and enthusiastic supporter of Mrs Thatcher. Stoppard and Ronald Miller, her speech-writer, were the only two playwrights that Thatcher could abide. Does Stoppard now regret his enthusiasm for Thatcher?

'What a strange question. My first response to Thatcher was that she dealt with the newspaper unions and that she found a way for that particular protection racket to be dissolved. I felt strongly about that and absolutely welcomed the dismantling of the print unions. Blackmail was not too strong a word to describe what was happening at 1 a.m. in the machine-rooms of newspapers. The fact that one consequence of Thatcher's actions was a new thrust for the Murdoch advance on civilisation is something I don't blame myself for not anticipating. The other thing I do recall is that in the period just before the arrival of Mrs Thatcher, politics had never been held in such low esteem. Everything was so hedged, so mealy-mouthed. I had a weary contempt for the to-ing and fro-ing of party politics. Then along came this woman who seemed to have no manners at all and who said exactly what she thought. She turned the political scene into a kind of Bateman cartoon, and everyone's eyes were popping and their jaws were dropping. I really enjoyed that, although I don't consider that period a good influence on my own world. It was essentially philistine.'

If, unlike the majority of his peers – Bond, Hare, Pinter – Stoppard found himself unable to commit to the left, or indeed to anything much at all, there was one political issue on which he knew where he stood. From the mid-1970s onwards, human rights in Eastern Europe – and the Charter 77 movement in Czechoslovakia in particular – became a passion. The passion manifested itself in plays such as *Every Good Boy Deserves Favour* and *Professional Foul*. 'I don't know how much my Czech origins accounted for the acuteness of my response and the sharpness of my interest, but here was an issue that I felt I could understand. There was no ambiguity about it. Certain things were right and certain things were wrong, and in that arena it was clear which was which. In Britain it was true, and remains true, that we live in a society where, to some degree, each side of an issue takes part of the other side – a democratic society is an infinitely elusive idea. In a totalitarian society, one is confronted by a more Platonic mix of politics and philosophy. In that situation, political issues resolve into moral issues. Here in Britain, I felt I was surrounded by people who were getting overheated about supposed curtailments of freedom; but it was all taking place within the context that everyone was free to write and say what they wanted. I thought this was a huge collective blindness about ourselves. We had this luxury of opinionating without penalty, while just two hours away by plane people were being locked up for mild dissent. I just found it offensive.'

It was in his role as a supporter of Charter 77 that Stoppard made the first of his return journeys to the country of his birth. It was 1977, 38 years after he had first left Czechoslovakia as a baby. He met and talked with the playwright Vaclav Havel, the Czech whom Ken Tynan once said Stoppard recognised as 'his mirror image – a Czech artist who has undergone the pressures that Stoppard escaped when his parents took him into exile'. But it would be almost another 20 years before Stoppard would return to confront himself.

Later, when I'm thinking about my conversation with Stoppard, the image of a dead man in the sea comes to my mind, and on his features are superimposed those of a small boy – Tomas Straussler, the child who was lost with his father. Another image is of a faded Kodak sepia photograph that Stoppard has described to me, which apparently depicts two little boys in a garden with their mother leaning against a tree. There is another photo too which shows the brickwork of a small house in Czechoslovakia. It is a house that Stoppard and his brother recently visited.

I imagine that house, and I think of the long journey of the boy called Tomas Straussler to the very English playwright called Tom Stoppard, and three apparently unrelated, but I think probably connected, thoughts arise. One is of the Tin Man in *The Wizard of Oz* and that moment when he cries: 'Now I know I've got a heart, because it's breaking.' Another is of *The Invention of Love*, where the aged Housman confronts his lovelorn 22-year-old self and helplessly declares: 'I wish I could help you, but it's not in my gift.' Finally, I think of that aching, poignant dance down the centuries that comes at the end of *Arcadia*, and of the terrible despair of that play that so insistently tells us that the past is dead and closed to us for ever, and that we can never really know what happened there. ●

· ·

14 May 1999

Libby Brooks

Every day I write the book

Last week, *Observer* writer Kathryn Flett was leafing through a glossy magazine while she waited to pick up a takeaway. There, in a 100-word review of her forthcoming book *The Heart-Shaped Bullet*, her life in print was summarised something like this: 'Columnist Kate meets gorgeous Mr Right, they get spliced, he leaves her for someone else, she shouts a lot. Then meets Younger Man, who is Destined to Leave Her, he does, she has a breakdown and checks into a glamorous clinic.' 'And I just had to laugh,' she says, forcing out a weak chuckle, 'because the fact is that nobody is going to care as much about this as I am.' Since the spring of 1997, Flett has laid the breakdown of her marriage and its devastating aftermath open like a wound, through her newspaper column and now in this more substantial medium. The book is many things – delicate, guileless, occasionally hilarious, worried like a scab and compulsive like a car crash. It is an exhausting read, and her unhappiness sticks in the mind like glue.

But primarily this is an ugly book, for the same reason that the most beautiful woman looks dreadful in a meanly lit public toilet. Midway through her dark night of the soul, Flett turned on the lights. And she chose to see our faces as we watch her fall to pieces. She relies, she says later, on everybody else being as honest as she is.

Flett married in September 1995. Seventeen months to the day later, her husband moved out of their flat in west London. He had fallen in love with another woman, to whom he is now married. The book charts her attempts to comprehend the failure of the marriage, in particular assessing the impact of her parents' abusive relationship on her own romantic assumptions. She later embarks on a fresh relationship, which ends abruptly. This second rejection precipitates her nervous breakdown. She is treated as an in-patient for clinical depression. She asks her fellow patients to choose their own pseudonyms for their appearance in her memoir.

But a life does not unravel in a vacuum. 'Nobody is going to care as much about this as I am.' Unless you are Eric, her ex-husband, at best the wearer of sociology lecturer shoes, at worst 'The Tin Man', emotionally retarded, commitment-phobic, who announces to friends that the marriage is over 'as if he were rescheduling a couple of appointments'. Or 'The Boy' ('just too young, too handsome and too bloody lots of things, really, to be with me'), whose sweetly pompous e-mails are reprinted without his permission. Or her father, who is exposed in print as a wife-beater.

Why? 'I was astonished by the response that I got to the column. As a journalist you get used to writing into a vacuum. I didn't want the only record to be this one-sided soap opera-ish story.' Flett's butterfly collector approach to memory is a constant throughout the book – key moments must be captured on video, her wedding service 'gone, all of it', simply because it was not committed to tape.

'The more I learned about myself and the relationship, the more naïve and self-deluding it would have been to pretend that I hadn't played a part in the demise of the marriage, and it would have made a very dull and dishonest book. Although this sounds rather unlikely, I was trying to give Eric a bit more respect.' Why? 'On a wider level, I think my generation are very bad at committed relationships and I wanted to explore why that might be, using my marriage as a metaphor.' She sighs. 'I sound like an egomaniac. I had to feel as though I was producing something that was going to go away from me and the people involved, and out into the world to reflect other people's lives and really stop being about us.'

Sprawling in the tidy, bloodless lounge with her white rescue dog from Battersea, Possum, she is nervously reflective. Her dark crop frames a pale face. The bracken eyes would rather be elsewhere. She looks so young. She fills the room with the bruises on her old heart. She has the most beautiful smile and in other circumstances she must be captivating.

Many argue that Flett is parody on a plate: the shrewish avenger, the patho-
logical solipsist, the pitiably banal product of our equivocal relationship with
the piss-and-tell school of lifestyle journalism. But, respect it or damn it, the
book is weighty with contemporary resonance. The snapshots of a love in pieces
are compulsive.

But pain is not a competition and honesty is her best policy. Though thick
with self-analysis, the book is not self-justifying. The only explanations are those
she is searching for herself. And God is in the detail. Flett writes best when
she applies a tender eye to the minutiae. But for those she writes about, the
devil is in there too. This is not a vengeful book. Her treatment of others is
questing rather than cruel. But she fails to accept that the very act of inclusion
is invasion enough.

'I don't think I have invaded other people's privacy because I haven't gone
inside their heads. I've presented my life, and it's only where I've touched them
or they've touched me.' She pauses. 'But I have to believe that, don't I?' She
sent her ex-husband a proof copy, which he returned the following day along
with a note which said that he and his wife had decided not to read it. 'I would
imagine that he wants it to go away so that he can get on with his life.' Her
relationships with her parents are stronger as a result of confronting the truth
of her childhood: 'On a personal level, whatever comes out of this process my
small family and I are talking about things and actually healing old wounds.'

It seems absurd that she has so little conception of her capacity to affect
others. The spurious privacy distinction and an insistence that she has not
overstepped the mark smack of denial. Is Flett essentially a narcissist who cannot
envisage people as anything except players in her own tragedy? Or is she simply
supremely naïve, lacking any appreciation of her own power? There is a third
explanation which speaks to a deep contradiction in how she views the act of
writing itself. Does writing about the thing make it more true? 'Possibly for
me . . . yes. I am pathologically a writer.' She gurgles. She has always written
thus. 'As a child, a way of controlling life is by documenting it, feeling that
you own it somehow. Certainly now when things get chaotic in my head I find
it useful to set them down.' Powerful, but not an act of therapy. It was not
cathartic, she insists. 'No. It was just fucking hard.' She remains friends with
'The Boy', she tells me, although she is aware that he would rather she had not
written about him. So why did she, when the book refers to an explicit promise
that their relationship would be off-limits. Indeed, she writes of a 'dark little
running joke' that 'The Boy' would remain out of print so long as he did not
dump her while she was writing the book. 'He broke his promise first,' she
whispers.

But why? 'It finished the book. It wasn't the end of the story that I wanted,
but I'd had another relationship, I'd been in hospital, I came out and there was
a book to finish. He was in it because that was how the plot went.' The plot.
Her life. She insists that much was left out, and that 'after the last full stop,

everything else is mine. You can't know everything about me.' Both in print and in person, she repeats self-assessments like incantations, one step ahead of those who would judge her. Her conversation is littered with caveats.

What is evident is that she was unable to control the process of writing; that, as she became increasingly vulnerable and broken, the book gathered a momentum of its own.

'I signed for the book within seven months of my husband leaving, and several months before finishing the column,' she explains, 'although at that stage I was expecting to write a different sort of book.' Constantly writing about emotions, in particular unpacking her childhood demons, exacted a price. 'I was on the slope towards having a breakdown and I think that writing the book precipitated me towards that place.' In the book, her awareness never quite settles into insight. But that was then. Less than a year on from completion, Flett talks of the writer of the book in the third person. 'She's definitely a me that's contained in there, and after the last sentence I'm coming from a different place. She was a more naïve, more trusting person. She might have been a nicer person.' Amidst the sound and fury generated by this book, it is easy to forget her impressive career credentials. A pioneer of style journalism, she worked as features editor and fashion editor on the *Face* before becoming the award-winning editor of men's magazine *Arena* between 1992 and 1995. All by the tender age of 31.

'I'm 35, I'm single, I'd be lying if I said I looked forward to a life of doing circuits of Paddington recreation ground with Possum and carrying on being a spare part at dinner parties.' She sounds at once bemused and resigned when she admits that the book is now indelibly marked on her 'emotional and professional CV'. She says that she has written her own death warrant. 'It'll be a very intriguing sort of man who'll have the guts to say: "Never mind the book."' I want to get past this, she says. I want to get better. She is still receiving treatment from 'the people with letters after their names'.

'I'd love to have a relationship that was everything that a relationship could be, and I'd love to have kids, but at the moment I know that I'm not able to give and I'm terribly, terribly wary. I've just got to do a bit more growing up, I suppose. I can no longer treat happiness as an end in itself. It's the difference between me and the woman who thought she'd be wandering around in a middle-class haze with small and attractive children, that sense of it being bestowed upon you by the god of happiness. It's not something you can go and get, it creeps up on you in small moments.'

In time, this interview may become part of Kathryn Flett's plot as well. It will be read by her colleagues, who work two floors above the *Guardian* office. It will be scoured by ex-lovers and nosy acquaintances in search of further revelations. It will be dismissed at dinner parties. It might be mocked by other newspapers. Circles, in circles, in circles.

I didn't know how to greet her when we met – a professional handshake, a colleague's kiss, a sympathetic hug? I kissed her goodbye. She has very soft cheeks. And afterwards I felt dismal. Because I didn't want to know all those things about all those people. ●

9 March 1999

Adrian Searle
Splash bang dollop

No reproduction can truly prepare you for the awesome physiological and psychological effect of Jackson Pollock's best work, the so-called 'drip' paintings he made between 1947 and 1950. These are the paintings on which his reputation as an artist ultimately rests. And no amount of critical hyperbole can prepare you for just how awful much of what led up to this work really is. Be prepared for the best and the worst of Pollock at the Tate Gallery's retrospective, which opens on Thursday. The show has been cut down to 122 works – around half the canvases, paintings and drawings shown recently at the Museum of Modern Art, New York.

This is a disappointment, in that we miss so much of Pollock's most fertile period. My first sensation on walking around was that too much emphasis had been given to his difficult gestation as an artist, and that his three or so years of great work between 1947 and 1950, and his subsequent faltering recapitulation and decline, are represented as a foreshortened and frightening descent.

But it really was like this, and the mythic, tragic aspect of Pollock as the live-fast, die-young Wild One of Abstract Expressionism is unavoidable. It is part of Pollock's greatness (a word I don't use lightly). And anyhow, there are six or seven works here that probably say everything that needs to be said about his achievement. The rewards of his best works are endless: they are paintings without end, to which one wants to return again and again.

Pollock was born in 1912 and died at 44 in 1956, when the car he was driving crashed into a tree, killing the artist and one of the two women passengers. Pollock's end is like a bad novel, or the undoubtedly bad movie his life is about to become. His studied inarticulacy, his abusiveness to women, the alcoholic binges, the punch-ups, the outbursts and self-recriminations and self-doubt which destroyed him are true to a morbid fiction of artistic behaviour, an American existential myth.

Pollock was no role model as a man. It must be said too that a great deal of his early work, from the early 1930s to the early 1940s, is terrible – the first half of the exhibition is an almost unrelievedly painful record of perseverance against ineptitude, a struggle for identity, ambition overcoming seeming insurmountable difficulty. Pollock's problems, personal and artistic, unmade him as a man and made him, all too briefly, as a towering artist.

Pollock was eight years younger than fellow Abstract Expressionists Willem de Kooning and Arshile Gorky, both of whose works had a superficial maturity by the late 1930s. Both too were Europeans – Dutch and Armenian respectively – while Pollock, Wyoming-born and West Coast-raised, struggled against different odds for an independent artistic identity. While Gorky (a self-mythologiser if ever there was one) could say urbanely: 'I was with Cézanne for a long time, and now, naturally, I am with Picasso', Pollock's development was an archetype of oedipal struggle, a perfect example of Harold Bloom's theories of poetic usurpation: Pollock wanted to kill Picasso, but at the same time Picasso was the father figure he never escaped.

Pollock the artist was formed out of a mish-mash of influences: Thomas Hart Benton's xenophobic American regionalism; Albert Pinkham Ryder's overcooked and eccentric old-masterisms; the muscly proletarian heroics of Mexican muralists Siqueiros and Orozco. Masson and Miro and Michelangelo are in the mix too, undigested and indigestible. All art has to come from somewhere, and Pollock's came from an America which was, through the 1930s and 1940s, almost nowhere on the international art map.

Whatever one might surmise about Pollock's psyche – and commentators constantly return to it – his overriding problem as a would-be painter was his cack-handedness, his bludgeoning lack of feel for paint, his lack of a subject to meet his imagination and his needs. Pollock's difficulties as a painter led him on terrible detours, into vague mythological and Jungian references, but they constituted the very thing he had to overcome. Early apologists, like Frank O'Hara, wallowed in the symbolism as a way to avoid the problems of paintings like *Guardians of the Secret* and *Pasiphae*.

Only when he speeded up the application of paint to such an extent that it overcame the sullen inertia of his touch, and when he actually stopped touching the painting at all, did his paintings finally develop into something marvellous. Ditching overt figuration helped too, though it was always in and under the surface somewhere, however much he masked it. All those palimpsests of over-laden imagery; the impacted, overpainted moves and countermoves of his moiled surfaces; the cartoon flailings of his loony figures; the press of bodies and body parts into crudified walls of paint were aspects of a necessary failure. If he hadn't been so bad, he would not have become so great.

The 'drip paintings' appear to escape from his difficulties, although they too may be seen as a figuration of inner turmoil, and to literally embody it as the trace of the act of painting. They are unprecedented. I think of Pollock painting in the late 1940s. The enamel paint, scooped out of a can with a brush, is stringy and viscous. It runs like syrup in a continuous thread. It flows from the brush on to the canvas on the floor. It isn't so much poured as drooled, flicked and arced, ejaculated across the space between the brush in his hand and the canvas beneath it. Its trajectory is always somewhat uncertain; the paint lands as though it were still in mid-flight, still on the way somewhere. It still has energy and direction as it hits the canvas.

The paint is driven by gravity and the propulsive energy of the artist's wrist, his arm, the punch he puts into his shoulder, the twist of the torso. The action is sometimes like the follow-through a fly fisherman performs when punching a line out into the wind, and sometimes it is like a choppy, locked-elbow table tennis block and return. Sometimes it is a jerky twist of the wrist, slathering with wetness and spray. When he puts enough energy into that blind stroke in the air, the arc of paint breaks up into droplets, each with its particular slipstream trail. You can see the direction they were travelling in when they hit the canvas, catching on the nub of the raw cotton, skidding slightly on the thinner paint already on the surface. It has partially soaked into the weave. Sometimes the colour is close in warmth and tone to that of the canvas – a bit darker or lighter, so that the painting appears to have grown from the surface itself. There are earthy browns, industrial greys, metallics and whites, with the tan colour of the canvas sometimes showing through and around the edges of the canvas.

He leans out to reach the centre of the unrolled bolt of cotton. Scoop and flick, scoop and arc. Breathe in, breathe out. The painting seems to breathe back. Take one step, then another. There are several syncopated rhythms here, superimposed on the trace of yet earlier rhythms. The layers go down, but the effect is visual and visceral rather than musical. There's a kind of elastic tension building up, as each layering both cancels what went before and adds something more. Sometimes he'll superimpose an earlier colour, so that you can't exactly read the succession of layers, at least not optically. What is building here is a kind of resonance, a squeezing and trapping of space between the layers.

Look into the surface, as you'd look into water, and you see that there are great deeps in the gaps in the skeins. Yet from a distance, or out of the corner of your eye, all the layers flatten out, and everything seems to catch the light and glisten. Looking at the surface face on, up close, the surface disappears, the paint apparently hovering in an indeterminate space. I feel I could stick my hand into these particles and blobs and streamers and swirl them around.

The artist can see his paint-spattered shoes, his paint-smeared hands, the can and the brush filthy with paint. The painting at his feet goes in and out of focus. Enamel paint reeks, and he can taste the reek through the cigarette smoke. 'Is this a painting?' Pollock once asked his wife, the painter Lee Krasner. Pollock's paintings were something as yet undefined.

This is how I imagine Pollock painting, how I know him from Hans Namuth's famous photographs, how I imagine I know him from my own experience as a young painter, a 20-year-old belatedly method-acting the broody but sensitive deep and dark stance. Pollock's appeal (separate from the appeal of his paintings) has an adolescent streak. Looking at the painting, raised up on to the wall and evenly lit, one sees it not as Pollock saw it as he painted it. Pollock painting and Pollock's paintings are different things, even if, by their nature, the cumulative act and the object itself seem inextricable.

I think of the painter's body in motion and the painting taking shape, and as I step towards the surface, so that a section of the painting entirely fills my field of vision, I feel something happening to my own body. It is a sensation of immersion and exhilaration. The painting has been dry since before I was born, but I feel its liquidity, as though it were still being made as I look, as though it were still taking shape around me.

The feel of these drip paintings is not at all homogeneous: *Autumn Rhythm* has a faster pace than *Lavender Mist*. *Summertime* seems to furl and unfurl and helix through itself in a sedate rolling movement as I watch – I feel like I'm watching something in flux rather than looking at something static. *Number 32*, from 1950, is a painful wrung-out black, a wrenching sobbing web, tarry on the matt canvas. I feel the endless emptiness of the space between and beyond the black, not the dull background of unpainted canvas but nothingness itself. Which is where his handprints are, in *Number 1A*, 1948, trapped between the loops and splats and the blankness beyond.

The violence and delicacy of the best Pollocks go right through me. I want to defend their presence heart and soul. The space he created in these paintings is more like a discovery of a natural phenomenon than an invention, and these works go on being vital and intangible and indefinable and utterly compelling to this day. •

29 May 1999
Alex Brummer
The business of ethics

Sixth-formers around the country are currently benefiting from the wisdom of some of Britain's top business leaders working closely with senior rabbis. The idea is to provide students, many of whom are contemplating careers in the rough and tumble of finance and business, with an ethical compass to guide them through a complex thicket.

The programme, assembled by the Jewish Association for Business Ethics, enjoys the intellectual support of the Chief Rabbi, Professor Jonathan Sacks, and reaches deep into biblical and talmudic sources to understand the ethical approach to concepts such as fair trading, property and the concept of the jubilee year, which occurs at the end of every seven cycles of seven years (the fiftieth year) and during which debt is forgiven.

The upsurge of Jewish interest in the study of business ethics is no accident. A group of senior businessmen – including Pentland Group chairman Stephen Rubin (who made his fortune from Reebok shoes) and Stephen Zimmerman of investment managers Mercury Asset Management – became concerned about the negative media image of some Jews in business in the mid-1980s and early 1990s.

The trial of the Guinness four, for instance, carried anti-Semitic undertones, which elements of the tabloid press could not resist playing up, even though the person at the centre, Ernest Saunders, was only partially Jewish and had converted to Anglicanism. Similarly, the Maxwell scandal was largely seen as a Jewish conspiracy – not helped by the old rogue's burial among the heroes of the Jewish people on Mount Zion in Jerusalem.

Such events did nothing to enhance the image of Jewish business leaders, even though some of the most meticulously run companies in the UK – like Lord Weinstock's GEC – were under Jewish stewardship.

It was thus partly to address the past that the Jewish Association for Business Ethics has pushed its 'Money and Morals' programme for schools. Within the last month, business leaders from the association held a 'board meeting' for 75 sixth-formers from the JFS comprehensive in Camden Town, Clifton College and Immanuel College to illustrate the dilemmas faced by directors told to sack senior and loyal staff to please shareholders – a very familiar situation.

The ethical approach to such problems is outlined by Jonathan Sacks in a new Institute for Economic Affairs paper, 'Morals and Markets'. Sacks tiptoes through the sacred texts to find insights into the writings of Friedrich Hayek and to understand better the talmudic input into Max Weber's *Protestant Ethic and the Spirit of Capitalism*.

The abuse of property rights by a ruler, Sacks observes, is 'one of the great corruptions of power'. Judaism is a religion born out of the slavery in Egypt and the longing for redemption. It is underpinned by concepts of private freedom and economic independence. Judaism is also a classless religion, which accords equal recognition to those who toil with their hands and those deploying professional skills. This concept is embodied in the Shabbat evening liturgy, which sings of the value of work: 'When you eat of the value of hands, you are happy and it shall be with you.' There is no aristocracy in Judaism – despite the efforts of some of the great Anglo-Jewish families to create one – but there is an obligation for the richer Jew to help his poorer neighbour, not simply through alms designed to absolve the conscience but by making loans or offering a business partnership, thereby allowing the less well off to establish themselves.

Perhaps most relevant to the business dilemmas faced today is the Jewish concept of fair trading. Among the first questions a soul is asked in the next world is: 'Did you deal honestly on business?' Much of the body of Jewish law is taken up with the concept of fair trading, the idea that it is wrong to gain at someone else's expense.

Sitting in the Richmond synagogue recently, as the rabbi read from the final portions of Leviticus in biblical Hebrew, I was struck by how relevant the concept of the jubilee year – when debt is forgiven and mortgages cancelled – is today, as the West moves to deliver loan cancellation to the world's poorest countries. The wisdom of the Torah still provides a guiding light at the dawn of a new Christian millennium. ●

· ·

19 June 1999

John Ezard

Line on the occasion of a laureate's first words

'It's an unforced, musical poem which handles a royal occasion with some dignity,' Elaine Feinstein said. 'It's quite a decent poem. But what more do people expect from a poet laureate?'

That, last night, was the sympathetic and in some quarters repentant mood of the British poetry world about Andrew Motion's official debut as Laureate on the most dreaded of all modern literary subjects, a royal wedding.

A month after his appointment was dismissed anonymously by one poet as 'a piece of shite', it was be-understanding-about-Andrew's-awful-job day.

The director of the Poetry Society, Chris Mead, who had read the wedding poem in advance, said: 'I think it's important that these poems speak for themselves,' and declined to comment further.

Peter Porter, who had not seen it, said: 'It's very difficult for any laureate.' Another poet, who is a friend of Motion's, said beforehand that he only wanted to comment if he liked the verses. After seeing a faxed copy, he said: 'I can't offer any constructive comment.'

Ms Feinstein, an admired poet and translator of poetry for more than 30 years and a fellow of the Royal Society of Literature, said: 'I think Andrew Motion has been subjected to some quite unfair treatment by journalists and fellow-poets.'

Among other writers, who asked not to be named, the view was the poem was 'a decent attempt', its name bravely echoing Edmund Spenser's celebrated *Epithalamion*, written in the heyday of Tudor court poetry.

But it was seen as tending to collapse in the third verse, on wedding vows. 'A bit *Desiderata*-ish, that,' said an Irish writer, comparing it with an American inspirational prose-poem which begins: 'Go placidly amid the noise and haste . . .'

In a long interview due out in the magazine *Poetry Review* next month, Motion concedes that the laureateship is a completely no-win situation. 'I'm damned if I do, damned if I don't,' he says. 'I've thought about that and the flak-taking. For a poet like me, it is quite a test to write about public things. I have to find a private way to tackle them. I decided there was something so interesting and creative to do for the whole community of poets that I'd take the risk. One of the odd things [since my appointment] is that I now feel there's another Andrew Motion going round in the newspapers who is barely recognisable. There was a lot of begrudging during the first week . . . Then it steeply turned round, with much more friendly things being written.'

Among his ambitions in the post, he says, are to raise money to provide places where poets can work uninterrupted, to edit regular poems about national events and to produce a 'gigantic' poetry anthology for schools.
Epithalamium St George's Chapel, Windsor

Epithalamium
St George's Chapel, Windsor

One day, the tissue-light through stained glass falls
on vacant stone, on gaping pews, on air
made up of nothing more than atom storms
which whiten silently, then disappear.
The next, all this is charged with brimming life.
A people-river floods those empty pews,
and music-torrents break – but then stop dead
to let two human voices make their vows:
to work – so what is true today remains the truth;
to hope – for privacy and what its secrets show;
to trust – that all the world can offer it will give;
to love – and what it has to understand to grow.

Ted Heath gives Baroness Margaret Thatcher an enigmatic glance at the Conservative Party Conference, 1998

Martin Argles

Politics: arts of the possible

....

25 March 1999

Hugo Young

Tortuous questions

Shining through the House of Lords' final verdict on General Pinochet is a single, revelatory truth. A lot of static crackles round the judgement. The second batch of Law Lords found refuge in a point which the first had hardly considered. As a result, the politics of extradition will take over from the law. But the heart of the matter remains. What three Law Lords decided in November, six more have agreed in March: that a former head of state cannot claim sovereign immunity in a foreign court from trial for certain crimes he committed or supervised when he was in power.

When the first hearing reached that conclusion, it was regarded as aberrant. And it was certainly surprising. Those who didn't like it offered insidious explanations. Two members of the court, it was noted, were South Africans: a serious disablement. And one of them, by his reckless failure to declare an interest, poisoned the decision of the whole tribunal, with the result that the case had to be heard again. The second hearing, unique in the history of the legal system, put in jeopardy the entire standing of the Lords as our court of indisputable finality.

On the central issue, such anxiety can now be set aside. There is no confusion. Lord Hoffmann's dreadful blunder, far from being the start of an unravelling of both the case and the court, turned out to be the pretext for reinforcement of a vital point. No fewer than nine Law Lords have said that Pinochet, as a former head of state charged with torture, can claim no immunity from extradition. The opinion is no aberration. In this, moreover, Britain's top court is a global pathfinder. During the second hearing, a search was made for any other domestic court in the world that has refused immunity to a former head of state in such situation. Not one, apparently, has ever done it before.

So the Law Lords have saved their court. In addition, the extra time and the armies of counsel helped produce a set of speeches more fully reasoned and more subtly copious than first time round, which will add weight to the international role they can be expected to play. Lord Browne-Wilkinson's, in particular, was a model of de-obfuscation. The new limit placed on Pinochet's predicament – that he cannot be extradited for alleged crimes dating from before December 1988 – is of no significance to the future impunity of travelling former despots. They risk being detained and tried, at any rate if they come to Britain. This is a definitive assertion of the primacy, in certain circumstances, of international human rights.

We come, though, to the new departure, on the basis of which the Law Lords almost seem to be seeking a different outcome as far as Pinochet himself is concerned. The 1988 cut-off point was barely argued in the previous courts. It rests on the claim that extradition for torture, from Britain, was not legally available until the international Torture Convention became part of British law, which it did late in 1988. Any crimes Pinochet committed before that, all Law Lords but one asserted, should be struck out of his extradition charge sheet. The eight judges who had previously heard the case at different levels, including those who opposed the general's extradition, all dismissed this point as empty. But it is now the given law, with which the Home Secretary has to deal.

For his is now the decision. To cut out everything Pinochet did before 1988 is to cut out a lot of crimes and alters the factual basis on which Jack Straw made his original decision to let extradition proceedings begin. Their lordships made a lot of this, time after time urging him to look again at what he had done. The 'drastically reduced charges', said Lord Browne-Wilkinson, changed the picture. Perhaps this was just a reminder to Mr Straw that, if he didn't look again at the case and review his own decision – which some lawyers say he doesn't have the power to do – he might face review by the judges. What its iteration sounded like was a plea for clemency.

This will be amplified by others. The old political pleadings will resume. Well, I can hear them say, Pinochet is an old man. He was always a friend of Britain. He has been given a disgracefully hard time, thanks to an officious Spanish magistrate who has vastly overreached himself in the charges he thought he could bring. Now that the strict illegality of extradition has been shown in all but a handful of cases, the minister's decision, if he reaffirms it, will be sheer vindictiveness, if not proof that those student days in Santiago make him devoid of impartiality. Thus will sing the piety of Latin America's new discovered champion, Lord Lamont.

The claim that while many torture charges are unconscionable, a single torture charge can be excused and forgotten, exposes a startling moral imbecility. Such relativism can perhaps be explained, but surely never excused, by weight of expectations: the belief that, when scores of crimes are eliminated, those that remain somehow lose their critical mass.

Yet in any other circumstance, a single charge of torture, if disclosed by an extradition claim and if in all legal respects fully in order, would not be deemed insufficient simply because it was alone. Torture doesn't acquire immunity, as an international crime, merely because there isn't enough of it. And actually, while urging Mr Straw to look again, some Law Lords took this point. Even if the charge sheet was confined to crimes committed after the cut-off date, Lord Hope acknowledged without demur, 'the allegation is that [Pinochet] was a party to the use of torture as a systematic attack on all those who opposed or who might oppose his government'.

The residue of these uniquely lengthy hearings is that Pinochet, when everything is pared down to strict law, is charged with a handful of extraditable offences, from the consequences of which he has no immunity. Torture, and conspiracy to torture, late in his time, stand against him. The most thorough judicial process ever conducted in this country has concluded with a clear assertion of international morality and how it should be enforced. Half-ducking the particular implications of this general rule, the Law Lords were behaving in a very British way. Leave Pinochet to the minister, they said. Let him think again. But the minister too has Britain's reputation in his hands. Where they have found a path, he should follow – or let this proclamation of the limits of tolerable evil be subverted by the compromising habits of a politician. •

....

13 January 1999
Simon Hoggart
A case of leaves on the brain

John Prescott's use of the language may be infectious. Yesterday one of his understrappers, Dick Caborn, drew himself up to his full height and replied derisively to remarks made by a Tory, Bernard Jenkin. 'That question shows a marked lack of ignorance!' he shouted. What was weirdest of all was the way that the sycophants on the Labour backbenches laughed long and greasily, as if this were a riposte Oscar Wilde could have relished.

A short while later Hilary Armstrong was asked about rate-capping, which she referred to as 'rate-crapping', a felicitous neologism worthy of the master himself, not merely school of Prescott.

As for the Deputy Prime Minister and Secretary of State for Transport and the Environment himself (he has almost as many titles as Michael Heseltine once did), he was on robust form. Or so we were supposed to think.

It is a myth cultivated by, among others, Mr Prescott that he is a rough, tough, no-nonsense sort of fellow who has no time for the sound-bites and evasions used by what he contemptuously calls 'the beautiful people'.

But a myth is what it is. He actually adores a good sound-bite. Last autumn he made a speech attacking the privatised railways that was packed with them. 'It's time to give the red light to the rail industry and demand, "All change!"' was one. The speech was full of windy threats and brought cheers from Labour delegates who had arrived three hours late on Virgin trains.

His remarks returned to me yesterday morning as I stood wet and freezing for the best part of an hour waiting for various privatised trains which didn't turn up. The fact is that, in the 20 months since Mr Prescott took responsibility for the service, it has steadily degenerated. You can watch it continue to do so, week by week. Hordes of commuters staring desperately at information screens, like famished voyagers on *The Raft of the Medusa* scanning the horizon, was something you used to see occasionally. Now it's three or four times a week.

Mr Prescott's response is more bombast, which turns out on examination to mean extra bureaucracy in the future. Yesterday he announced a new railways regulator, a new franchise director and a new strategic rail authority! The effect might have been greater if he had not announced precisely the same many months ago, since when things have gone on deteriorating.

There has been a rail summit. On 26 November, we were told, Mr Prescott and John Reid, the minister directly responsible for transport, met the train operators 'to identify problems'. (I can identify them for free: it's a bunch of greedy bastards running a lousy service.) But that's not all. 'On 21 February there will be another rail summit in London ... with a view to getting the improvements required,' Mr Prescott vouchsafed.

Meanwhile, the buccaneers ruining our railways must be quaking at Mr Prescott's latest grim threat: 'There is to be a shadow strategic rail authority', its chairman to be appointed later this month.

Oof, take that, you brigands! It's lucky Mr Prescott wasn't running the country at the time marauders and corsairs were seizing laden merchantmen in the Spanish Main.

'Something must be done, Your Majesty.'

'Fear not, Sir Francis, I shall appoint a shadow strategic Spanish Main supervisory committee and your troubles will be gone!'

Richard Ottaway asked whether, if the Jubilee Line were not open for the millennium, Mr Prescott would resign. Labour backbenchers laughed uproariously at this suggestion. For a minister to resign, not because of sexual malpractice or financial finagling, but because he'd failed to deliver his election promises! Whatever next? •

· ·

8 March 1999
Roy Hattersley
Smile, Gordon

P eople whose judgement I normally respect persist in telling me that I am one of Gordon Brown's natural allies. Rightly, they take it for granted that I admire his intellect and applaud his industry. But they argue that I should take my support a step further.

'Gordon,' they say, 'is, unlike the Prime Minister, a proper Labour man', and I should applaud him both for the way he respects the Labour Party and for his attempts to fulfil that part of its destiny which requires a serious attack on poverty. They even go so far as to say that he believes in a more equal society – citing as evidence for their claim two redistributive budgets which taxed the rich and helped the poor by stealth.

I shall certainly applaud if the forthcoming budget taxes child benefit and uses the extra income to assist low-income families. I understand the arguments against and concede that the collection will be complicated. But if, by raising extra revenue, he can take the weekly payments to over £15, the help provided for families in need will more than justify the marginal damage done to the principle of independent taxation for men and women.

Labour MPs who oppose such a progressive move are a throwback, not to the extremism of the 1980s, but to that decade's debilitating desire to support fashionable causes.

Presumably intelligence as well as ideology will prevent Gordon Brown from endorsing the most extreme proposals for funding the care of the elderly. I now have some experience of the subject. It relates, I hasten to add, to my mother rather than to me. She has both a house and a bank account. The idea that, when her contribution to the cost of care is calculated, one should be taken into account and the other ignored, is economic illiteracy. They are just different forms of capital.

Fortunately the issue does not arise with my mother. But if her house was left untouched, while the state paid all the bills, the Exchequer would be helping me not her. Taxpayers would be underwriting my inheritance.

Yet I suspect that the Chancellor is sympathetic to some of the house-owners' arguments. I heard an elderly lady on the radio asking why she, who had been prudent all her life, should be required to sacrifice her hard-won savings while elderly layabouts receive state hand-outs.

The Protestant ethic burns brightly in the Chancellor and those who subscribe to that view are notoriously liable to confuse the rewards that come from hard work with the duty to punish those who work too little. Reading the predictions of next Tuesday's budget, I wonder if Gordon Brown draws a fiscal distinction between the deserving and the undeserving poor. The only decent criterium for help is need, however it came about.

I am absolutely certain that he subscribes to all those Victorian saws with which Ford Maddox Brown surrounded his most famous painting: 'Seest thou a man diligent in his business? He shall stand before Kings.'

Like Gordon Brown, I know work to be the great purifier, the great healer, the great redeemer. But unlike him, I believe that our mutual conviction is shared by most of the adult population.

Half of the Chancellor's tax and benefit proposals seem built on the premise that what is left of the unemployed have to be bribed or bullied into jobs. Some of them may, because, having got out of the habit, they need a stick or a carrot before they return to harness. But *Coronation Street* enthusiasts know that there is only one Les Battersby in Weatherfield. Everybody else wants a job.

Our different view of the human condition illustrates the great divide between Gordon Brown and me. The Chancellor is, or always seems to be, essentially pessimistic. He may predict – and will probably achieve – an increase in national prosperity during his years at the Treasury. But what he predicts is always an Eldorado in which the gold shines no more than lead. He gives the impression that, were he Foreign Secretary, he would be positively opposed to the gaiety of nations. I do not want him to joke his way through every difficulty.

Though Denis Healey's sense of humour was the government's not very secret weapon 20 years ago, I just want Gordon Brown to look, and behave, as if he is driven onward by hope, rather than apprehension. His stern resolve to avoid the easy options is to be applauded. Indeed I wish he were sterner with the very rich and forced some hard choices on them as well as on the poor. But socialism is essentially a product of optimism.

Men and women are perfectible. We were not expelled from the Garden of Eden because of the inherent sin within us. Economic conditions made it impossible for Adam to resist the apple.

I want a Chancellor who is as clever and as dedicated as Gordon Brown but also believes that a millennium is not a silly celebration in December but an attainable condition of universal happiness.

If I have misjudged the man he can prove me wrong by smiling, just once, during the budget statement. ●

. . . .

3 August 1998

Madeleine Bunting

Real politics: go to the Muslims, go to the Catholics

As a teenage rebel, I changed my first name; a matter of no importance to anyone other than my irritated teachers, my baffled family and, 17 years later, my local Social Security office. After several lengthy telephone calls, they asked me to come in for a 45-minute interview on the change of my name.

My point is not directed at Alistair Darling on the inefficiency of the welfare state. The experience at my local DSS was a bitter illustration of where the welfare state has failed, and where it is struggling with issues beyond its remit. At 10.30 a.m., the office in Hackney, one of the most deprived areas of western Europe, was full of people waiting; dozens of different nationalities were represented. You could not speak even to a receptionist until your docket was called, yet it took me a while to find a docket dispenser. There were 20 people waiting ahead of me. The large room was silent except for the crying children. People avoided each other's eye. An elderly, ill, white man was racially abusing a black receptionist.

I was impressed that the DSS had bothered to track me down after 17 years, but what horrified me was the stench of angry humiliation. These people are my neighbours but, suddenly thrown into a room with them, I realised how a car in a city enables you to select your community; neighbours become virtually meaningless.

My community is no longer geographical. I negotiate the anonymity of a city by establishing a network of work, friendship, family and leave the rest. Ease of transport opens up wider access and enables us to avert our eyes from what is virtually on our doorstep. How do you open up communication and stitch together the social fabric of a neighbourhood from an enormous diversity of ethnic groups? In what way could the Bangladeshi grandmother establish common cause with the Irish single mother? There is no rallying ideal of citizenship as in America.

The welfare state, that crucial interface between government and subject, has never been about empowerment but about entitlement. Even the terminology of 'service' and 'client' identifies the passivity of these welfare recipients. Only in the NHS has it ever succeeded in embodying a concept of solidarity. Britain's welfare state, under both Tory and Labour governments, has been entrenched in concepts of paternalistic hierarchy. And, from a high-rise tower block in Hackney, the highly disciplined, centralised New Labour appears only another permutation of that model. Add to that a bitter local history of factional politics and it is hardly surprising that voter turnout in Hackney is low, and there's so little interest in politics.

The conclusion of Neil Jamieson, of the Citizen Organising Foundation, which works in six areas across Britain, is that the most powerful form of social capital left in many areas of east London is the faith communities. He points to the East London Mosque in Whitechapel, which attracts more than 1,000 men every Friday for prayers, or one of the cavernous Catholic churches which can also see more than 1,000 people cross the threshold on a Sunday.

Jamieson, himself a Quaker, draws on that rich dissenter tradition of political activism. The idea behind Telco, The East London Communities Organisation, which he has set up and to which he has recruited more than 40 member organisations, is unapologetically imported from American-style community organising.

Telco has just sent Abu Hassan of the East London Mosque on a training course with a Mexican community organisation in Texas. But the rhetoric is reminiscent of radical left-wing politics of the 1970s; Jamieson believes in 'actions' and 'struggle'.

He argues that it is in face-to-face encounters that social solidarity emerges and seemingly insurmountable barriers of prejudice and stereotyping are overcome. Remember demos and banners? It is in the struggle and the victories – sometimes small, sometimes big – that people learn self-confidence and skills of leadership that they never believed possible of themselves.

The 'struggles' are over the issues that directly affect the communities involved – from pedestrian crossings to demanding a quota for local people of the thousands of jobs in construction in Canary Wharf and on the Millennium Dome;

from education to health, planning and transport. The emphasis, says Jamieson, is demanding face-to-face meetings between Telco members and the people who determine their lives – for example, the chief executive of the health authority, their MPs or a director of one of the big City banks.

Yet this is a form of civic association – social capital – which has the secular, liberal left wing squirming uncomfortably. In all the trendy discussion about mutuality and fostering civic spirit, there is a real wariness of getting religion involved. For example, Charles Leadbeater managed to write a whole pamphlet for think tank Demos on 'Civic Spirit' and the importance of mutuality without mentioning a religious institution once. Yet churches, mosques, gurdwaras, temples, synagogues – for all their decline in membership – remain the biggest mutual institutions of civic society.

Of course, the wariness of mobilising faith communities for political ends is, in some ways, understandable. A paternalistic liberalism chokes on the idea of an empowered Muslim community that will not necessarily facilitate women's participation, or a Catholic community lobbying for the closure of an abortion clinic. Mutuality is not all apple pie and Neighbourhood Watch schemes. But what makes Telco and the sister organisations of the Citizen Organising Foundation in such places as Bristol and the West Midlands such a fascinating experiment is that they are using institutions which reach into, and attract immense loyalty among, some of the most deprived communities in the country to inculcate concepts of citizenship and political participation. Then they are building alliances between those faith communities in a complex task of getting those of different religions to respect each other.

It's a brave attempt to answer the questions posed in the Social Security Office in Hackney. ●

....

28 April 1999
Francis Wheen
Wheen's World

Some Conservatives have long had their doubts about Peter Lilley, and his sudden discovery that there are more things in heaven and earth than are dreamed of in free-market philosophy has confirmed their worst fears. 'He lives in Islington, you know,' one muttered to me, implying that Lilley's tribute to publicly funded health, education and welfare could be attributed to a surfeit of polenta and squid ink.

Margaret Thatcher is reported to be hopping mad. (Is she ever not?) Other ex-colleagues are more puzzled than angry. Now that even Labour has adopted the private-is-best creed, they say, the Tories should be claiming the credit, not disowning the policy.

Tempting though it is to sit back and enjoy the bickering, the Blairites should be warned. Peter Lilley is not a fool. He was the first right-wing minister to realise that the game was up for Thatcher and her poll tax; and he told her so. 'Coming from such a source, this upset me more than I can say,' she confesses in her memoirs.

As you may recall, the campaign against the poll tax began in Scotland, not least because the ludicrous levy was imposed there in April 1989, a year before its introduction in England and Wales. Now the Scots are again leading the way, this time in a crusade against the Private Finance Initiative. Can it be that history is repeating itself? This, I'd suggest, is the likeliest explanation for Peter Lilley's advice that Tories must 'openly and emphatically accept that the free market has only a limited role in improving public services like health, education and welfare'.

It may seem unlikely that such a dull acronym as PFI can arouse popular passion. 'PFI means paying more for less,' Dr Jean Shaoul, an accountancy expert from Manchester University, wrote in *Public Finance* magazine a couple of months ago. 'The consequences for the public, both as service users and taxpayers, are enormous. Yet the initiative is going ahead with little public debate and even less informed scrutiny.'

Not any more. The PFI is now a big issue in the Scottish election campaign, having been wrenched from the pages of professional journals and on to the front pages of mass-market tabloids. 'Fewer nurses, fewer doctors and fewer hospital beds,' the Scottish *Sunday Mail* declared recently. 'That's the shocking price the NHS will have to pay for handing over almost £1 billion of taxpayers' money to a private consortium.'

One of the most potent examples of these PFI deals is the Royal Infirmary of Edinburgh, which is being built at a cost of £180 million by a group of private companies known as Consort. The new hospital, on a remote greenfield site, will 'rationalise' the services now provided at four city-centre locations, which are to be sold off to developers. Like every hospital commissioned under PFI, the infirmary will have fewer beds (869 instead of 986) and fewer staff than the institutions it replaces. The beneficiaries will be Consort, which, when the PFI contract expires after 25 years, will own the hospital outright and have recovered all its capital costs from the government.

Labour ministers, in their innocence, regard PFI as a wondrous alchemy that produces something from nothing. Look, they exclaim, we're building all these new hospitals and it doesn't add a penny to the Public Sector Borrowing Requirement! But this is mere sleight of hand. The PFI disguises borrowing by hiving it off to the private sector at far higher interest rates. And who pays the interest? You do, with money that would hitherto have been recycled in the NHS. It is like taking out a mortgage from a loan shark to buy a house which you already own and then discovering, 25 years down the line, that the property has been repossessed by the lender anyway.

Whom will the voters blame when they realise that they are being fleeced? It is true that the PFI was introduced by the Conservatives in 1992. However, as Dr Shaoul points out: 'The initiative was struggling until the incoming Labour government cleared the obstacles in its path.' In the 18 months since a 'Treasury Taskforce' was set up to coordinate the scheme, more than 50 significant projects worth a total of £4 billion have been signed; another 30 are on the way. Annual spending on PFI already amounts to more than 1 per cent of total government expenditure – a figure that is likely to rise alarmingly quickly, given New Labour's evangelical zeal for 'public–private partnerships'. As the hospitals' debts and losses rise, the NHS will have to divert more and more of its resources to bailing them out.

Like a credit-hungry consumer buying top-of-the-range television sets through ruinous hire-purchase agreements, the government seems blithely unaware that there's no such thing as the never-never, merely a delayed day of reckoning. ●

Kate Illingworth, a retired teacher from Bristol, woke up a couple of weeks ago to find herself infamous. A huge article in the *Times* identified her as one of 'a trio of experienced political activists' who had organised the 'conspiracy' to bring down Chris Woodhead. The other two were Christine Purkis, another former teacher, and the actor Tony 'Baldrick' Robinson.

Since then it's been a case of infamy, infamy, they've all got it in for me. A few days later, Melanie Phillips of the *Sunday Times* noted that 'behind Mrs Woodhead was a trio of Labour party activists, [including] Kate Illingworth . . .' Last Sunday, sources close to Chris Woodhead told the paper of their fear that Cathy Woodhead was being manipulated by Illingworth. The *Sunday Times* also claimed that the story of Woodhead's affair with Amanda Johnston had been 'touted around newspaper offices' by Cathy and Kate for months.

There are a few tiny problems with this theory. Until Cathy Woodhead broke her silence in the *Mail on Sunday* recently, complaining that her ex-husband had incited her to lie on his behalf, Kate Illingworth had consistently refused to speak to journalists about the story. She has not seen Tony Robinson since Christmas, and Christine Purkis hasn't spoken to Robinson for a year, which must have made it rather hard for the three of them to formulate their plot against the Ofsted chief.

What about Kate Illingworth's 'manipulation' of Cathy Woodhead? She produces her phone bill for the last quarter, which shows that between 15 January and 14 April she made precisely one telephone call to Cathy. 'I haven't actually seen her for about two years,' she adds.

Nor is she any kind of Labour activist. Though her membership has now lapsed, Illingworth did belong to the party for 16 years 'but, to my shame, I never went to a single branch meeting'. She did once deliver a branch newsletter, however.

If there is a conspiracy at all, it is the one organised by Chris Woodhead's supporters to smear his critics. For Woodhead, unlike his former wife, has friends in very high places indeed. They include the Prince of Wales, plus two shadowy figures who are believed to be long-term Labour activists. Their names? Tony Blair and David Blunkett. ●

....

16 April 1999
Michael White
Stepford jibes

Parliament was back from its Easter break this week. But apart from that defiant Lords' vote on gay sex, would you have noticed? Its marginal role in the Balkan war serves only to highlight a painful truth. The executive branch of government goes from strength to strength, but the legislative branch is proving a quiet disaster.

This is becoming the Forgotten Parliament. This week backbenchers protested (again) about being ignored by the broadsheets and the BBC. The debate was itself largely ignored. Ditto the report proposing a second 'mini-chamber' for uncontentious debates, as if two ignored forums will be better than one. What do they have to do to get attention? Take their clothes off, like the Yorkshire WI?

Yes, there's a war on. And the repackaging of power, up the line to Brussels and down to Edinburgh and Cardiff, also serves to diminish a deliberative national assembly. So do modern media habits and Blairite attitudes such as an impatience with Old Brit institutions. But what is really killing the present Commons is mere numbers, the debilitating mathematics of the biggest election landslide this century. What many people instinctively felt in the small hours of 2 May 1997 has turned out to be true. The Blairistas' historic victory has proved pernicious.

It raised expectations of Labour omnipotence after years of trying to lower them. That is the government's problem. Potentially much more serious, it also left Parliament full of new MPs. There were simply too many Labour members (418) to have much influence or leverage, too few Tories (165) to make the system work, too few Lib Dems (46) to matter – even though there were more than for 60 years. No balance of power for Paddy after all!

Little wonder that when Fiona Jones was for a time ousted from her Newark seat, accused of electoral fraud, the one statistic not mentioned in press reports was how it would affect Labour's bloated majority. If two busloads of Blair's flock went over a cliff in a Millbank-run photo opportunity it would scarcely matter.

Arithmetic thus combines with New Labour management style to marginalise Westminster, which currently functions at full-ish power for about two days a week (Tuesdays and Wednesdays), when committee quorums can be filled. Thursday is as quiet as Friday used to be; most Fridays feel like Saturdays. There is a ghostly feel to the old place.

Margaret Thatcher also enjoyed huge majorities, but faced an energetic and experienced Opposition, not to mention her own troublemakers, left and right. In 1997, 117 MPs retired (pensions are better now, another factor) and a further 132 were defeated, the biggest exodus this century. Almost two years on, many MPs remain too cowed ('Big Brother is paging you,' as a Fabian Society wit put it) or too complicit to challenge the government, as all governments must be. Some resent the Stepford MP jibe, and it is true that the class of '97 contains clever, hard-working and conscientious souls, busily doing good as they always did.

The Awkward Squad also survives, the Benns and Dalyells, augmented by younger troublemakers who do not want jobs (Bob Marshall-Andrews, Lynne Jones). When the government finally makes a hash of something big (Kosovo perhaps?) they – and the Tories – expect a parliamentary revival.

Meanwhile, much of the heart has gone out of the place. 'I'd like to vote with you, but it won't make any difference to the result and will finish me with the Whips,' MPs tell the old lags. 'Some members now behave like employees,' complains a very respectable Labour ex-minister. 'We are supposed to represent our constituencies at Westminster, not the other way around,' says one exasperated Tory.

Some argue that the Commons is now being run for the benefit of New Labour MPs who have families or constituencies in south-east England and want to go home to them at night. Hurrah, say the 119 elected Sisters and the New Men; tiredness and adversarial politics late at night, fuelled by the joys of the Strangers Bar, do not make for better legislation or accountability, any more than do hereditary (mostly elderly Tory) peers.

The modernisers preach the virtues of 'big tent' inclusiveness and the non-partisan, pre-legislative scrutiny of bills. Their pollsters tell them voters are switched off politics, especially the yah-boo kind. That was how Blair justified his unilateral imposition of a single 30-minute PM's Question Time, now widely disliked. Like recent procedural reform, the changes seem executive-driven.

Parliament is relevant when it asks the questions that should be being asked in pubs and on *Newsnight*, questions which are not always on-message. But parliamentary politics is a bit like sex: the real danger is atrophy through lack of use. It would be an irony if, as the Strasbourg parliament finds its proper vocation, the locals in SW1 lose the plot. ●

....

13 February 1999
Smallweed

People sometimes wonder that Tony Blair, so smiling and agreeable to most of the nation, reserves his sharpest public disfavour for groups closest to home, like the unions and the Labour Party. This is a wicked calumny. There are other groups too whom he finds it equally hard to love and respect. The House of Commons for one. It's a Commons tradition that ministers, even prime ministers, don't stamp on select committees which dare to be critical.

So Blair's instant contemptuous dismissal of this week's report on the Sandline affair – quite apart from the fact that he made it to Jimmy Young, not to the Commons – puts his backbenchers on the spot. Whose side should they take when the issue comes, at last, to the Commons? Fortunately we have an impeccable guideline to help them decide. 'The first duty of an MP is to defend the rights of Parliament against any government that threatens those rights.' Said by a red-haired chap with a beard, whose name I forget, in the Commons debate on the Scott report. I knew we would need it sooner or later if Labour got in.

Dame Judi Dench, having done with Victoria and Elizabeth, laments she has few more queens to enact. Before long she'll be down to 'Boudicca, with only one breast'. But our dame is too doom-laden. In the pages of Edward Gibbon, I came across Zenobia, Queen of Palmyra and the East, who falls heavily into my category of People Largely Unknown to Otherwise Informed Deipnosophists.

'If we except the doubtful achievements of Semiramis,' the great historian writes, 'Zenobia is perhaps the only female whose superior genius broke through the servile indolence imposed on her sex by the climate and manners of Asia.' Her beauty, salivatingly described in these pages, was said to match Cleopatra's. Succeeding her murdered husband, Odenathus, she extended his empire by conquest even to Egypt, but was defeated in war by Aurelian and captured while fleeing on the most fleet of her dromedaries. She lived out the rest of her life in comfort and opulence in a villa 20 miles from Rome, 'insensibly sunk into a Roman matron'. I see Dench as the later Zenobia, with the earlier Zenobia played in flashback by Julia Roberts to ensure the movie is shown in America.

Our Readers' Editor apologised the other day in 'Corrections and Clarifications' after somebody used the term 'knob' to apply to a member of the nobility. We should have said 'nob', he contended. I wonder at this fellow's assurance. If Smallweed made a statement as bold as that, a spate of letters would arrive from various universities saying I was in error, and that using 'knob' to mean somebody well-to-do was perfectly proper practice.

As in this case, I happen to know, it is. The term 'knob' as short for 'nobility', or, as they would have said, 'knobility', derives from the habits of a tiny, enclosed community which flourished in the seventeenth and eighteenth centuries in and around the town of Knebworth in Hertfordshire. They cherished their own peculiar practices as faithfully as the Amish, and none more so than the tradition of attaching an unsounded 'k' at the start of every word beginning with 'n'. Because the 'k' was unsounded, the rare outsiders who penetrated the community never noticed that it was there. But then a historian called Knollys, who had left the community to pursue an academic career – insisting to those who sought to deter him that there could be no higher calling than knowledge – recorded its peculiar terminology in a monograph now held at Knottingham University.

Despite their primitive ways, the principal local families – the Knappers, the Knills and the Knights – were people of substance. The Knatchbulls, who lived at the Hall, even owned a Kneller. Most earned their livings at trades like knitting and knife grinding. Men and women alike wore a distinctive dress of knickerbockers and knapsacks; a man over middle age would customarily carry a knout or knobkerrie. In religion, they followed Knox, and their favourite king, celebrated each year with a feast in the knave of the chapel, was Knut, whom they pronounced Newt.

But the forces of centralisation eventually did for them. One day in September 1788, Knollys returned to the village. At first the inhabitants greeted him with their usual courtesy. But the great world outside had turned the historian's head. Flourishing a knational knewspaper, the first they had ever seen, he told them in brutal terms that the world was changing. The 'k' attached to words beginning with 'n', he declared, was kno longer knecessary. Their kindliness turned to anger. Denouncing him as a kne'er-do-well and a knincompoop, they drove him out of the town. But the young of the village absorbed what he said, and bit by bit the tradition began to die. I'd be tempted to say it would never return, but I'm stayed by the stern injunction which, according to Knollys, Knebworthians were wont to address to each other daily: 'Knever say knever.' •

....

10 May 1999

Martin Walker

Alice would have felt quite at home here

Each of the three main European institutions has just made a complete ass of itself, and the common factor has been that besetting Brussels sin of *folie de grandeur*, the madness that comes from power, or at least the perception of having it.

Your European commissioners reporting for no duty at all, sah!!

The latest folly comes from the European parliament, which was about to go into next month's elections with a sporting chance of being taken seriously by the voters after forcing Jacques Santer and his hapless commissioners into mass resignation. But since any parliamentary assault on the commission for fraud, corruption and mismanagement is a classic case of the pot calling the kettle black, MEPs were obliged to clean up their own tawdry act by finally ending the long-running scandal over their travel expenses.

Every time I run into an MEP strolling from his Brussels home to the parliament offices, I wonder whether he or she has billed the taxpayer for a first-class return airfare from the constituency. This has been a frequent practice, since MEPs' expenses claims are not checked. It has also taken place with a nod and a wink from the parliament's authorities, because each MEP is paid the same as an MP from his or her national parliament. This puts the Italians and Germans on £80,000 a year, and the Greeks and Spaniards on £20,000. Fiddling expenses evened things out a bit.

The reform plan was kicked off by Tony Blair at the Cardiff EU summit last year, and pushed hard by Labour MEP Pauline Green as leader of the Socialist group in the European parliament: to pay MEPs the average of what all the national MPs received. This kept the Brits at about the same level, boosted the incomes of the Greeks and Spaniards and hit the Germans and Italians.

Pauline Green was so confident that this would pass that her spokesman issued a press release last week boasting of the clean-up. He spoke too soon.

The Germans and Italians revolted, and so MEPs are now heading for the polls while stuck with the indefensible practices of the *ancien régime*.

Jacques Santer has gone the way of Louis XIV; his Marie Antoinette, Edith Cresson, still queens it in Brussels, with two full-time chauffeurs at her service. Like the rest of the nominal ex-commissioners, she is still on full pay and allowances. By the time she goes in September, Mme Cresson will have raked in some £80,000 since she grumpily signed the resignation statement.

If the new commission president, Romano Prodi, wants to prove his commitment to reform, he ought to padlock her office doors, transfer her chauffeurs and block her salary payments – and defy her and her wretched dentist to take him to court for the money.

Can't do that, my dear chap, say the old hands. Prodi not actually installed yet. Abuse of power. Breach of law. And all the other cogent reasons for doing nothing which got the Brussels old guard into such a stagnant, arrogant mess in the first place. Brussels currently feels like Europe through the looking glass. Alice would feel quite at home. The commission has supposedly resigned, but nothing has changed. The 20 ex-commissioners still meet each Wednesday, run their offices, make speeches – and the chauffeurs still take them to the airport for foreign trips as if nothing had happened.

The only one who seems to realise the world has changed has been Martin Bangemann, Germany's pudding-shaped industry commissioner. I can forgive him for spending so much time on his yacht after he confessed his relief at no longer having to defend the 'bullshit' of the commission's formal position on the banana row with the Americans.

The Americans also play a central role in the third daftness which bedevils the European institutions. This time the blame falls on the Council of Ministers, where the EU's 15 foreign ministers airily assumed that Europe would take over the civil administration of post-war Kosovo. Yet they failed to consult Nato or even the Americans, who are providing most of the air power which might just get us all into that post-war situation. The Americans are rather cross about this, although one might have thought they were accustomed to Europe's delusions of grandeur by now.

The Americans have discreetly told the EU to forget it. The post-war dispensation will be in the hands of the UN, and the US thinks it would be far more sensible to entrust Kosovo's civil administration to the OSCE (Organisation for Security and Cooperation in Europe), which includes the Russians and Eastern Europeans and Serbia's neighbours, as well as all EU members.

Obvious really, unless you inhabit that curious Brussels biosphere in which ex-commissioners still serve, MEPs still ride the gravy train and EU ministers think they decide foreign policy. •

27 January 1999
Jonathan Freedland
Our mightiest democrat

He was a drunk with appalling table manners, a loud mouth and a giant-size ego. Both his marriages failed, he died in penury and he was condemned by his peers as a 'loathsome reptile', 'a demi-human arch-beast' and 'an object of disgust'. And yet this man, whose birthday is on Friday, could hold the key to Britain's political future – and to Tony Blair's greatest dilemma.

For 29 January marks the two hundred and sixty-second birthday of Thomas Paine. Nearly two centuries after his death, Paine's words remain the clearest clarion call for democracy ever fashioned. Even now, his urgent, radical voice, whether in the *Rights of Man* or *Common Sense*, can stir the heart, almost shocking in its relevance to today.

He was against monarchy, aristocracy and superstition. He wanted the mysteries so beloved by the élite to be swept aside, making way for a system of government understood by every citizen. He was a militant for equality, a scourge of privilege, an enemy of heredity. His prose was as egalitarian as his politics, his style sparkling in its simplicity. Take his riff on the irrationality of inherited power: to Paine, the House of Lords and the monarchy were 'as absurd as an hereditary mathematician, or an hereditary wiseman, as ridiculous as an hereditary poet laureate'. We don't allocate those jobs by bloodline, so why the highest offices of state?

He was a man of action too, a player in the two great revolutions of his time, writing the manifesto of the rebel Americans in 1776 and winning a seat in the French National Assembly a decade and a half later.

Yet Thomas Paine is nearly forgotten in his own land. There is a statue in his Norfolk hometown of Thetford – located, inappropriately enough, on King Street. There used to be a Rights of Man pub nearby, and there's still a Tom Paine Society (with Michael Foot, the editor of his collected works, its president). But the great Briton's face adorns no banknotes, his name lines few streets. Paine is honoured in America and France, but in Britain his standing has not much improved since the chilly day in December 1792 when he was convicted *in absentia* of seditious libel and banned from ever coming home. Like the old ditty ran:

> Poor Tom Paine! There he lies
> Nobody laughs and nobody cries
> Where he has gone and how he fares
> Nobody knows and nobody cares.

In a bid to end the amnesia, Britain's republicans will gather on Friday to drink Paine's health and to launch in earnest the Common Sense movement, dedicated to heeding his call two centuries on. What they, and I, believe is that the days of forgetting have gone on long enough; London should take its place alongside Paris and New York, and raise a statue of Thomas Paine. There's an obvious space for it: the long-empty plinth at Trafalgar Square would suit old Tom just fine. But there should be a more vital memorial; Paine is too bubbling with life to be confined in marble or bronze. Instead his ideas should be enshrined in today's politics.

For progressives who have given up on the old Marxist canon, Paine offers an alternative – a rebuttal to those who say the age of ideology is over. His ideas, formed in the dusk of the eighteenth century, stand as a coherent creed for the dawn of the twenty-first.

He is almost irresistibly right-on. In Pennsylvania, he moved to make that state the first to emancipate the slaves. In France, he pleaded with the Jacobins to spare the life of Louis XVI, arguing that no human being was evil enough to merit the death penalty. He sketched out a plan for child benefit, free education and universal pensions. He wanted a written constitution and was appalled by the existence of extreme poverty and wealth side by side, 'like dead and living bodies chained together'.

It is an inspiring set of ideas, underpinned by the liberating belief that each generation can 'begin the world over again', unburdened by the outdated conventions of the past. He believed that the people should be masters of their own fate, sovereign in their own nation. They could, at last, put away childish things, including the fairy-tale institution of royalty.

Last week we heard endlessly of Tony Blair's grandest project, the realignment of the centre left. After Paddy had gone, how could Tony hope to bring Labour and Liberal Democrats together to keep the Conservatives in permanent exile? Most answers concentrated on the mechanics of Lib-Labbery, the business of committees and Cabinet seats. Few worried much about ideas, the commodities we are now told have been banished from politics.

Yet a quick read of Thomas Paine proves that ideas could solve Blair's problem. For Paine was the original liberal, a believer in minimal government and maximum social freedom. He yearned for equality of opportunity, but had no hang-ups over equality of outcome. He embraced the free market – aware the alternative meant handing greater muscle to the central state – but despised privilege for tilting the playing field. He sought genuine meritocracy, with rewards for those who displayed talent and hard work – and none for the 'nobility' of the aristocracy. He wanted to rein in central government, replacing it with local control. He sought a civil society of enterprise and equality, not a feudal one dominated by one caste with all power hoarded at the centre.

It reads like a blueprint of liberalism, still relevant for today. By his actions, Blair has embraced several of its key tenets anyway. He too trusts in the free market and is wary of intervention by the central state. He too is bent on removing heredity from Parliament (if not palace). But so far New Labour has always argued those positions in the language of grudging electoral realism: the voters won't let us do anything else. Paineism offers another path, a liberalism of principle, adamant in its demand for both freedom and equality. If Labour adopts that as its creed, there would be no place for pacts with Charles Kennedy or deals with Menzies Campbell. The Liberal Democrats would simply become redundant, their best ideas – liberty and democracy – gobbled up by Labour. There's no need to call Peter Mandelson; the game plan's already been written – by the man whose birthday we should all celebrate on Friday. ●

....

5 May 1999

Ewen MacAskill

Fear and loathing mar campaign

Politics is dirty in Paisley. Two years ago a heavy mortise lock crashed through the kitchen window of Nancy Allison, the Labour provost of Renfrewshire. Recalling the incident last week, as glaziers dealt with another act of vandalism, she said the lock had been wrapped in a leaflet saying 'For Nancy Allison: vote Scottish National Party.'

Who was responsible? The 65-year-old provost, who is retiring at the election, did not know who was behind this and a host of other incidents since, and was reluctant to speculate, but what provides an insight into the vicious nature of politics in Renfrewshire is that any number of individuals could have been responsible.

In a troubled town, whose Ferguslie Park area has become synonymous with drugs, guns and deprivation, hatred between Labour and the SNP is deeper than anywhere else in Scotland. The police have been regular attenders at Renfrewshire council meetings, called in to escort unruly SNP members out at the request of the ruling Labour administration. But relations within the Labour Party have been even worse, descending to a level of personal abuse and acrimony unparalleled in Britain, brought to a conclusion only through expulsion and resignation.

Expectations for the Scottish parliament, at least among those who have long campaigned for it, are high. The SNP in Renfrewshire is more uncompromising than elsewhere in Scotland. The leadership is fundamentalist, a long way from the cheery and relatively sophisticated politics of Alex Salmond. Jim Mitchell, its deputy leader on the council, who has been among those ordered out of the chamber, is a gut nationalist who said the English 'had been screwing the Scots for long enough. If we had been some other part of the Commonwealth, we would be independent by now. Our misfortune is to live next to the English.' Bill Martin, standing for the Scottish parliament as SNP candidate for Paisley South, chose for the last four digits of his telephone '1314', the date of the battle of Bannockburn, when the Scots defeated the English.

Since the beginning of the election Mr Salmond has been accusing Labour of fighting a negative campaign. He has overlooked the SNP's campaign literature in Renfrewshire, almost all of which carries the headline 'Points for Sex Offenders', a claim that Labour is to give priority on council housing lists to paedophiles.

The SNP leaflet is tame in comparison with one from Paul Mack, a former Labour deputy council leader who has fallen out with his colleagues and is standing as an independent in Paisley South. Mr Mack's scurrilous leaflet, which includes a personal attack on Mrs Allison, is the subject of a court order. Mr Mack, who has been ordered out of the council chamber 10 times, is scheduled to appear in court on Friday, an unusual beginning to a career as a member of the Scottish parliament in the unlikely event of his being elected.

Mr Mack is being supported by another Labour maverick, Tommy Graham, MP for Renfrewshire West. Mr Graham is not loved by the Labour hierarchy, one of whose members described him this week as a malign force. Mr Graham was expelled by Labour last year after an allegation that, as part of political manoeuvring, he had claimed to have a compromising photograph of a gay trade unionist. Mr Graham disputes the charge.

Labour's investigation into Mr Graham began after the furore that followed the suicide of the Paisley Labour MP, Gordon McMaster, soon after the election. His constituency office is on the edge of Ferguslie Park, in a street scarred with barbed wire. He said he had had 31 death threats.

He sees himself as the innocent party, the victim of internecine warfare in Paisley, stitched up over petty rivalries and for his battles against the remnants of the ultra-left grouping Militant, which was banned by Neil Kinnock. He decried the violent reputation that Paisley had gained, but later went on to make detailed allegations linking politics and the drugs world, and recounts gun incidents. He had supported the creation of a Scottish parliament but was under no illusions that the kind of battles witnessed in Paisley would be avoided in Edinburgh. After a honeymoon period, he predicted, it would 'disintegrate into political mayhem'.

On the other side of the barrier from the SNP and Labour dissidents is the official Labour candidate for Paisley South, Hugh Henry, a former schoolteacher and social worker who has had the difficult task of holding together the minority administration on Renfrewshire council. Out canvassing, he recalled that his worst moment during these last few hard years had been abuse from an SNP supporter in the council chamber who shouted he was a child molester, which was bad enough in itself but made worse by the presence of his young daughter in the chamber.

Mr Henry is liked by the Labour leadership, which believes he has achieved much in cleaning up council politics. That Donald Dewar, the Scottish Secretary and likely first minister of the parliament, likes Mr Henry is remarkable, as Mr Henry was a member of Militant. In his case, the Labour leadership has been prepared to forgive, putting his Militant days down to youthful indiscretion.

Paisley South is regarded as an SNP stronghold, though probably not strong enough to prevent Mr Henry taking it. He has found support for what Labour has achieved over the past two years, but there were also voices expressing disillusion, and there was a well of sympathy for the SNP.

Paisley has seen some of the worst excesses of Scottish politics but is also home to a new generation of politicians who will shape the Scottish parliament. Wendy Alexander, standing in Paisley North, is one of a group, now in their thirties, who 12 years ago formed Scottish Labour Action, a pressure group aimed at ensuring the party did not renege on its promise to deliver a parliament. About half a dozen of that group can expect to be elected, and some are almost certain to find themselves in Mr Dewar's first cabinet. The person eventually to replace Mr Dewar could come from that generation.

Ms Alexander, brought up in the Renfrewshire village of Bishopton and until the election a special adviser to Mr Dewar, rejected the idea that the Scottish parliament will be Paisley on a bigger scale. She gave two main reasons: the new voting system that will see proportional representation used on the British mainland for the first time, and the number of women, expected to make up more than 40 per cent of the members, which she said would be a higher percentage than any other legislature in the world.

Idealism and realism will clash in Paisley tomorrow, and again when the parliament is up and running. The hope is that those elected will prove to be of a higher calibre and show more restraint than many of their counterparts in Paisley. •

27 March 1999

Leader
A nation divided

None of the usual rules apply. The old battle lines have become blurred and confused. Suddenly it's Red Ken the Bomber versus Lord Toff the Peacenik. A Labour prime minister takes to the airwaves urging support for our boys in action, while Tory grandees plead for restraint. Ken Livingstone backs Nato and Washington. Lord Carrington, a former secretary-general of Nato, wishes Britain would stop playing America's poodle. The *Daily Mail* is deeply sceptical of the Nato operation; the *Guardian* more supportive. So who's on the left and who's on the right? And, after Kosovo, what do those terms even mean?

The truth is, Kosovo has divided Britons – and along none of the usual lines. The Nato onslaught has provoked an extraordinary reaction on radio phone-in shows, in MPs' mailbags and all the other instant outlets for public opinion. People are debating this mission in a way they rarely argued over the war in the Gulf or the peacekeeping effort in Bosnia. Even Britain's own war in Northern Ireland has seldom sparked quite so heated a public debate.

Why has this happened? Might it be because no side has a monopoly on truth? You don't have to be a heartless bystander to object to the nightly – and now daily – bombing raids on Belgrade. You might loathe Serbia's war against the Kosovo Albanians just as much as any of the gung-ho interventionists – it's just you fear this is the wrong type of intervention. You might agree with Tony Blair's insistence to the nation last night that we would be guilty of 'unpardon-able weakness and dereliction' if we did nothing – it's just you wish we would do something else, like send in ground troops rather than rely on the easier option of air strikes. That's not an illegitimate position – even if it smacks a little of ideal-worldism rather than a pragmatic acceptance of the best available course of action. What it does reveal, however, is the inherent messiness of the Kosovo dilemma, one that does not easily reduce to black and white.

For that reason, the right and left have not divided along party lines. In the days of the Cold War, choosing sides was a simpler business – no matter how far away the battle raged. The right sided with America and the 'pro-democracy' forces; the left opposed the US and backed the 'anti-imperialist struggle'. But no such gloss is available here. The Serbs and Kosovars are not proxies for the US and the old Soviet Union. This time we have to think for ourselves.

So other factors have come into play. Instead of left and right, old and young has become a key determinant. The Second World War generation – Denis Healey, Tony Benn, Lord Carrington – have led the opposition to the Balkan mission. Are they informed by a historic empathy for the Serbs, a sense of solidarity with the nation which stood up to Nazism? Or are they driven by the calculus of comparison, believing that whatever atrocities Slobodan Milosevic is guilty of, they pale alongside the Nazi evil which obliged their generation to go to war. Ranged opposite them are Messrs Blair and Clinton, the voices of the baby-boom generation. One would have thought Vietnam would colour their judgement, pressing them to steer well clear of any potential quagmire. Instead they are keen to strike – though only from the air – aware perhaps that the Cambodias and Rwandas of recent history were possible only because the strong governments of the West did nothing.

But the public is not yet convinced. Mr Blair said last night that the 'longest hours' in a PM's life are the ones waiting for news of the service personnel he has put in harm's way. Beyond that anxiety, he has another challenge: he somehow has to lead an uncertain nation in a war they do not yet fully support. These may well be his toughest days. ●

. . . .

28 June 1999

Michael White

Benn's declaration of independence

The news that Tony Benn is to end his parliamentary career at the next election is not all good news for New Labour. With a characteristically mischievous flourish, Mr Benn made it clear that he will not be retiring to write his memoirs. 'I want more time to devote to politics and more freedom to do so,' he said.

As if to make his point, the 74-year-old MP gave a barnstorming speech about the welfare state at a 250-strong 'pensioners' parliament' in Nottingham. Alan Simpson, MP for Nottingham South, who was at the rally, said: 'He played a stormer. He has always thought the Lords is undemocratic and often expresses fears that this is what the Commons is being reduced to. You are going to see a rejuvenated Tony Benn. This is not so much a retirement as Benn's declaration of independence.'

Just to underline that declaration, Mr Benn promised 'to work closely with all those, outside and inside parliament, who want to see the Labour Party recommit itself to the causes of social justice, democratic socialism and peace'.

In the agenda of the 1990s that translates as defending the universal basis of the welfare state, challenging globalised capitalism and running a campaign against what he sees as quasi-imperialist actions by Nato – with or without UN sanction – towards countries like Iraq and Serbia.

His outspoken opposition to the war in Kosovo has won him new friends – and confirmed the view of old enemies, who see him as a mixture of upper-middle-class romantic and calculating populist who campaigned ruthlessly to end MPs' exclusive rights to pick Labour leaders because it was the only way he could win that prize. It may have eluded him, but no Labour figure since Aneurin Bevan has aroused such strong feelings on both sides.

In the circumstances it was not necessary yesterday for him to indicate whether he would be available to serve in the House of Lords. Apart from his ideological differences with New Labour, he is the only man alive who has fought three by-elections to establish his right not to be a peer. 'Don't be silly,' he replied when asked about a life peerage yesterday.

In a ground-breaking three-year campaign in 1960–63, the then Anthony Wedgwood Benn, whose older brother, Michael, had been killed in the Second

World War, refused to succeed to the hereditary title of Viscount Stansgate. The title had been given to his father, an ex-Liberal who became a minister in Britain's first Labour government. Bristol South-East voters re-elected their MP when the election court repeatedly debarred him as a peer and the law was eventually changed.

As with later Benn campaigns, the results were not always foreseen. Two Tory MPs also renounced their peerages, one of whom, the Fourteenth Earl of Home, ended up in the Commons as prime minister.

By the mid-1980s, when Michael Foot handed over the Labour leadership to Neil Kinnock after a bloody internal war with the Bennite left, it was fashionable to blame him for helping Margaret Thatcher consolidate her rule by making his own party unelectable. Mr Benn had insisted on fighting Denis Healey for the post of deputy leader, even though the party leader, Mr Foot, asked him not to. He lost by a tiny margin, but the fight contributed to the creation of the breakaway SDP and Mrs Thatcher's victory by 143 seats in the 1983 election. He remained unrepentant, despite losing his Bristol seat, insisting that more people had voted for a socialist manifesto than ever before.

That same manifesto was called 'the longest suicide note ever written' by Gerald Kaufman and few MPs have ever been indifferent to Wedgie, as he has long been known. Harold Wilson accused him of 'immaturing with age' and Tony Crosland, a close personal friend, is supposed to have said: 'Nothing wrong with Jimmy [his nickname for Mr Benn], he's just a bit cracked.'

That did not matter to the man who had seen government from the inside in 1964–70 and 1974–9 and concluded that Labour was betraying its activists, its voters and its history.

Having joined the Tribune Group – he promptly split it – he became a pillar of the Campaign Group and a passionate advocate of grass-roots, participatory politics in the age of focus groups and spin doctors.

'All progress has always come from outside Parliament,' he insisted yesterday.

Mr Benn's public image has changed sharply over the years. He was a moderniser in the 1950s – 'the Peter Mandelson of the 1959 campaign,' he once claimed – and a pipe-smoking ministerial technocrat under Harold Wilson in the 1960s. In the 1970s he moved steadily left to become a thorn in Jim Callaghan's side, though he never resigned, and infuriated left-wing MPs with his pragmatic decisions. It was under his rule as energy minister that the oil industry escaped regulation by the health and safety executive.

'When Tony was a minister he did one thing, in opposition quite another,' one old sparring partner recalled last night. In the heyday of Thatcherism, Mr Benn became the bogeyman of respectable society when aligned with the hard left and Arthur Scargill against Neil Kinnock's early modernisation.

The rise of New Labour – Liberals in disguise, he says – has marginalised Tony Benn and he may have personal reasons for announcing his retirement before reselection of MPs starts in the autumn. His wife, Caroline, has been unwell and only last week he passed the family torch to his son, Hilary, whose maiden speech as MP for Leeds Central he watched with unabashed fatherly pride.

Nowadays even Tory MPs express respect and admiration for Tony Benn's devotion to Parliament and his brilliance as a speaker – even when, as over Kosovo, they violently disagree with him. Now that Enoch Powell is dead and Michael Foot retired, only Ted Heath has his range or breadth, and no one has his passion.

Tony Benn has had years of practice at avoiding the status of much-loved elder statesman. He will go on causing trouble. 'I have planted quite a number of little acorns and they have grown into oak trees,' he said yesterday. He is still planting. •

1 February 1999
Polly Toynbee
Rich farmers are merrily milking the system

This time of year the Chancellor is casting greedy eyes around in search of painless new taxes for his budget. Gordon Brown has done brilliantly at raking in sizeable sums from places people don't understand (pension funds) or from fat cats they hate (privatised utilities). But if he is looking around for other unloved fat cats, I recommend he turns his gaze upon the vast, totally untaxed profits made by landowners who sell green fields for new development. Few people realise that they pay no tax on their gigantic profits.

The Urban Task Force, chaired by Richard Rogers, is currently searching for carrots and sticks to persuade developers to use derelict city sites instead of green fields: 1,700 people a week are pouring out of cities for outer suburbs, country or villages, usually moving to brand-new developments. The task force is seeking ways to reverse this trend, to breathe new life into cities and save the countryside from further depredation. The Chancellor would be working with the grain of that policy if he made country landowners pay their fair share of tax on their windfall capital gains.

At present, through a curious tax loophole, landowners pay no Capital Gains Tax on the colossal profits which have been earned by no sweat of their brow or entrepreneurial risk, but by a local authority planner's signature on a piece of paper redesignating farming land for development. You could make an excellent case for giving the local authority most of the landowner's profits to compensate the local community for the extra building on their doorsteps. But that probably smacks of a little too much Socialism for this government. No, this more modest proposal is just to make landowners pay the same taxes as anyone else on their capital windfalls. Most people would be astonished to hear that they pay nothing.

The Chancellor could collect an estimated £1 billion if he turned his eye upon this advertisement that appeared recently in the *East Anglian Daily Times* (just one among many such): 'Farmland Wanted Urgently. To obtain capital gains tax roll-over relief on the proceeds from selling part of his farm for house building development, farmer must reinvest up to £5 million prior to next budget. Any locations and acreages considered. Reply in confidence . . .'

This is how the scam works. A landowner has 50 acres of farmland which, to his great good fortune, are suddenly included in a local development plan. No NIMBY, he's overjoyed to welcome a prime plot of executive homes into his back yard. His agricultural acres, yesterday worth a mere £150,000, are now sold for £5 million. He has made an overnight capital gain of £4.85 million, on which any ordinary punter would expect to pay £1.94 CGT. But he won't have to pay a penny. Through a loophole designed for quite other purposes, he is allowed to reinvest the whole sum in buying vast acres, whole extra prairies, tax-free.

How can this be? It springs from a perfectly sensible tax law allowing a farmer to relocate by selling one farm and buying another without getting hit by CGT. The same applies to anyone selling a business. They can immediately reinvest the money in another enterprise without paying any CGT. It's a reasonable way of encouraging entrepreneurs to keep their money in business, with flexibility to move from one enterprise to another. But when it comes to land values inflated overnight by planning permission, none of this makes any sense at all. It's unfair and it has a counterproductive effect on the use of land.

It encourages farmers to sell and to buy gigantic tracts of land they can't possibly manage themselves, sell off any farmhouses and put it into the hands of management companies who do no good to the countryside or local communities. As the frantic tone of the above advertisement suggests, it inflates farm land prices, making it even harder for genuine small farmers to stay on the land and keep the countryside picturesque. As farmer Oliver Walston's brilliant recent television series, *Against the Grain*, proved conclusively, we don't need mega-farms and subsidies for high production no one can consume, but small unproductive farms subsidised, if necessary, to keep the country looking good.

At a conservative estimate, the Treasury loses at least £1 billion a year by failing to levy CGT on these landowners' windfalls. There used to be a Development Land Tax under the last Labour government, designed to discourage greenfield building, but it was generally judged a disaster because it simply brought development to a halt, with builders holding their breath and waiting for a Tory government to remove it (which they did). But to apply ordinary CGT to these land sales would not be a punitive tax, simply the same tax on profits paid by any other property or share owner. The money could be earmarked to encourage developers into derelict city sites.

In the run-up to the budget, it's worth listing the many perks and reliefs that go to the better off, usually forgotten in the great cacophony of criticism of the benefit system. (This one loophole for a handful of landowners is worth a quarter of the entire estimated Social Security fraud.) The middle-class welfare state is subtle, complicated, well hidden from view and rarely discussed in polite society, but we can hope it is being hotly debated within the Treasury just now.

Here are just a few examples of the perks for the better off: £1.8 billion on Mortgage Tax Relief, £1.7 billion on Married Couples' Allowance (mainly benefiting middle- and upper-middle-income families), £1.05 billion in tax forgone on private schools' charitable status, £450 million on private health's secret subsidy. The self-employed escape with some £2 billion through clever accounting on top of the colossal £5 billion they are officially exempted from National Insurance for no clear reason. Most transport subsidy goes to better-off commuters, not to poorer workers who travel least. Then there's the huge £8.9 billion tax subsidy to occupational pensions, again benefiting mainly the better off.

Not all these should be cut, but they form the middle-class welfare state which we should never forget in the often warped debate about how much we tax and spend. Meanwhile, this exemption for landowners is certainly ripe for the Chancellor's pruning hook. ●

....

8 October 1998
Anne Perkins
The 'Ann and Mo' shows

First it was Mo, now it's Ann. In barely a week, the Labour and Tory conferences have elevated the two women the parties' image-makers most long to get their hands on into potential party leaders. Last Tuesday it was the Northern Ireland Secretary Mo Mowlam: Blackpool's Winter Gardens rocked with the affectionate cheers of the party as Tony Blair paid tribute to her part in the struggle for peace. Straggly hair growing back after chemotherapy for a brain tumour, her round face split in an unusually self-conscious grin, and she became St Mo in an instant. Around her on the platform, the coming men and women of the party, like the immaculate Patricia Hewitt and the dapper Mike O'Brien, have the impact of dummies in a Principles shop window.

And this Tuesday it was Ann Widdecombe, Tory health spokeswoman, the one they used to call Doris Karloff, who slayed 'em at Bournemouth, flailing about among the Ikea furniture on the conference platform, ignoring teleprompt and lectern with the same unapologetic conviction she had when she was a

Martin Argles

Ann Widdecombe: a star rises at the Conservative Party Conference, 1998

Home Office minister defending the decision to manacle women prisoners in labour.

'I did think it would be quite interesting, because no one had ever tried to make a speech that way before, but I wasn't expecting it to be as massively great as it was,' she said with mild satisfaction yesterday. 'I don't think Mo and I really have much in common,' she added, 'except that we are both quite informal and we say it as we see it.'

And, conference-darling status apart, the most obvious thing about the two women is how different they are – politically, natch, but in style too. Widdecombe, brisk sometimes to the point of prickliness, against the easy, cuddly expansiveness of Mowlam. In debate, where Mowlam has a difficult decision to defend, as she has on prisoner release, she always starts by acknowledging there are two sides to the argument (though she did famously once tell Ian Paisley to 'fuck off'). The Widdecombe approach, by contrast, is uncompromising; rational argument delivered at top volume. They're about the same age, but where Mowlam is now (recently) married with two stepchildren, Widdecombe is celebrated for her celibacy. 'A prude and proud of it,' according to one tabloid headline.

But despite the differences there are similarities too in the way they managed to bring their respective party faithful to collective climax. The most obvious is their spectacular unselfconsciousness about their appearance, a trait which clearly endears them to audiences longing to identify with leaders rather than worship them. Received political wisdom says such casualness is an electoral liability: after all, being endearingly unselfconscious about his appearance never did anything for Michael Foot, the man who terrified Fleet Street by wearing a dufflecoat to the Cenotaph on Remembrance Sunday. But for Mowlam and Widdecombe, their evident ease with themselves plainly makes them instantly attractive.

What the affair of Foot's duffle coat (he always denied it was a donkey jacket) did, by showing how powerful a negative image can be, was to trigger a whole generation of embarrassingly self-conscious politicians. It cued the painfully manicured politics of the 1990s, a time when Alastair Campbell, the Prime Minister's press secretary, could in an earlier incarnation as the *Mirror*'s political editor, write an article in praise of Labour's 'beautiful people' and Robin Cook could dismiss speculation about a leadership challenge with the quip, 'Come on, you know I'm too ugly to be leader of the Labour Party.'

Now the 'Ann and Mo' shows illustrate how alienating that approach is, even for the party faithful. One of the key indicators in opinion polls is whether or not a party's leaders are 'in touch' and 'understand my problems'. It gave an early indication of Mrs Thatcher's demise, and confirmed everyone's suspicions about John Major's chances. With the polls suggesting voters are beginning to find Labour becoming more distant, maybe they should ponder the lessons of the party conferences.

The message sent out by the rumpled Mowlam and the ample but nowadays increasingly tailored Widdecombe is the one politicians most covet and least often earn. The way they look reinforces what they say: they sound honest, genuine and uncalculating, people with convictions – which are far more important than dreary matters of style.

Nothing in politics, of course, is ever quite that straightforward. What, after all, could have been better timed than the episode which simultaneously propelled Widdecombe into the public eye and terminally sank her ex-Home Office boss Michael Howard's bid for the Tory leadership? And she carefully paved the way for her own political comeback in the Shadow Cabinet, playing down the personal antagonism without ever going back on her devastating indictment of Howard. Widdecombe is no political innocent.

Nor, unsurprisingly, is Mowlam. The Unionist cause in Northern Ireland is particularly hostile to her. At one stage in the peace talks the Unionist leader, David Trimble, protested privately, 'She can't walk in a straight line.' Julia Langdon, who is writing a biography of Mowlam and knows her well, says: 'She makes herself slightly more scatty than she is to make herself more endearing. It is part of the artifice of being a politician. But several people have said to me that the Good Friday agreement could not have been achieved without her character. She is also quite without fear.'

Fearlessness is a rare commodity, but it is one which Widdecombe has too.

It is impossible to imagine circumstances which would throw her. She rose sublimely above the black propaganda put out during her row with Howard, when efforts were made to portray her as a sad spinster yearning for a lover. It marked the start of her rebirth as a feminist icon. (Not something the Tories in Bournemouth would necessarily recognise.) But Widdecombe did admit among the dozens of interviews she has given recently that she would love to have had children, a remark guaranteed to be heard sympathetically in what claims to be the party of the family. It was also a rare admission of regret from a woman whose trademark is to have no regrets.

Mowlam has won sympathy (and admiration) too for the typically matter-of-fact way she has coped with illness and the aftermath of chemotherapy, in particular her habit of flinging off her wig either as a gesture of matiness (with some visiting American journalists) or frustration (during the peace talks).

They might be basking in the adoration of their parties, but they're not universally popular at the very top. Mowlam has always been a moderniser, but relations with Tony Blair were strained by the peace talks, and are decidedly chilly with Gordon Brown, who dropped her from his shadow team. But that continuing antipathy between her and Brown adds a bit of zing to the suggestion increasingly heard around Blackpool last week, that 'if Tony fell under a bus, don't assume it would be Gordon who'd take over. There's a lot of support for Mo.' And how Howard must chew his pillow at night to hear Widdecombe talked of as a potential leader. Yesterday she was typically noncommittal about her long-term prospects after Tuesday's triumph: 'You're only as popular as your last speech.' •

The five men charged but never convicted of the murder of Stephen Lawrence being pelted with eggs after leaving the inquiry

Crime and punishment

20 February 1999

Duncan Campbell
Met's man tackles racism

If there is a portrait of Geronimo on the wall and a volume of Camus on the bookshelf, this must be John Grieve's room at Scotland Yard. The deputy assistant commissioner of the Metropolitan Police has a degree in philosophy, a fascination for the history of American Indians, and enjoys reading Harold Pinter, Bob Dylan, Tom Stoppard and James Lee Burke.

But Mr Grieve's new role is far from fictional; it is deadly serious. Appointed last August by the commissioner, Sir Paul Condon, to head a new task force on racial and violent crime, Mr Grieve came to the job after a number of successful operations as head of the anti-terrorist branch. He had been the director of intelligence at the Yard, head of the drugs squad and one of its best-known detectives.

As a young undercover man he had been familiar to the denizens of the underground paper *International Times* as a chap with long, lank hair called DS Grieve. Since then he has tackled the Provisional IRA and drugs gangs and organised crime in London, but he says his current adversary, racism, is as tough as any he has faced.

There is much damage to be limited as a result of not only the Lawrence case but also others such as those of Michael Menson, initially thought by police to have killed himself, and Ricky Reel, drowned in suspicious circumstances, and a catalogue of grievances over deaths of black people in police custody, revived most recently by the death of Roger Sylvester in Tottenham.

Mr Grieve's unit consists of a core of a dozen officers and a further 20 attached to teams in north and west London. They already have their hands full.

'Naïvely, I thought we would have had a gap at the end of the Lawrence inquiry,' he said. 'I didn't realise it would be so difficult and so unremitting.' So did he feel that the criticism of the police had been unfair? 'Good Lord, no,' he laughed.

He had recently been to see *The Colour of Justice*, the dramatised version of the Lawrence inquiry edited by *Guardian* journalist Richard Norton-Taylor and shortly to be shown at the Victoria Palace Theatre – just around the corner from Scotland Yard. 'But I think you are seeing a watershed.' The new unit, the links being built with the families of those affected by racial crime and a less defensive approach were starting to work, he believed.

Since he took over in August more than 400 people have been charged with racially motivated crimes. Last July there were 62 such charges, in November 141. Posters sent to all Metropolitan Police stations encourage officers to report racial crime and intelligence reports on such crimes have trebled.

'The vast majority are harassment, abuse, excrement through the letter box, graffiti,' said Mr Grieve. 'The same families appear over and over again.' He believed most of it was disorganised racism, some of it perpetrated by very young children backed up by their families, but not orchestrated by racist groups such as Combat 18.

'There is a lot of racism in society, and at some stage we are going to have to confront what is happening. We should take our hiding over what we did wrong, but a much more mature debate has to take place.'

While the police had been justifiably criticised over Stephen Lawrence, the wider racism in society that bred his killers was not being addressed. Some press coverage of asylum seekers, portraying them as ungrateful scroungers at the least and violent criminals at worst, was 'dangerous, risky stuff'. Sight was being lost of the true objective of the murder investigations: 'to lock up some racists'.

Police failure to communicate properly had been part of the reason for the recent distrust of police explanations on deaths of black people in custody, he said. 'People expect us to give definitive answers very quickly, and if we don't, it's a conspiracy. Sometimes these answers are not available.' Like journalists, police officers found the words 'I don't know' hard to use.

Most immediately, Mr Grieve's concerns are the Menson and Lawrence murder investigations. He now believes that Ricky Reel was not murdered but met his death by a tragic accident.

His team checked out all known racists on the final bus journey that the attackers were believed to have taken but could find nothing to support either a murder or a manslaughter charge, he said. Last month the Commons home affairs select committee on police recruitment and training was told by Paul Wilson and David Michael of the Black Police Association that many senior officers, such as John Grieve, were sympathetic to change and to fighting racism, but such feelings were often not communicated further down the line.

Mr Grieve now has the task of doing that, of translating the Met's fine words and commitments into actions and also convincing a wary black community that the police mean business and the lessons have been learned.

He will need all the leadership skills of Geronimo and all the imagination and vision of Camus. ●

. . . .

6 January 1999

Tessa James
Grassed up by mum

'You have the right to remain silent . . .' The rest was a blur as I burst into tears. Jack and I were driven to the police station and we began the process of filling in forms before being taken to a drab, functional interview room. Suddenly, all the scenes I had watched thousands of times on TV dramas were a grim reality. There was the tape machine, the bare, grimy walls, the uniformed officer – and my ashen-faced 16-year-old son, trying desperately to look nonchalant and almost succeeding.

Three weeks ago, I reported Jack to the police. Or, as he puts it: 'My own mum shopped me to the pigs!' Said with a mixture of wounded pride and bravado, I am told.

What is it that drives a mother to turn in her son? Some might expect extreme circumstances: a long history of drug addiction, violence, or an attempt to protect a mentally ill child from himself. Sure, Jack is going through a 'difficult' phase: he can react with anger, verbal abuse and furniture-kicking when he doesn't get his own way. But he had no criminal record and, to the best of our knowledge, no drug habit – though he admits to sharing a joint with a mate a couple of times a week.

It had been a quiet Sunday evening and life in our house was calm. Jack was out at a friend's, his younger sister was tucked up in bed and my husband, Bob, went up for a bath while I watched TV. Then Bob went into Jack's room in search of a calculator. Instead, he found an envelope containing the identity cards of another young man. Student cards, video shop, building society credit cards – and a library card issued the previous day in the next town, where Jack had been to the skate park.

Questioned about it, Jack offered no explanation, hotly denying all knowledge of the existence of these cards. They had, it seemed, beamed in from outer space. When we explained that credit card theft was serious and that if he had found them or been given them, it was still a crime, he just shrugged and told us to eff off. When I said the police would have to be informed, that the cards' owner would be losing sleep over it, he yelled: 'Go on then, call the pigs! You're my mum, great, shop me if you like.' Jack then lay low in his room, watching TV, while his dad and I, in a state of shock, debated the next step. After some time, I rang the police. Two officers were round in minutes, and so began the questioning, the formal arrest, the taped interview in police custody and the release on bail of our teenage son.

After the interview, the policewoman turned off the tape and asked Jack if he was all right. He nodded and she told him: 'You have a good mum.' It was quite common for parents to shop their kids, she told us, in an effort to nip any criminal behaviour in the bud. But most arrived at the station swearing and yelling at their kids and spent the interview hitting them around the head.

I hoped Jack had got the message, though for the next 24 hours he pointedly ignored me. I was the Enemy, the mother who had betrayed her son. He then stayed in for two whole evenings, which is unheard of. He was cheerful and seemed happy to be around us.

It is now three weeks since that Sunday evening. During that time the fall-out has been devastating. We have had several appalling scenes and twice Jack has threatened to leave home, telling us that he has somewhere to go. Yet he comes in at a reasonable hour and continues to spend more time in the house. Last week, after the row to end all rows, he suddenly snapped out of it, talked cheerfully to us and put up a shelf in his room: hardly the action of someone about to leave home.

It seems unlikely that Jack will be charged with theft as there is no evidence – he will most probably be charged with handling stolen goods. It is more than possible that he is shielding someone else and we have been told that while he will receive only a caution if he admits the offence, it is vital that he doesn't admit to anything for which he isn't responsible in an effort to shield someone else. If he continues to refuse to cooperate, he will drag us all through the strain of a court appearance. We hope and pray that time to think and, perhaps, to feel afraid will help him decide to tell the police what happened. We have told him we love him, will support him, and that all he needs to do is to tell the truth. For now, all we can do is wait.

Tessa James is a pseudonym. ●

23 January 1999
Duncan Campbell
Hand over fist

In September 1967, Jimmy Boyle was having a lunch-time drink with friends in the British Lion pub on Hackney Road in east London. There seemed, thought Boyle, to be an unusually large contingent of local factory workers in overalls, and the barman was behaving oddly. Suddenly, the 'factory workers' jumped up from their tables, pulled guns from their pockets and grabbed Boyle. He had been captured and was to be taken back to Scotland to stand trial for murder.

Pinioned by the arms and legs, in a pub swarming with armed police and with all the exits covered, there seemed no way he could get free. Yet Jimmy Boyle escaped.

Escaped, not in the sense that he managed to throw off the arresting officers, but escaped, in the end, the fate that seemed inevitable at the time: of a lifetime in jail, in trouble, or both. Escaped so far that today, more than 30 years after that interrupted pint, he is an internationally renowned sculptor, a prize-winning writer, a drugs counsellor, a wine expert, the subject of a proposed musical and, as of next week, the author of a published novel, *Hero of the Underworld*.

The Glasgow underworld has had many heroes. In fiction, there was Johnnie Stark, the Razor King, the hero of *No Mean City*, the classic novel of pre-war Gorbals gangland, when, as its authors, A. McArthur and H. Kingsley Long, observed: 'Battles and sex [were] the only free diversions in slum life.' In real life, there was James 'Razzle' Dalzell, who was murdered in 1924, and such a committed heavy that at parties he would dance only with fellow gang members because he considered dancing with women to be effeminate. And there was Dan Cronin, the legendary Gorbals street-fighter and a hero to the young Boyle, even though he died when the latter was just a six-year-old doing little more wicked than playing truant.

Jimmy Boyle was born into that same Gorbals in 1944. His father was a well-known robber who died in his thirties. One of Boyle's earliest memories of him is of waking up next to an apparently lifeless body swathed in blood-soaked bandages; the man was so heavily mummified that the young boy was unsure who it was, his father or some friend lying there recovering from a battering by rival heavies. His mother was an industrious woman who supported her brood of boys by working as a cleaner, first of the corporation trams and then of the homes of the Glasgow bourgeoisie.

These days, Boyle's oldest brother, Pat, is a talented classical pianist, and gay, which probably required as much courage in the Glasgow of that time as any gangland showdown. The other two brothers, Tommy and Harry, whom Boyle describes respectfully as 'grafters', live in the US, where they work as a plumber and a painter-decorator.

Jimmy was the one who trod in his father's footsteps. As a boy, he soon graduated from stealing sweeties to taking cash from pockets. His first detention – for breaking into chewing-gum machines – came at 13; he wept bitterly and asked for his Ma when sentenced. The tears dried swiftly, however, and by 20 Boyle was a local hard man, collecting debts, either with violence or with the threat of it. In the next couple of years, he was twice arrested for and twice cleared of murder, and by 23 he was on the run in London and under the protection of the Krays. After his capture, he was jailed for the murder of fellow villain, Babs Rooney, having refused to name the friend who he said had actually done the deed. Then came life imprisonment, constant conflict with the prison authorities, rebellion and solitary confinement, before he was moved to the experimental special unit at Barlinnie Prison.

The unit had been the idea of Ken Murray, a senior prison officer, and Alex Stephen, a civil servant, who argued that there had to be a better way of dealing with 'uncontrollable' prisoners than chaining them up or injecting them into zombified passivity. The unit, which opened in 1973, was staffed by volunteer prison officers and run on democratic lines, with prisoners allowed a voice, which provoked consternation among the more conservative elements in the prison system. Prisoners were allowed access to teachers and art materials, and encouraged to express themselves without violence. The unit was shut down in 1995, with a variety of reasons – staff unhappiness at 'prisoner power', high costs – advanced for the closure. Two less radical units for difficult prisoners now operate at Peterhead and Shotts prisons.

While at the special unit, Boyle experienced a remarkable redemption, learning both sculpture and the pointlessness of life behind bars. His autobiography, *Sense of Freedom*, followed in 1977, while he was still inside. In 1980, he wed Sarah Trevelyan, a psychiatrist and daughter of the former film censor, who had read his book and started visiting him in jail. Two years later, having been in prison or on the run for all but 12½ months between the ages of 14 and 38, Boyle was paroled. He embarked on a career as a sculptor, which was so successful that he was able to set up the Gateway Exchange in Edinburgh, to help young people with addiction problems.

Rich enough material for any novel, you might have thought. But Boyle's new book is not an updated version of *No Mean City*, or celebration of the Gorbals and of gangster culture. The hero of the title, far from being a charismatic wideboy, is a former inmate of mental institutions who links up with other outcasts and misfits to steal a prize bull from under the noses of local gangsters. The story has everything from necrophilia to rat kebabs – it is not for the squeamish.

'A lot of the motivation for the book came from the Thatcher years and Care in the Community,' says Boyle, perching on a stool in the studio at his Edinburgh home. He had seen the headlines about people with mental health problems coming out of institutions and committing violent acts, but knew from his work at the Gateway that there was another story to be told. 'What is the real underworld of society? The so-called "glamorous" underworld I've been through, and it's all pretty sad and sordid. I'm more interested in an underworld of people who are disenfranchised and dispossessed. To be honest, I was never the glamorous, successful criminal that people say. I was a failure in life and a dunce at school. That's the reality.'

He is bemused by the fascination with the memoirs of old villains such as Mad Frankie Fraser. 'I could never do what they're doing. The best of luck to them if they get a few quid for it – it's better than pulling someone's teeth out. But to think that you have a guy making money out of how he's tortured people, as opposed to saying: "That's a part of my life I'm not very proud of." It's bizarre. It's capitalism eating itself.'

He'd love to be able to put his own past in a drawer. 'It's an albatross around my neck, particularly in relation to my own kids. A couple of weeks ago, I was asked to give a talk to the police because I'm on the [Edinburgh Lord Provost's] Commission for Social Exclusion. I agreed on condition that it remained confidential. The cops being the cops, they leaked it, so I'm taking the kids [he has a young son and daughter] to school, and there's the *Daily Record* billboard outside, saying: "Outrage at Killer Boyle". It hurt me, because I don't want the kids crippled with my past. For me, it's a source of great pain and, when I see that, it makes me question why I stay in Scotland.'

But stay he does, because he loves his adopted home of Edinburgh, which has long been lumbered with a reputation as the repressed, genteel cousin to rumbustious, good-hearted Glasgow.

'There's a lot of mythology about Glasgow friendliness – and I can say that as a Glaswegian living in Edinburgh. When I came out of prison, I had to distance myself from my past. It was important to do that in a physical sense, and Edinburgh's such a beautiful city. We looked at moving abroad, or to London, but Edinburgh is a very difficult city to leave.' He is not bothered now, he says, by his past catching up with him. 'Taxi drivers ask: "Are you never worried that someone will hit you?" And I say: "Always." But it's a fantasy. I'm the one that got away.'

The ones that did not get away he met at the Gateway, which encountered local opposition when it was set up. 'There was the usual *Daily Record* headline – "We don't want your ex-junkies, we don't want your ex-cons" – but within two years, with people like Billy Connolly lending support, it changed. Unfortunately, most of the kids who used the place and successfully came off drugs became HIV-positive, and I spent the next two or three years seeing these kids through to their deaths, including three brothers, not one of them over 25. It was: "What do you want to wear during your funeral? Where do you want your LPs to go?" That sort of thing.'

The Exchange has now metamorphosed into the Gateway Trust, which operates from the same building in which Boyle has his studio, distributing funds to organisations in the same field.

But back to the book. 'What I'm trying to do is say what happens to someone when they come out from a long-term institution. It's a person struggling to come to terms with life outside. I was trying to take that person to a pretty low level, and see how they go on to build a life. My release was very different, because I was coming out to something. I was trying to look at coming out to nothing.'

Although the novel is far from autobiographical, there are many echoes of *Sense of Freedom* and Boyle's own incarceration. Had they not stirred the old demons? 'Had I not sorted myself out – been broken down and rebuilt as a person – then I would have been opening up things I hadn't looked at before. But I'd looked at them when I was in the special unit; I'd come through all the pain of what I had done. And it was very painful, the worst part of my confinement. But through eight years in the unit and two back in the main prison, I was able to look at that and deal with it, so now I've moved on and it's not earth-shaking. I have changed as a person, but it's been a long, harrowing journey, not an overnight change. I had nightmares for 10 years after my release. I had a recurring one about being back inside, with my kids looking in at me. It was dreadful, but I haven't had it for four or five years.'

The book has already elicited generous pre-publication comparisons. Steven Berkoff says: 'Jimmy Boyle is becoming a satirist in the vein of Jonathan Swift with a touch of William Burroughs.' Helena Kennedy, QC, suggests: 'He interweaves Monty Python grotesque with the horror of Ken Kesey's *Cuckoo's Nest* and the raw violence of Jack London's abattoir.'

'Joe Orton goes Trainspotting' might be another comparison – all those corpses and bent coppers against a grim, Caledonian backdrop. But the author who comes most to mind is one who wrote a hugely powerful book about institutional violence, official sadism and the defensive powers of excreta back in 1977: Boyle himself, in *Sense of Freedom*. Here, for instance, is the hero of *Hero of the Underworld*: 'They're under the impression that, because I'm here in solitary, I long for the company of other human beings. Ha, if only they knew I much prefer my company to theirs.' Later in the book, he falls in with an Irishman, Sligo, who regales him with tales of his homeland:

> The feeling of actually belonging anywhere is something that I don't actually have. All those years of isolation in The Institution had resulted in my own self being broken down, fragmented into a million pieces, only to be resurrected in this new form. Although that long period of being alone provided me with a new belief in myself . . . it also affected my relationship with everything else. It had wiped out any longing I might have had for my home, my community or citizenship for that matter.

Today, although devoted to and protective of his family, Boyle still identifies with the pleasures of solitude. 'I love being on my own. That is something that will always remain with me. I'm quite disciplined. It is the one thing I learned.' His day begins with a four-mile run around Inverleith Park, past the Gothic towers of Fettes School, where Tony Blair was educated, and past, as it happens, the home I grew up in in the middle-class heart of Edinburgh. On his return – in boots, to build up the leg muscles – it's into a steam bath, breakfast with the kids, stack up a load of CDs (everything from classical to The Verve) and on to the sculpture.

He started off working in clay when he was in the special unit, but now his work is in bronze, Portland stone or marble. He uses only a hammer and chisel, which gives the work a distinctive, muscular quality. It has been favourably reviewed in France and the US, but less effusively in Scotland, where it's suggested that the publicity it receives has little to do with its quality.

All the same, it is the sculpture that allows him to lead the life he does, with the Edinburgh home, a place in France and a collection of fine wines. There have been exhibitions in Australia, Moscow, Romania, a big one to come in Barcelona, and sales to US corporations and Russian industrialists. 'I have to keep pinching myself that it has got so mega-successful. I do limited editions that sell from £7,500 to £11,500, and every piece here is off from the end of next week,' he says, looking around his studio.

Travelling abroad, where he is known only for his sculpture, is another form of escape. In Moscow, he was the subject of a major interview in the sort of set-up normally reserved for visiting heads of state. 'There were about 30 journalists, and it went on for three and a half hours. There was not one reference to my past, which was great. It was unbelievable. Their manners as journalists, the way they deal with you, is so different from here. One woman asked: "Mr Boyle, please don't be offended by this question, but could you describe poverty in Britain, so we can compare it to poverty here?" I said: "I know some of you are great admirers of Mrs Thatcher, but I'd like to put straight what she did to our country." It was the same in Australia, America and South Korea: no reference to my past. Mind you, I'd have to be able to read Korean to be sure.

'That's what I love too about France: the freedom of anonymity. The only disturbing thing in America is that a lot of people don't know where Scotland is. They think it's a town in England. Some people know – they've been to Edinburgh and they play golf – but with others you mention Scotland and they say: "Uh?" And that is in New York. Then you come back here and it's "Killer Boyle". That's why I don't sell to anybody in Scotland or touch the Scottish galleries.'

In his homeland, Boyle's rehabilitation, writing and release provoked vastly different, if predictable, responses: the bleeding hearts, as they were portrayed, versus the bleeding obvious. The *Sun* called him 'Scotland's Most Notorious Murderer', the *Mirror* 'The Baby-faced Killer'. The press turned his wedding into a circus, and a reciprocal resentment is never far from the surface.

Twenty years ago, young Labour MPs, Robert Kilroy-Silk and Robin Cook among them, were fighting Boyle's corner, arguing for parole, while Conservatives were hostile and sceptical of the notion of allowing the likes of Boyle access to art materials and visits from strangers. There remains a lingering resentment at his success, at the fact that it all went so damned well for him, that his marriage flourished and that he didn't end up back behind bars. Little might those Labour politicians have imagined that, one day, a prosperous Boyle would be a major contributor to Labour's fighting fund at the last election.

He remains unashamedly supportive: 'It was a great joy when Labour got in, and I'm weary of their supporters who keep having a go, saying they've sold out. They've been in for less than two years. I spend a lot of time saying: "Have patience; judge them after five years." Labour's its own worst enemy. I think they're doing a brilliant job.'

There is already talk of adapting *Hero of the Underworld* for the cinema. Boyle has nearly finished his second novel – about the theft of the *Mona Lisa* and its arrival on an Edinburgh housing estate. Then there is, would you believe, Boyle the musical: a US company is looking to raise £5 million to adapt *Sense of Freedom* for Broadway. Boyle wishes the producers well, but has reservations about any personal involvement. 'I met the guys involved. I said: "I'm delighted, but leave me out of it."'

There was even nearly an acting career. He went along to the casting for what is provisionally entitled *The Match*, a comedy movie about two Scottish pub teams who play each other for the right to have the only establishment in the village. 'I did an audition for it. It gave me a lot more respect for actors – it's bloody daunting!' He had to pull out, which seems a pity as he is built like an old-fashioned Scottish right-half, but then his only interest in football over the years was cheering the defeats of Aberdeen, to wind up the prison officers at Peterhead.

Boyle reads little fiction himself – he's currently in the middle of Christopher Reeve's account of his riding accident and subsequent paralysis. 'I'm not a great novel reader, unless it's a classic like Dickens. For me, it's got to have a meaning to it, like the sculpture. I've never read Irvine Welsh or the other new Scottish writers. I'm delighted to see they're all doing so well, but it's just not my thing. In relation to Welsh, I suppose I've seen enough of drugs first hand.'

Most closely, he has seen it through James, his son by his first marriage, who became a heroin addict while Boyle was in prison and who was knifed to death in 1994, aged 28. He takes responsibility for what happened: 'I was never able to make up for those absent years, no matter how much I tried.'

Boyle remains pessimistic about what is happening in that world he left behind him. 'It's 31 years since I was convicted. It was a pal of mine who murdered Babs Rooney and, although 31 years have passed, nothing much has changed. If you take the Stephen Lawrence case, those boys are bound by that same subculture of not grassing. For me, it was the reverse: I went to prison and did life for something I didn't do. People ask: "Do you not hate the guy?" but we were pals and I wore that silence like a badge of honour. I was a good guy and I wouldn't grass, but it's mental, crazy; it's so sordid.

'What I had to live with wasn't remorse about what I had done, because I hadn't done it, but with the stupidity of it all. Until we attack that subculture, we'll never make any progress on attacking crime.'

The special unit at Barlinnie is long gone: 'They made it clear they would never allow what happened in the special unit to happen again. They see me as one of their failures – the way they describe it is that I beat the system. They won't even let me into Scottish prisons.'

It has been a strange journey. The man they wanted to keep inside for ever is now kept firmly outside, even when his message to the young men serving time today is that there is nothing life-enhancing about doing life. The British Lion, where Boyle's physical freedom was curtailed all those years ago, has been less successful about escaping its past. A rather depressing pub with a 'No Travellers' sign in the window and a Metropolitan Police Pubwatch sticker on the door, it has just had its one-armed bandit done in by one of the two-armed variety.

In a *Guardian* questionnaire in 1991, Boyle – Most admired person: Gorbachev; Most despised person: Le Pen – was asked how he would like to be remembered. As a leopard that changed its spots, was his reply. Out of the Lion came the leopard. It is not giving the plot of *Hero of the Underworld* away too much to say that its last line might also be taken as a motto for Jimmy Boyle: 'The ultimate revenge lies in making the positive decision.' ●

· ·

25 February 1999
Vikram Dodd
'The police treated me like a suspect instead of a victim'

Duwayne Brooks is not asking anyone to feel sorry for him just because he witnessed the brutal murder of his close friend, Stephen Lawrence. What stokes his anger is the way the police and the rest of the criminal justice system treated him, and to his mind systematically tried to undermine and destroy him.

Duwayne, the main eyewitness to the murder, still fears for his life, but says he is more scared of the police than the gang who killed Stephen.

Now that Sir William Macpherson's report is out, the debate has started about what precisely institutional racism is. For Duwayne, that debate is a side issue. He knows the devastating effects, which drove him to the edge of madness. His first experience of the prejudice running through the Lawrence murder came within seconds of Stephen's stabbing. Having dialled 999 for an ambulance – he did not ask for the police – Duwayne begged a white couple for help. They initially ignored him and later said they thought Duwayne was going to rob them.

Stephen Lawrence spent most of his last hours alive with Duwayne, a close friend since the age of 11. They had met briefly at lunch time and later were at the house of Stephen's uncle to play video games. At 10 p.m. Stephen decided to head home and started his final journey. Duwayne went with him.

On the day we met, Duwayne wore a crisp white shirt and tie. He was tired after his day's work as an electrical engineer. He looks slightly younger than his 24 years and has a piercing stare that searches for any sign that you are even thinking of stitching him up. During one long answer attacking the police he noticed that I had stopped writing and said: 'There's no point me talking to you if you aren't going to write down what I say.'

He exudes a mix of world-weariness and childlike righteous anger at his six-year ordeal. His lawyer gets him a glass of squash as he begins detailing his nightmare. 'At the scene the police treated me like a liar, like a suspect instead of a victim, because I was black and they couldn't believe that white boys would attack us for nothing. They tried on the night [of the murder] at the police station to get me to say that the attackers didn't call us nigger. They described me as violent, uncooperative, intimidating. They were stereotyping me as a young black male. They didn't care about what I told them. They weren't bothered that Stephen was lying there dying.'

Duwayne believes his life is in danger from the suspects, against whom he is the main witness. But he fears the police more: 'The suspects and their associates are more of a threat to my family and friends. The people that present the most threat to me is the police. They do things and get away with it. They commit crimes and murder,' he says referring to black deaths in custody. 'The Lawrence case shows what the police do when they want to cover up a crime. They collude together, they cover up for each other, they throw away vital evidence.'

Duwayne has needed extensive counselling to get over the debilitating effects of post-traumatic stress disorder: 'The police treatment made it worse. Since they did not see me as a victim I wasn't referred to a specialist. It made me feel very insecure, made me have unbelievable bouts of paranoia because the police did not want to arrest the murderers.' He says police waged a campaign to blacken his name: 'I was repeatedly stopped and searched after the murder. When the police found that I had no criminal record they used other means to try and discredit me.' At one of three identity parades officers accused him of stealing cans of soft drink.

He still maintains he correctly identified two suspects, Neil Acourt and Luke Knight. But that identification was undermined, the public inquiry heard, by Detective Sergeant Christopher Crowley. After driving Duwayne home from a line-up, Crowley made a statement claiming Duwayne told him he was unsure of those he had picked out. Duwayne denied it, but in any trial the defence could use Crowley's statement to attack Duwayne's credibility.

Duwayne was crushed when the judge at the Lawrences' private murder prosecution refused to allow him to testify before the jury, ruling that his evidence was unreliable. Duwayne, suffering from post-traumatic stress, had appeared muddled about important details in front of the judge.

At the public inquiry Duwayne discovered that during this trial he had been guarded by an officer, Detective Constable David Coles, who was alleged at the public inquiry to have a corrupt link with Clifford Norris, the gangster father of one of the suspects. 'I was shocked and frightened. My life would have been at risk if the prosecution had continued.'

In one of those ironies the Stephen Lawrence case keeps throwing up, Duwayne Brooks faced a full criminal trial before any of the five murder suspects. He was arrested and charged by the Crown Prosecution Service with violent disorder after a protest march following Stephen's murder. The judge stayed proceedings on the grounds of abuse of process. 'I was distraught. They tried to fix it to convict me,' Duwayne says.

As well as fear, Duwayne has to wrestle with guilt, partly blaming himself for Stephen's death. Duwayne and Stephen were at Well Hall Road in Eltham, the murder scene, because they had got off a bus. Duwayne had wanted to stay on the number 286, but Stephen wanted to get off and take a bus which would get him home quicker. Stephen won out. They were waiting on Well Hall Road for another bus when the attackers spotted them.

Duwayne said: 'I had the stronger personality. We wouldn't have changed buses if I had bullied him to stay 10 more minutes on the 286 bus and change in Blackheath instead. If I had made him stay longer on the bus, he would have got home safe.'

Sometimes it seems that Doreen Lawrence also partly blames Duwayne for what happened to her son. In her statement Mrs Lawrence told the inquiry: 'He [Stephen] had been quite strict about being home on time, but after the influence of Duwayne, where Duwayne was allowed to come and go as he pleased, it was different.'

Duwayne's relationship with the Lawrences is strained, but he refuses to discuss it. But he has testified in court and made statements every time he has been asked to.

Six years on he compares the sacking of two Essex police officers for maltreating dogs to what happened to the officers in the Lawrence case. Duwayne said: 'An officer can kick a dog and be expelled from the force. In the Stephen Lawrence case they perverted the course of justice by throwing evidence away and nothing's been done. They treated us worse than dogs. The establishment recognised a dog's life was more important than Stephen's.' •

....

25 February 1999

Leader
Let this be his epitaph

He was not a famous or great man, just a boy with bright dreams for his future. He did not have mighty friends or high-powered contacts, just a couple of stubborn parents who refused to be pushed aside. He did not set out to be a leader of men or to turn the world upside down, but Stephen Lawrence has done something for which he will never be forgotten: he has given his country a chance to change.

The report into his death, published at long last yesterday, marked a moment rare in our national life. It forced us all to take a long, uncomfortable look in the mirror, to examine not just the people we pay to protect us but ourselves. As the Home Secretary said in an admirable statement to the House of Commons yesterday, Sir William Macpherson's searing report 'opened our eyes to what it's like to be black or Asian in Britain today'. As Jack Straw conceded, it contains some painful truths, all of which we now have to face – 'each and every one of us'.

We cannot load all the blame on to the Metropolitan Police, or even its commissioner. The officers who turned a blind eye to justice, failing to pursue Stephen's killers, are, along with the killers themselves, not aliens; they did not land in Eltham from Planet Racism. They are members of our society; they grew up in it, they are rooted in it. If they are a problem, then so are we. This is why the Macpherson report is a volume of shame. It depicts a police culture riven with prejudice and ignorance. It reveals a company of men, and some women, who regarded those with black or brown skins as less than fellow citizens, perhaps even less than human beings. Their suffering was valued less, the life of one of their sons was valued less. Doreen and Neville Lawrence's enduring contribution to British life has been to expose that fact to all of us – and to refuse to take it. They forced us to look at the conduct of those who police our society in our name. So the sight of the Lawrences at their press conference yesterday, seated apart, their faces worn down by grief and struggle, was doubly heavy. The heart breaks, not just for them but for what we have done to them.

The Macpherson report has given us a chance to make amends, to make what Jack Straw called a 'watershed' in the relations between Britain's races. It lays bare a history neatly summarised by the churchman who told the inquiry that over 30 years black Britons have been consistently over-policed and under-protected. Overall, Macpherson is thorough and wise – and a devastating indict-ment of the 'pernicious and institutionalised racism' running through the Met as well as the 'flawed and indefensible' police work the inquiry discovered everywhere it looked.

Reform in the police has, regrettably, always been scandal-driven. Will this latest scandal produce equally rewarding results? There were several initiatives announced by Mr Straw yesterday which reformers could embrace. First and foremost the police – along with other public services – are to be brought within the ambit of the 1976 Race Relations Act, as they should have been from the very beginning. This will allow the Commission for Racial Equality to begin its own inquiries into deaths in custody, discriminatory use of stop and search, or stations suspected of harbouring racist officers. This is an accountability that is long overdue, but to be totally effective the Race Relations Act will need amending to restore to the CRE the original powers which have been sub-sequently curbed by the courts.

Then there is to be a new police disciplinary regime beginning from April, under which police officers will not be able to retire early to escape prosecution. This is a start, but Macpherson was calling for something much more substantial than this, including an independent investigation of police complaints and a code of conduct which would ensure that racist acts by police officers would be a dismissal offence. An immediate inspection of the Met has been ordered by the Home Secretary, with HM inspectors ordered to apply a much stricter level of standards than applied in earlier reviews.

Mr Straw had already signalled his intention of setting much higher targets for the recruitment, retention and promotion of ethnic minority officers for all police services. Two decades ago in the wake of the Scarman inquiry, visiting Americans could not believe Britain was still trying to police black communities with such tiny numbers of black officers: a mere 0.5 per cent in the Met. Two decades ago America had several forces where 40 per cent were black and half a dozen led by black chief constables. Twenty years on just 2 per cent of police officers in England and Wales are from ethnic minorities. Straw is insisting this rises to 7 per cent nationally, and even higher in areas of high concentrations of ethnic minorities.

Sensibly, the Home Secretary is referring to the Law Commission the daunting and dangerous Macpherson proposal that the Court of Appeal should be given power to permit prosecution after acquittal where fresh and viable evidence is presented. The Commission will be fully aware of the dangers which such a proposal holds. The principle of a person not being tried twice for the same offence is one old and ancient concept which should be protected.

The Met itself pointed yesterday to its more rigorous anti-racist training and its new specialist anti-racist squad, which has doubled the number of people being charged with racially motivated crimes since last August. But what was missing yesterday was just how much closer supervision will be applied to officers on patrol and involved in investigations. No other professionals work with so little supervision or with so much discretion. Tighter supervision is crucial. Doreen Lawrence rightly asked what would be done to ensure the officer on the beat behaved properly.

What of Sir Paul himself? He escapes serious criticism in the report, though there is a strong implication that he was not sufficiently sceptical of the first Barker review of the investigation. There is a plausible view that Sir Paul has escaped lightly. The buck inevitably stops with the Commissioner, and this is some buck. It may be argued that Sir Paul has been at the helm of the Metropolitan Police for some six years now and that he cannot evade responsibility for the catalogue of incompetence and racism described by Macpherson. Sir Paul's acknowledgement of institutionalised racism within his organisation was belated and accompanied by a certain amount of semiotic self-justification. Against that should be set a general acceptance that Sir Paul has a long and public record of fighting racism within his force, and also his courage in tackling police corruption – often in the face of considerable hostility from his own officers. His resignation would have had a certain symbolic cleanness about it. But if he is to stay, he must surely realise that yesterday's report was a beginning, not an end. In the 10 months he has left he has much to prove. All the fine work of Macpherson will have been wasted unless it inspires extraordinary efforts by the police to win the confidence of the black community which it patently lacks at the moment. That fight should start today and, yes, the buck really does stop with Sir Paul. ●

25 *February 1999*

Gary Younge
Alabama tactics

In the American Deep South they used to call it reckless eyeballing – the accusation that a black man dared look a white woman in the eye.

In 1993 it cost Ali Ibrahim his life. The 21-year-old Sudanese refugee was walking along the road in Brighton with two friends when a white man accused him of looking at his girlfriend. The row spilled into an alleyway. The man pulled out a knife and plunged it into Ibrahim's heart. The man who had fled civil war in Sudan collapsed and died on the streets in Sussex.

Quddus Ali, aged 17, was walking down Commercial Road in Stepney, east London, when eight white youths beat and kicked him into a four-month-long coma. He is permanently brain-damaged. In the Deep South they used to call this lynching.

Two racially motivated attacks against young men for which nobody has been convicted. Both took place in the same year that Stephen Lawrence was murdered. Yet neither Quddus Ali nor Ali Ibrahim has become a household name. There have been no films in their honour nor any hand-wringing statements from the dispatch box.

What was it about the stabbing of one young black man almost six years ago which has focused attention on racial injustice and police incompetence? The media have had a great deal to do with it. In this story they had a simple narrative of good and evil that fitted into the framework of their own racial bias and which they felt they could sell to their readers.

On the one side were his alleged murderers – violent, criminal and boorish – as alien and hostile to the respectable mainstream as you can get. 'Racist thugs,' wrote the *Sunday Telegraph*. 'A gang of racist thugs,' said the *Mirror*. 'Five lowlife thugs,' wrote the *Mail*.

On the other side was the Lawrence family and their late son. Unlike Ali Ibrahim, Stephen was not an asylum seeker. He had never been in trouble with the police. He did not have an outlandish haircut, nor was he from a one-parent family.

It is telling that the only thing most people know about Stephen Lawrence is that he was an A-level student who dreamed of being an architect. 'He was young and bright and black' and 'a hard-working sixth-former with everything to live for,' wrote the *Daily Mail*; he was 'not involved in drugs in any way,' wrote the *Sunday Telegraph*.

His parents were similarly respectable and accessible. They speak English and are of Christian stock. 'The word most commonly used by friends and neighbours to describe his family was "ordinary",' wrote the *Telegraph*. 'They were kind and pleasant.' 'Their next-door neighbours are white,' the *Telegraph* explained in another article. 'The Lawrences have white friends.'

So Neville and Doreen Lawrence became Everyman and Everywoman who happened to find themselves in the eye of a judicial and political storm. They were everything that the white establishment had ever demanded black people should be; they could not be explained away with the usual stereotypes.

The very sight of them – Neville is tall and broad; Doreen slight and gentle – conveyed a sense of proud yet solemn reserve. Into this patronising mould was poured their grief. They suffered the loss of their son 'with a dignity that has won them great respect,' wrote the *Mail*.

Their profile in the press was partly due to a political agenda. Marc Wadsworth, former leader of the Anti-Racist Alliance, which played a huge role in supporting the Lawrences during the first year after Stephen's death, says he played to the value systems of the newsdesks and the public. 'We were saying Stephen Lawrence was like you. He wanted to be a decent citizen.'

There is a precedent for this in the frail form of Rosa Parks. Parks was the woman thrown off a bus after she refused to give up her seat to a white man in Montgomery, Alabama, in 1955, sparking the boycott which launched Martin Luther King to fame. But she was not the first to break the segregation laws. E. D Nixon, who organised the boycott, said: 'We had three other people prior to Mrs Parks arrested.' The others were considered unsuitable. They came from the wrong part of town. One was a single mother.

There is no suggestion that activists in the Stephen Lawrence case were cynical enough to reject other murder victims because they did not have Stephen's popular appeal. But they pitched their campaign in a way that would attract the widest number of supporters. •

. . . .

25 February 1999

Letters
How to root out racism

I worked with, but not for, the Metropolitan Police from 1983 to 1989. Officers clearly presumed that as a young white male I shared their attitudes and values. I heard outrageous racist and sexist remarks on a regular basis. Upon asking if an alleged rapist in custody was black, a detective inspector said to me: 'Aren't they all?' I was also informed on numerous occasions that women police officers were a waste of resources and 'only good for a shag'. A detective constable informed me: 'If it wasn't for blacks there wouldn't be any crime in London.'

Much of the racist/sexist braggadocio one hears routinely in police stations is the consequence of the pervasive macho culture. Military-style uniforms and ranks such as sergeant aid this mindset. I did meet some highly professional, highly motivated, intelligent and sensitive detectives, but they were not thick on the ground.

Our police are generally recruited from among those who do not star academically; they are conservative types and conformist. No 18-year-old declaring strong political views would get past the first interview. Young police officers must show they can take orders to the letter and without question. Curiosity about police policy or even thinking for yourself is strongly discouraged.

Police recruits understand all too clearly that maintaining the status quo and behaving unremarkably is the only way to the top. Regular attendance at the 'right church' secures lots of Brownie points.

Our police do not put a very high premium upon crime prevention because there's no promotion in it. An experienced detective will be described as one who has 'nicked his share'.

The courts are seen as too soft, magistrates have the wool pulled over their eyes and the criminal justice system is seen as long-winded, and a gravy train for lawyers (with some justification).

Before Paul Condon decides what to do about the current crisis, he and the Home Secretary might do worse than spend some time deciding exactly what it is the police service is supposed to be doing.

Name and address supplied.

Charlotte Raven asks how the Lawrence Five 'would know about Enoch Powell' ('The Lawrence case in black and white', 23 February). In south-east London, this question must strike people as monumentally naïve. In 1993, the year of Stephen Lawrence's murder in Eltham, the British National Party still spread racist propaganda throughout this area from a base in Welling in the London Borough of Bexley. This base was not far from the Eltham comprehensive school which some of the Five attended – nor, as it happens, from the police station which handled the Lawrence murder. In face of strong and persistent local and national protest, the Tory Bexley Council at that time refused to close the BNP base (a highly fortified shop, draped copiously with barbed wire, in a Welling shopping parade). It was not until the council elections of 1995 that a new Lab-Lib Bexley Council promptly shut it down. By that time, Stephen Lawrence had been dead for over two years.

Betty Shreeve
Bexleyheath, Kent ●

25 February 1999

David Pallister

'All get chivvied up' – street violence that is a way of life

Violence and racism came as second nature to the boys accused of killing Stephen Lawrence. Even as they entered their teens, the Acourt brothers and their friend David Norris were out of control. Knives and other offensive weapons were essential accessories on the street. 'Come on,' Neil would say when the gang went out looking for action, 'all get chivvied up.' His idea of a joke was to terrorise his friends with demonstrations of overarm stabbing. When Norris was a child his father and uncle were already gun-carrying drug smugglers.

Like many of the local people who followed Millwall and tolerated or supported the activities of the National Front and the British National Party, the boys hated black people. Besides football and occasional fishing, they filled their boring lives with television, smoking cannabis, vicious racist banter and hanging about looking for trouble.

Jamie and Neil Acourt, 16 and 17 at the time of the murder, fancied themselves as tough boys. The menace, the swagger and the slicked hair were straight out of East End criminal mythology; they liked to be called the Krays.

All but Norris lived on the adjacent Brook and Progress estates, minutes away from where Stephen was stabbed in Eltham's Well Hall Road. Because of the local authority's 'sons and daughters' tenancy policy, the area has remained almost exclusively white working class, with a high rate of youth unemployment.

Gary Dobson and Luke Knight lived with their parents; the Acourts shared a shabby semi with two elder brothers, pit bull terriers and an occasionally absent mother. Norris and his mother enjoyed more spacious surroundings a few miles south in a Chislehurst mansion, now in danger of being confiscated by Customs and Excise following his father's conviction for drug importation and possession of guns in 1996.

The Acourts and Dobson went to Crown Woods secondary school in Greenwich. At the age of 14, the delinquent Jamie was permanently excluded and moved to Kidbrooke secondary to join his friend Luke Knight. But Jamie lasted only 10 months. Once he was found with a monkey wrench in his bag. Another pupil claims he brought in a replica handgun, later found by the police at his home. He was finally thrown out after an assault on a black pupil.

Norris also got into trouble at Coopers school, a predominantly white, middle-class comprehensive in Chislehurst. He was expelled at the age of 13 in September 1989 for constant defiance and disobedience and sent to a special referral unit.

Outside school, the boys began to get into trouble from about 1990. They were regulars at the Orchard youth club on the Brook estate. Neil Acourt and Norris were expelled after the letters NF for the National Front were painted six feet high on the wall. They were part of a gang which forced one isolated Asian family to leave after persistent harassment.

As their collection of weaponry increased, the boys began indulging in greater levels of violence, with at least three allegations of stabbing. They had plenty of time on their hands after leaving school, as only Dobson had full-time work as an apprentice bricklayer. The Acourts did casual work as draymen at an uncle's bottling factory.

In June 1992 two brothers, Darren and Terry Witham, complained they had been attacked in Chislehurst High Street by a gang including Norris, Jamie Acourt and Luke Knight. Norris was charged with stabbing Darren and Jamie with having an offensive weapon, in this case a truncheon.

Despite police protests, the Crown Prosecution Service discontinued the case just before Stephen's murder. It has now emerged that Darren's father was approached by an intermediary, offering a bribe of £5,000 if Darren withdrew his allegation. Mr Witham refused, but it was a pattern that was to repeat itself. A month before Stephen's death, Norris, with Neil Acourt offering encouragement, allegedly stabbed a local white youth, Stacey Benefield. After the attack was brought to the attention of the police by the same informer who first named Stephen's killers, Norris and Neil were charged with attempted murder. Neil was discharged at committal but Norris was sent for trial and acquitted. Evidence before the inquiry revealed that, once again, money was offered to Benefield to drop the case. He took the first £2,000 with the offer of a further £5,000, but refused to change his story. We now know that the man who tried to save Norris's skin was his father, Clifford, who had been on the run since 1988.

Even after Stephen's death, the violence continued. In the summer of 1994 Jamie was arrested and charged with a stabbing in a local nightclub. At his trial he pleaded he acted in self-defence and was acquitted.

The boys' violent reputation, and the criminal associates in their extended families, meant that few people were prepared publicly to denounce them. But fear alone does not explain why the people of Eltham failed to come forward as witnesses.

While there were more than a dozen tip-offs, some anonymous, the unsavoury truth is that these teenage boys grew up in an area where racism was deeply engrained in the local white community. ●

· ·

12 May 1999

Chris Arnot

25 years for a murder he didn't commit

Andrew Evans scans the menu with a furrowed brow and asks: 'What's cheesecake?' On being told that it's a pudding, he goes back to perusing the options and asks for 'something simple, like a bacon sandwich'. Easier said than done. He could have strips of grilled chicken or steak on ciabatta bread, or smoked salmon and scrambled egg in a bagel. But bacon sandwiches are not on the menu, so staff are unable to access a price through a till strictly controlled by a computer ordering system. Eventually, Evans settles for an 'all-day breakfast', although it's three in the afternoon in a Nottingham café-bar.

Such places were unheard of in provincial England in 1972, when he was sent to prison for life for a crime he didn't commit. His was the longest miscarriage of justice in British legal history. He was 17 when he walked into a police station in Staffordshire and confessed to the murder of a 14-year-old girl in Tamworth. At the time, he had just been discharged from the army because of his asthma and was taking Valium for depression. Images of the girl's face came to him in a nightmare and, in a muddled state, he assumed that he had been responsible.

There were key aspects of his story which didn't tie in with the facts and he would later retract his statement and plead not guilty. Too late. By the time he emerged from the Court of Appeal a free man in December 1997, a quarter of a century had elapsed. The callow youth was now a man of 42 with grey hair and the beginnings of middle-age spread. He had gone in confused, depressed and barely literate. He emerged a prolific reader, a keen listener to Radios 4 and 3, able to write music and confident enough in his abilities at maths and English to teach fellow prisoners.

This transformation was largely due to his innate intelligence and resilience. Benign influences within 12 of Her Majesty's Prisons are far outweighed in his memories by the constant threat of violence from inmates and the terror of lying awake listening to night-time screams.

As he sits waiting for his late breakfast, his eyes are constantly darting from side to side as though expecting attack from behind. 'I must be getting better,' he says, ruefully, 'because at one time I'd have had to sit where you are, with a wall behind me.'

He had no illusions that life on the outside would be easy, but he remains staggered by the lack of preparation he received. 'If I'd been a murderer,' he says, 'I'd have had professionals on my case 24 hours a day. But because I didn't do it, they didn't want to know.'

He had to wait for his first £100,000 compensation from the Home Office, and legal representations are continuing for a proper settlement. So friends raised the £2,000 necessary to book him in immediately for 10 days at Ticehurst Hospital in Kent, where Terry Waite had gone for counselling following his release in 1991 after almost five years as a hostage in Beirut.

It was at Ticehurst that Andrew met Sheila, a psychiatric unit administrator. She went out of her way to help him overcome what might seem simple problems, such as opening a bank account when he had no identification. 'She was there for me,' he says, 'and I rushed into a relationship.' Understandably, perhaps. He had little experience of women before he was locked away and his youth was stolen from him. 'With Sheila, I was trying to do everything and ended up with nothing,' he admits. The relationship ended after a holiday together in Goa.

Back in England, he struggled to come to terms with what had changed in 25 years. Buses had become one-man-operated, requiring the correct change and causing him to curse the inventor of the 'ridiculously small' 5p piece. Supermarket shelves groaned with the sort of choices that didn't exist in 1972. 'It freaked me out,' he says.

'I kept expecting somebody to tap me on the shoulder and say: "Oi, put that back." And the money? 'Well, I'd expected prices to go up, of course, like the cost of coffee in prison canteens. But it still comes as a shock to pay £100 for a week's groceries.'

He is, though, enjoying cooking and eating good food. For 20 of his 25 years inside, he was a vegetarian – partly for moral reasons and partly to avoid gristly meat and what he calls 'cockroach-enriched cabbage'.

Out on the streets, he noticed another change. 'There's no eye contact any more,' he says, 'as though people are anticipating aggression. I was walking through the middle of Nottingham one night when I saw this bloke attacking a woman. Everybody around was moving away. When I went back to help, he'd cleared off and the girl was in tears. I gave her £20 to get a taxi – at that time I was spending money like water – but the woman I was with told me I shouldn't get involved. People keep themselves to themselves much more than they did.'

Evans lives alone in a rented bungalow in a pleasant part of Nottingham. 'I couldn't hold down a job at the moment because I keep having these fits when I just curl up in a ball and sob,' he says. At other times he can enjoy simple pleasures, like watching the history channel on cable television, going for country rides on his motor scooter and revelling in the view from his bedroom window – a gravel drive, trees and distant fields. 'No barbed wire, searchlights and locked gates.'

What he calls his '*pièce de résistance*' is his flush toilet. 'You never forget the smell from a plastic bucket in the corner of your cell in summer,' he says, 'or the stench of 100 prisoners emptying their piss-pots.' At least hygiene standards improved during his time inside. 'At the Verne [in Dorset] there were three toilets between 20 on a landing. That's not too bad.'

He would still be there now were it not for a chance meeting with Steve Elsworth of Greenpeace, who had gone to the Verne prison to give a talk. He returned one visiting time and took detailed notes while Evans poured out his story. Elsworth passed on the details to two Midlands-based Carlton Television producers, John McLeod and Allister Craddock. They featured his story, first in 1994 on *Crime Stalker* – fronted by John Stalker, the former assistant chief constable of Greater Manchester – and again in 1997 on a documentary called, appropriately enough, *The Nightmare*. Throughout, they worked closely with the human rights organisation Justice, whose lawyers would eventually secure Evans's release.

'I owe them all a great deal,' he says. 'I'm now becoming more comfortable with other people. But I've also become more and more aware of what they've known and what I've known over the past 25 years. It's only over the last few weeks or so that it's begun to dawn on me what I've lost.'

A *Thirty Minutes* documentary on Andrew Evans's first year of freedom will be shown in the Central region next Tuesday at 7.30 p.m. ●

. . . .

1 May 1999
Rory Carroll
A balmy evening that ended in death

It was a balmy evening and Old Compton Street was even more crowded than usual. The drinkers spilling out from pubs on to the pavement to catch the sun's dying rays were relaxed. It was like the first day of summer.

Work was over and for once the forecast was good for the bank holiday weekend. Tourists and theatregoers mingled with London's gay community, who had made the street their own. Restaurants and cafés wafted their smells of cooking into the air, but most were there for a drink.

Rush-hour traffic wound its snail-pace way past either end of the street. Hairdresser's and cake shops were getting ready to close. Neon signs in the few surviving sex shops were starting to wink.

By 6.30 p.m. catching a barman's eye was difficult. But the jostling, packed atmosphere was what made Old Compton Street so special. And it was what would make the bomb so devastating.

Yesterday's gay *Pink Paper* warned of the need for vigilance after two recent

Victims of the nail bomb attack at the Admiral Duncan

Neil Libbert

bombs had targeted minority communities, but this was Friday evening and many workers were carrying bags. Just like the man in a yellow baseball cap, blue and yellow T-shirt and blond goatee beard who entered the gay Admiral Duncan pub. He was seen leaving the pub empty-handed. It is not known if he was the bomber.

At 6.37 p.m. it happened. A sound like a massive crunch. It split the air, drowning out everything else. In less than a second, the inside of the Admiral Duncan was transformed into a scene from hell.

A white flash, then a blast shook the building and hurtled hundreds of nails everywhere. Windows splintered, showering shards. Eyewitnesses said there were a couple of seconds of stunned silence before the screams began. Through a cloud of dust and smoke staggered dozens of bleeding, choking, mutilated people.

'They had cuts on their bodies and their skin was peeling off,' said Don Crowm, 55, a signpainter. 'They were just lying on the ground. Most of them were in pain.' Another witness, Tony Howard, said: 'The injuries were horrific. There were bones sticking out of legs, people's faces were burned – it's difficult to describe, it was so horrendous. The whole of the front of the pub was blown out. I stayed with one man whose leg was partially blown off. You could see the bones in his leg. I just tried to apply pressure and tried to stem the flow of blood.'

Kia Biebelheimer, an American student, said people were walking and running around dazed by the blast: 'They were weeping and crying, in a state of terrible shock. It was awful.'

Through the front of the pub, now a blackened hole, had been hurled several customers, most unrecognisable. It was as if a madman had thrown a bucket of blood everywhere, said one witness.

It was like a Vietnam War movie, said one man who was in the pub with family members. 'I was just leaving, on my way out, when there was a large explosion at the back of the pub. There was a fellow that went over the top of my nephew. I don't know if the fellow has lost his leg or not. It was in an awful state.'

Jeremiah Henderson, 47, said: 'The building shook when we heard the explosion. I ran outside and I saw a man lying on the ground with his jeans shredded and there was smoke everywhere.'

Floorboards at the nearby Groucho Club vibrated from the blast. The two parties in progress ran down the stairs and into the chaos below.

'Most people were running to get away but I saw that most of the wounded had their partners kneeling beside them. They wouldn't leave their sides,' said Maureen Freely, a *Guardian* writer.

Trembling fingers from 20 callers dialled the emergency services within two minutes. They were on the scene within minutes, but for some victims it was too late.

The bomber had chosen his target well, said David Capitanchik, a terrorist expert from the University of Aberdeen. 'The nail bomb went off in a crowded, confined space, so fatalities are inevitable. The bomb was designed to do just that. In a small room crowded with people there is not much chance of surviving. It would be absolutely devastating. You would be lucky if you got out of that room without serious injury. It is not so much the blast itself, but the nails, shrapnel, broken glasses and windows.'

Sirens from dozens of police cars, ambulances and fire engines drowned out victims' wails. Fearing there could be more devices, police moved the uninjured behind a cordon in Dean Street.

A motorcycle paramedic, Ken Murphy, arrived on the scene within four minutes. Two men had suffered massive injuries and it was instantly obvious they were beyond help: 'They didn't look like human beings any more. They were not going to survive.'

Mr Murphy, 35, said 10 ambulances arrived within 20 minutes. The scene inside the bombed pub was surreal. 'There was a lot of moaning, a lot of people shouting to me. They were groaning, lying on the floor. They were serious injuries, flesh burns, amputation of limbs. There was tearing of flesh, tearing into the abdominal and chest cavities.

'People were calm. They knew what had happened straight away. It was just a case of people working together as a team. People were asking me for help.

There were bodies lying in the street. The vast majority were male, 20 to 30 years of age, fit, healthy chaps, and their lives have been literally torn apart.'

Despite pleas to step aside, many of the victims' partners were unable to leave. Stretchers, oxygen masks and blankets were distributed and a helicopter airlifted some wounded. Dazed but unhurt, Jean-Pierre Trevor, a film maker, turned his office into a makeshift hospital and mortuary. Shaking with emotion, he said police officers told him to black out the windows of the ground-floor offices of Image Makers, opposite the Admiral Duncan pub.

'I saw a priest running around trying to help people. I saw him bend down to a severely injured person who was covered in blood and start muttering words of prayer. It was just red blood everywhere, I saw a lot of red, a lot of people bleeding. I could not believe this had happened. Casualties were stretchered into our office, motionless people were just laid down. The ambulancemen asked us to cover up the windows. We were turned into a temporary mortuary.'

Stig Kolstad, 30, a Norwegian photojournalist, saw a body being pushed on a trolley: 'It was a terrible mess, it looked like a heap of paper.'

Rush-hour traffic hampered ambulances, which ferried 73 patients to four London hospitals. Surgeons were forced to make snap decisions. There had been more than two traumatic amputations – limbs lost in the blast – but it was feared that they would have to carry out many amputations. 'When a bomb goes off, if it's near you it shreds flesh. It's pretty horrible really. People have serious lacerations, deep wounds and there are some serious burns,' said UCH chief nurse Louise Boden. All the hospital surgery teams had been called in.

By nightfall the right-wing extremist White Wolves had claimed responsibility. Sir Paul Condon, the Metropolitan Police commissioner, promised they would be hunted down.

By midnight Soho Square had turned eerily quiet. Distilled water, empty drip bags, foil sheeting, blankets and dressings were strewn around. The square was empty. ●

· ·

9 June 1999

Leader

Mr Aitken pays the price

When we elect politicians to represent us at Westminster we enter into an unwritten contract. They, the politicians, speak, make laws and govern at our expense and on our behalf. In turn, we, the public, retain the right to scrutinise, criticise and, ultimately, unseat the politicians we have elected. That is the democratic bargain.

Jonathan Aitken was elected to represent Thanet as part of that bargain. In time, he rose to be a Privy Councillor and, as Chief Secretary to the Treasury, a member of the Cabinet. He became an elegant and articulate force in the land and was sometimes spoken of as a future prime minister. But it was never in doubt that the public which elected him had the right to be kept informed about his activities as a politician.

One means by which the public is able to monitor the performance of politicians is through a free press. The American founding fathers understood that well enough and enshrined the right to free speech as the very First Amendment of their Constitution. We have never gone that far, but there have been many Britons who have also fought for this freedom, from Milton and Wilkes through to Delane and Salman Rushdie.

One eminent judge put it well: 'We all recognise that an opinion-forming medium like the press must not be muzzled. The warning bark is necessary to help maintain a free society. If the press is the watchdog of freedom and its fangs are withdrawn, all that will ensue is a whimper, possibly a whine, but no bite. If the press is muzzled, you may think it becomes no more than a political pawn.'

The judge was the late Mr Justice Caulfield, summing up at the Old Bailey in a case in which Mr Aitken stood trial under the Official Secrets Act in 1971. Mr Aitken, then a journalist, did not conduct an unblemished defence. He confessed to telling a number of lies, to laying false trails and dumping the blame on others. But the judge saw clearly the greater fundamental principle at stake.

Mr Aitken was acquitted; it was a valuable fight. It was said that the judge's summing up – so robust in its defence of free speech and so favourable to Mr Aitken – was one reason that he was never promoted to the Court of Appeal.

In the early 1990s this newspaper wrote a number of articles about Mr Aitken as part of the democratic bargain outlined above. They included an examination of a weekend he had spent at the Ritz Hotel in Paris at someone else's expense while a government minister. Mr Aitken was given every opportunity to explain how and why he had come to accept this hospitality. He decided that he was under no obligation to do so. He lied.

Intrigued as to why a government minister should choose to lie to a newspaper over such a matter, we continued to write about him. He did not like what we wrote. He decided to break the democratic bargain and prevent us from writing about him. To that end, he employed the full armoury of the law to shut us up. He dressed this evasion up as a moral crusade. Calling television cameras to Conservative Central Office, he famously announced his mission: 'to cut out the cancer of bent and twisted journalism in our country with the simple sword of truth and the trusty shield of traditional British fair play'. We – and the rest of the British media – were muzzled.

Why on earth did he do it? The honest answer was that it was a reasonable gamble for a politician in trouble. The heat of democratic scrutiny was getting acutely uncomfortable. Mr Aitken knew better than most that Britain's defamation laws present an extremely effective way of shutting down criticism for those rich enough to play the game. The burden of proof is on the defendant; the plaintiff can, if he is lucky, dispose of a jury; and he knows that here (unlike in America or many Western countries) there is little or no protection for newspapers writing about the public activities of public figures. Plaintiffs appreciate the conditional free speech we Britons enjoy; they flock to London from all over the world to sue.

So Mr Aitken joined the long chain of libel litigants in our high courts – from corrupt eighteenth-century British politicians to the present-day Russian mafia. A less reckless figure would have omitted from his pleadings any reference to the weekend at the Ritz, but Mr Aitken deliberately included it as a cause of action. Having included it, he had to set about constructing a trail of lies in pre-trial statements, in affidavits and in evidence on oath in order to support it.

He persuaded his wife, his best friend and even his teenage daughter to contribute their own lies in order to buttress the central lie. The stakes could not have been higher. Succeed and (with his claim for exemplary and punitive damages) he would have cost the *Guardian* £2 million, and his political and business careers would have been back on track. Nothing would have been beyond him. Fail and . . .

Did Mr Aitken ever contemplate failure? What explains his rejection of the offer by the *Guardian* (miserably frustrated, as he intended, by his labyrinth of deceit) to reach a compromise settlement? Who can say? We now know that Mr Aitken's business in Paris that weekend was closely tied up with multi-million-pound arms deals involving his close friend, Said Ayas, and the Saudi royal family. For that to have become public would have been devastating for Mr Aitken, for the Saudis and for the government. He could not allow for the possibility of failure.

The rest is tortuous history. Mr Aitken's lie was – at the eleventh hour – uncovered. The libel case collapsed. Mr Aitken's marriage is said to have failed. He has declined to pay a penny of his debts, erecting new subterfuges and (carefully leaked) stratagems to throw off his creditors. He has lied to friends and yet more newspapers about what he was up to in Paris that weekend (remember the fake MI6 story run at gullible length by a tame newspaper – no word yesterday of how he 'lied for his country'). He encouraged his friends to savage the *Guardian* for its impudence. And yesterday, in that same Old Bailey court where he ringingly defended press freedom in 1971, he was jailed for perjury and conspiracy to pervert the course of justice.

Mr Justice Scott Baker rightly commented that this was 'no passing error of judgement [but] calculated perjury pursued over a period of time'. The involvement of his daughter was, he said, 'a gross and inexcusable breach of trust'.

One can debate the severity of the sentence. One can protest that our ideas about crime, punishment and rehabilitation are little more developed than our laws protecting free speech. But one cannot dispute that it was right for his crime to be properly acknowledged and appropriately punished.

Libel is often played as farce. Vain pop stars, self-important actresses and – yes – even editors can cut comic figures as they seek to protect their precious reputations in the mock Gothic majesty of the High Court. But the dishonest use of the libel laws to suppress legitimate reporting of the activities of people in public life is no joke. Lying on oath in court in order to scoop the damages jackpot and to silence an inquiring newspaper is no joke.

Mr Aitken ended his account of his 1971 Old Bailey acquittal by expressing the hope that no journalist or private citizen would ever again face legal action 'for publishing official information which is merely embarrassing or inconvenient to the government of the day'. Eighteen years later the valiant campaigner was jailed in the very same court for lying to suppress information embarrassing and inconvenient to himself.

It is undoubtedly a tragedy for him and for his family. But if his sentence teaches others the risks of abusing the democratic bargain which underpins all our liberties, then Mr Aitken may unwittingly have served the cause of free speech once more. •

∙∙

9 June 1999

David Leigh
Corruption unbecoming

Jonathan Aitken has been packed off at last to serve his time, and as one of those who investigated the former Cabinet minister, I'm certainly glad to see the back of him. Aitken's threats and lies had continued for five years – such a long while that in the meantime, as we all know, the sleazy Conservative government fell, to be replaced by Tony Blair's new dawn.

But some things don't change, and haven't changed in the least with his imprisonment – or even with the arrival of a regime in Britain of a different political colour. What the Aitken case was fundamentally about was not who actually paid whose Ritz Hotel bill all those years ago. It was about bribery.

We live in a country in which the culture of bribery has taken deep root. It is practised by some of the most famous firms in the UK, and connived at quite cynically by Whitehall. As Aitken is driven off to prison, British firms continue to arrange to pay bribes, and the new, shiningly ethical government with which we are blessed refuses to legislate to ban it.

VSEL, Yarrow, Marconi and Westland were all persuaded to agree to pay huge bribes to the Saudi ruling family in the hope of getting lucrative arms contracts while Aitken was minister in charge of these arms sales. This is not merely an unsubstantiated allegation. Companies involved admit it, and we

Mark St George

Jonathan Aitken leaving the Old Bailey after pleading guilty to perjury

possess details of the secret 'agency agreements' they signed at the time. The mechanics of those bribery agreements were organised by Aitken's close friend and business associate, the 'fixer' Said Ayas, who arranged for bribe money to go into a Swiss bank account. These deals were agreed during three-way meetings in January 1993 in Riyadh between Prince Mohammed, the Saudi king's son, Said Ayas and Aitken himself. They were discussed again at a discreet meeting between the three men in Geneva in September 1993.

That was what Aitken was so desperate to conceal that he lied about it when journalists first asked him in October 1993 what his 'private' trip had been for. And from that point, all his troubles began. The British firms involved – most of whom are now controlled by the arms giant GEC – are not really to be blamed for agreeing so readily to pay bribes intended for overseas officials. Their conduct was not illegal in Britain. Indeed, it was tax-deductible.

Furthermore, the Conservative government colluded with – indeed was implicated in – such bribery deals with the Saudis. Ministers stood up in Parliament in the mid-1980s and falsely said that no agents or intermediaries were involved in the gigantic series of Saudi arms contracts known as Al Yamamah. In fact, bribes were paid via middlemen at every turn.

This was all defended in private as justified 'in British interests' or for the sake of 'British jobs'. In reality, it grotesquely enriched a few corrupt foreign rulers and various other individuals, and enabled British firms occasionally to steal a march on their US competitors (who are forbidden by their country's laws to offer bribes; this means they have to be, if not more honest, then at least more careful).

All ancient history? Moss-encrusted Tory sleaze? I don't think so. Only last year, GEC (as they admit) signed a covert 'agency agreement' agreeing to make mysterious offshore payments if they got another multi-million-pound arms deal. It was for AS-90 howitzer turrets to modernise the Polish army, which is desperate to be accepted by Nato. The British government has been helping push such arms deals (so far unsuccessfully) on behalf of 'British jobs'.

Do they know the facts? If GEC ever agreed to publish this sordid little Polish document, it would be seen to contain specific reference to the possibility that foreign officials might be bribed.

This year, Britain at last ratified an OECD convention outlawing such bribery. But they have passed no law forbidding it (although they talk about doing so). And without an explicit law such bribes continue to be tax-deductible in practice, as the government's reports to the OECD concede. The anti-corruption organisation Transparency International say Britain's stance is 'unsatisfactory'.

It is distasteful that the habit of British bribery to get arms deals is now spreading from the Arab world to the newly liberated states of Eastern Europe. Even worse than distasteful, some might think. How about 'shameful'?

David Leigh produced the film Jonathan of Arabia, *which provoked Jonathan Aitken's 1995 libel action.* ●

Greg Dyke, Director General Designate of the BBC, board member at Manchester United, New Labour donor

Media matters

7 November 1998

Ian Mayes
First aid for the injured

. . . people who wrote to the newspaper were proverbially unbalanced.

T he thought with which William Boot consoled himself in Evelyn Waugh's *Scoop* (1938) after a disastrous mistake had appeared in his 'Country Diary' (great crested grebe had been substituted for badger) was still widely held when I became the readers' editor of the *Guardian* just a year ago.

Many letters of complaint were answered but many more, it's almost certainly true to say, were left in the deep litter on someone's desk for a week or two and then binned. The idea that the writers were generally deranged helped this process along. Very few errors were admitted and very few corrections were made.

Even before I began I had numerous warnings from colleagues to 'beware the green-ink brigade', conjuring the spectre of obsessive correspondents who would write at great length and persistently, typically covering their copious sheets in long-hand scrawled in green ink. I have seen one or two – and I mean just one or two – that more or less fit the description, *Guardian* readers all. It is a paradox that newspapers are afraid of the readers they court so vigorously. This chapter in my autobiography, if I survive to write it, will be called 'How I Learned to Stop Worrying and Love the Readers'.

In the past year, almost 6,000 of you have been in touch with my office, most of you to complain about something (occasionally, to the delight and astonishment of one colleague or another, I pass on a letter of congratulation). This week I had a meeting with the colleagues who help deal with these calls – many more, I think, than we expected at the outset – and I asked them what impressions they'd formed of the paper's readers. The first thing mentioned and that we all agreed on was your loyalty. Readers presenting quite serious injuries often end their calls, e-mails, faxes and letters by saying something nice about the paper and that, enraged or upset though they are, they won't stop taking it. Calls of this kind remind us of our responsibilities.

The provision of a point of reference, a number that readers who wish to question or complain can call, has clearly stimulated traffic. We have several regulars, some of them journalists on other newspapers, who, deprived of any opportunity to correct their own effusions (because their errors are never admitted), derive amusement from correcting ours. Many callers, older readers one suspects, now get a great deal of pleasure from 15 to 30 minutes of brisk error-hunting first thing in the morning and will call on the dot of 11 a.m. with the words: 'I suppose you've already got this one . . .' We have a class of caller, of whom we are not, to be frank, particularly fond, who, quite unable to imagine making a mistake themselves, can't point out a mistake made by someone else without a sneer or an angry shout.

No matter, all have contributed to the 'Corrections and Clarifications' column, in which over the year some 1,200 entries have appeared. It means that something like one in five calls produces a correction, a clarification, an apology. I say something like, because many of our mistakes are spotted by more than one of you and some by a great many. In a very real sense, readers whose comments are noted, whether or not a correction appears, are contributing to the conduct and regulation of their paper. We are sorry that so few of you get a direct acknowledgement – that's something that we would like to be able to do.

Many of the corrections we carry could be described, although not by me, as trivial. I try to select those that have some instructional value for us. I nearly always correct errors in the names of people, considering a wrongly spelt name to be in the first place a discourtesy and in the second the lapse of a basic professional practice. I carried a correction putting back a missing accent on a French word, and had a spell of correcting foreign words and phrases, simply to make the point that we very often get them wrong (so much so that some of you think we should avoid them altogether).

I correct only spellings that we repeatedly get wrong (supersede; practice/ practise; licence/license). These things pass at least three people, including the author, before they get into the paper. *Guardian* readers take a close interest in the language we use and will make only limited concessions to the frantic rush with which we put the paper together every day.

I don't regard this kind of thing as trivial. The fact is that the 'Corrections and Clarifications' column also carries entries which seek to redress serious wrongs. The main purpose and priority of the readers' editor is to jump to the aid of the injured. Our willingness to do this appears to be appreciated. It has led to a significant reduction in the number who have felt it necessary to have matters argued out between lawyers. Thanks for that. ●

. . . .

25 March 1999
Dukagjin Gorani
We run for our lives

N ato is bombing and things are going from bad to worse. Everything in Pristina is shutting down and, except for security forces, everyone is off the streets. No shops are working, and only a few cars are out. People are scared and families are trying to get together to figure out where they will stay. We have reports of heavy shelling on the outskirts and the population is moving towards the city centre, believing it is more secure there.

There is barely any information. During the day, a few journalist crews tried to penetrate the Drenica region, a stronghold of the Kosovo Liberation Army, through side roads, but they were turned back and apparently they were shot at. The area is completely blocked off and no one is really sure what is happening there, or in other small cities, such as Glogovac and Produjevo, where there have been offensives by the Yugoslav authorities.

Yesterday was the last day of publication for *Koha Ditore*. The Yugoslav authorities have fined us nearly $25,000 for publishing a public statement by KLA leader Hashim Thaci which was distributed by the Belgrade news agency, Beta. But Beta itself was not fined. Last week, three other Albanian-language papers were fined in a similar way and shut down, and a few days ago I was beaten outside our offices by police and could not get out of my bed for two days.

Like the other Albanian papers, we refuse to pay such a 'fine' to the Yugoslav authorities, which would only be a contribution to their repressive regime. So even if we had the cash, which we do not, we would not comply, even with a symbolic amount. Our publisher, Veton Surroi, said in his editorial that at least, through this fine, we confirm that we agree with the regime on one thing: we represent a threat to them. At least they got that right.

But frankly, in such a situation, the publication of *Koha Ditore* is a luxury phenomenon, a quirk. The time for such communications with daily newspapers is finished. (There are no Albanian-language electronic media.) Any kind of news that you can get is like a breath of fresh air. But there is no distribution and people are on the move. We cannot get the paper to the people. As for the English-language edition, of which I am the editor, all the foreigners have left, so I have lost my readers.

In any case, now it is simply a matter of priorities: how to preserve yourself, how to find shelter in the coming days. The newspapers can find other ways of publishing again, but for the present we are thinking of fundamental survival, of running for your life.

The population of Kosovo, in Pristina in particular, is completely unprotected from the Serbian police, military and – worst of all – paramilitaries. Armed Serbian civilians may also mount their own attacks on Albanian civilians. Yesterday bombs went off at cafés in towns. People may feel safer in Pristina. But we fear a direct attack on the city and it may be that 'the massacre' is yet to come. It may be launched now the air strikes have begun.

Local fighting in the villages will cause more people to flee. At the moment, the KLA is no match for the Yugoslav army and security forces, which have overwhelming amounts of troops and heavy weaponry. It is estimated that there are some 40,000 troops on the ground and active in Kosovo now. The KLA cannot match these numbers, much less hardware, and for the moment is taking cover in the mountains and other unreachable places.

But the army is not after the KLA. They are after the villages and 'ethnic cleansing'. They will of course target villages that have been KLA strongholds, but this is mostly just an excuse. What they are really doing is trying to create a Republka Srpska in Kosovo, and recent moves suggest they are intending to cleanse the north and north-east, and possibly parts of the east of Kosovo, as well as some portions of the centre.

This area includes the main mines, as well as some key Serbian religious sites. But the main aim is probably simply to use this 'new reality' on the ground as a bargaining chip. They are using the Bosnian model, only in a smaller area with a much higher density of population, and without any real opposing army. So the possibility for casualties is in fact higher.

Pristina might suffer the destiny of Sarajevo in Bosnia and be divided into two or three zones. It does not have as large a Serb minority as Sarajevo did, but already there are barricades cutting off certain areas, such as Dragodan and Sunny Hill, from the centre of the city. These barricades, such as the one on the way to my district, are manned by around 50 armed men each.

Air strikes will weaken the Serbian defences, but Slobodan Milosevic will never be persuaded by them to agree to the peace deal. Yet now the strikes have begun, the unleashing of reprisals on the urban areas is inevitable. Air strikes are needed, but without a strong involvement of group troops, the crisis will only deteriorate. A Nato deployment of ground troops is the only way to prevent a vast humanitarian crisis.

Meantime, we just run for our lives. Because of my profession, and being publicly exposed, I will change my place of residence and take shelter for now. I followed the statement by Tony Blair, the British Prime Minister. I am quite knowledgeable about what is happening in the British House of Commons. But otherwise we have no news. I don't have the slightest idea what is happening 500 metres from my house.

This article is taken from the Balkan Crisis Reports of the Institute for War and Peace Reporting. ●

· ·

28 April 1999
Polly Toynbee
We say their press lies, they say ours is as bad. Impasse

All day and night, with flags and whistles, the Serbians stand across the road from Downing Street protesting at the bombing. The occasional passer-by abuses them: 'Murderers, racists, rapists!' and a noisy altercation ensues. A girl is near tears as she asks how people can be so racist about Serbs. It's the fault of our media, whipping up this race hatred. No Serbs ever ethnically cleansed anyone, they just don't do that, Serbs are not those kind of people. Why does our press lie, day after day?

Conversation with them is like speaking through bullet-proof glass, no message passes through either way. They are watching the same news and they are reading the same newspapers and yet they see and read something quite different. They see nothing but Nato lies, just as we see the lies in Serbian news. In wars, truth is in the eye of the beholder. An elderly man thunders on about how this war was planned in 1870, part of the British Empire's grand scheme for world domination. In vain I try to tell him the British Empire is no more. Someone else says Nato wants Kosovo's oil. What oil? The Germans found it in 1914, but it's been cleverly hidden. Try saying that no one wants that godforsaken, dirt-poor, hate-ridden blot on the map of Europe. Rubbish! Of course the Americans want it! It's the geopolitical power point of the world, the vital crossroads between Europe, Asia and Africa!

Young, thoroughly anglicised, lived here for years, many of them anti-Milosevic before this – they don't believe a word of British journalism. Why, they ask, do we report what the refugees say without any independent corroboration? Of course Albanians invent atrocities, they would, wouldn't they?

Why, I ask in reply, can't Western journalists go into Kosovo to see for themselves? Ha! If you were allowed in you'd all just tell more lies! But, I protest, by keeping us out you force us to rely on refugee stories. Ah, I see, says one young man, so if I tell you that my seven brothers have been abducted by aliens, you'd put that in your paper too?

So do they truly believe all Kosovan atrocity stories are lies? Like Holocaust-deniers, do they honestly think the world has conspired to create false images of hundreds of thousands of people in extreme distress, a brilliant fraud? Yes, they reply, and they mean it. (They've seen *Wag the Dog*.) The Albanians, they say, are running from bombing, not cleansing. If Surrey villagers were caught in a civil war, they'd run away too, wouldn't they? No, these people won't, can't, don't believe either the magisterial authority of the BBC or the wide political diversity of the press.

No doubt they wouldn't believe the pictures so fatally missing from this war – the live satellite pictures of hundreds of thousands of starving refugees being shelled in the Kosova hills. Nor would they believe the pictures – if only there were some – of the ethnic-cleansing squads so chillingly interviewed by Maggie O'Kane (one of them spat her name and called her a liar). It is a salutary reminder that journalism, straight or crooked, does less to change hearts and minds than we like to think. After all, neither I nor you are likely to change our views by reading *Daily Mail* leaders, so why do we think others are so easily swayed? Lord Haw-Haw made no converts. For that reason it was a pointless act of folly to bomb the Serbian RTS TV station, a gift to Nato's many critics.

Many Serbs watch CNN, but it makes no difference. Nor would Nato's comical plan to force-feed them six hours of the BBC every day. Truth or propaganda, they will believe what they want to believe. We can only hope as small cracks appear that more of them, along with Milosevic's own deputy, will emerge who never did believe Milosevic or who have changed their minds. But the Western press is unlikely to do it for them.

In this armchair war, where even the high-altitude pilots are almost as far removed from the action as Nintendo players, journalists are key combatants, however unwilling. All who write about it from home or from the Balkans are players too, willy-nilly. Testing each other's nerve, leaders on each side read the enemy's press to guess their resolve.

No doubt Milosevic's team pores happily over a sheaf of daily cuttings from Nato's critics in Britain, France, Germany, Italy, Greece or the US. (His incomprehension of pluralist democracy means he will misread it badly.) His press, of course, reveals nothing, but we too grasp any slender sign of Serbian psychological weakening. We journalists who passionately support the war are thought slavish tools of Nato propaganda. Those writers who oppose it with equal passion could be accused of fuelling Milosevic's delusion that Nato's nerve is weak and will crumble first.

While bombing the TV station was a bad tactical mistake and all civilian deaths are tragic, I don't regard it as some kind of exceptional humanitarian outrage. Disgracefully, the National Union of Journalists' only statement since the war began has concerned that bombing: 'This is barbarity. Killing journalists does not stop censorship, it only brings more repression. It makes you wonder what the democratic values we are supposed to represent in this conflict are worth.' Unlike the International Federation of Journalists, the NUJ was not sufficiently moved to say anything about the murder of Slavko Curuvija, the dissident Serb editor, nor on the banning of the B92 radio station.

The press wallows in self-aggrandising myths that journalism *per se* is a noble calling and practitioners across the globe pursue some common truth. That's certainly not the public's view: the press is a low trade, except where it faces gross persecution. There is scant community of values across the British press between, say, the few liberal papers and the *Mail* or the many Murdochs, let alone with our Serbian brothers.

I snorted with laughter when I read some quotes assembled to celebrate World Press Freedom Day, such as De Tocqueville's: 'It would diminish the importance of newspapers to believe they only serve to guarantee freedom; they maintain civilisation.' Well! I'll settle for Wole Soyinka's more modest proposition: 'The greatest threat to freedom is the absence of criticism.' Nato briefers may sometimes lie, but Western diversity guarantees criticism whatever they say, while Milosevic silences his. ●

....

28 April 1999

Julie Burchill

A life more ordinary

Last week, at the suggestion of a Sunday newspaper, I wrote my standard hissy tract, begging the question (though not really expecting an answer): 'Why do good girls have to go bad?' In it I deplored the fact that, in the tradition of Anthea Turner posing naked with a snake or Kylie Minogue getting 'caught' with handcuffs in her hand luggage, Jill Dando could be seen on the front of the *Radio Times* posing in a leather catsuit.

The usual suspect phrases found their way in, of course. This was 'the call of the mild', 'the bland leading the bland' and the New Look seemed 'to owe more to M&S than S&M'. Miss Dando, I jeered, was obviously 'a woman so modest that she is engaged to marry a gynaecologist rather than let a stranger get an eyeful'.

I pointed out that, at her own admission, asking her mother to shorten her school skirt at 14 was 'the nearest I ever got to rebellion', and that her favourite photograph of herself showed her in a taffeta ballgown at the Vienna Opera Ball, dancing with her friend Cliff Richard. All in all, I concluded, she was about as convincing as a Bad Girl as Sir Cliff was as Heathcliff. With a stroke of good luck bordering on the criminal, the paper was full and the piece wasn't run.

Interestingly, I found that in the course of my efforts I could not manufacture even a simulacrum of dislike for Dando, of whom I knew nothing apart from the fact that she was massively successful on the sort of television I never watched, and that she looked like the missing link between a precious past royal bride and a dull putative one. I normally dislike clean-cut blonde women who appeal to the sort of men who fetishise about clean, white cotton underwear. But I had no feelings of antipathy towards her, and sudden and violent death seemed the last thing that should or would happen to such a bright and breezy Betjeman girl. My first reaction to the BBC1 bulletin was that it was a particularly horrible and effective joke. Then came the news programmes, and the drawn faces of colleagues, and I realised it was true.

'The oddest thing has happened,' I drawled to the only other person in the house: 'Jill Dando's been killed.' She sat down rapidly and gasped: 'Oh, no! But I really liked her! She was lovely!' It sank in then, how much people liked her, people you'd have as friends, not just your mum, who wished you were more like her. Like Princess Diana and Sharon Tate before her, they'd somehow managed to take out the one decent person in a profession full of rotters.

Two years younger than me, coming from very nearby my home town of Bristol, Jill Dando was a world away from my kind of journalism and my kind of life. My career was one of winging it, of the style press and powerful patronage and cocaine nights at the Groucho. Hers was old school, calm and measured, the slow steady climb through provincial TV to a more mainstream and solid kind of fame. Like finding a tarantula in a punnet of soft English strawberries, any idea of hit men and contract killing seems grotesque.

'Yes, but what does it mean?' we will be wondering from here to Christmas. Well, no one knows yet. But one thing is sure: whatever it was that killed her festered and bloomed darkly in the mind of the perpetrator, not the victim. Her secret was that she had no secret, no dark side. And in a culture steeped in psychobabble, when even cartoon characters like Batman and Spiderman cannot be brought to the screen without ludicrous research into their dark sides, the final taboo has become accepting the unsexy fact that someone's life could actually be as blameless as it appeared to be.

'Jill Blando', she once called herself, but this alone indicated that she was a woman of intelligence and humour. True, she appealed to a rather sad type of male journalist, but then no one can be blamed for their fans. Many wrote of liking her for what she wasn't — intellectual, frightening, overtly sexy — rather than for what she was, but this too says more about them than it does about her. After a predictable period as an old man's darling when she lived with her boss, some 15 years older than her, for seven years in her twenties, she was due to marry a man a few years younger than herself — the final sign that an Eternal Girl has grown up.

Like Diana, Jill Dando was perceived as an icon of cleanliness in a dirty world — perhaps even a more perfect, more truly English unspoilt Diana, unbroken by fads and fancies and psychics and playboys. She had pulled away in front of the rat pack of blonde rivals to Diana's tiara as they were revealed one by one to be too flighty (Anthea), too common (Denise) and too clever by half (Kirsty). In an England forever panicking about what being English actually means, it is not too fanciful to suggest that a certain sort of middle-aged, middle-class Home Counties man could look at Jill Dando's kind, sensible face mated with that long-legged grace as she fought crime in her silky sarongs and think, for a moment, that God was in his heaven and all was right with the world.

The clever-clogs tendency among commentators has found it somewhat unsettling that the Queen and the Prime Minister were so quick off the block with their condolences, but it makes perfect sense. Jill Dando was exactly the person whom both these strange, isolated, dysfunctional individuals project themselves as being; by hitching their wagon to her, as they did with Diana before her, they show us how well they can 'do' emotion and that they're just like us, really.

But they're not like us, and they're certainly not like her; such an open life, with so little to hide. It is a bitter irony that a woman who was always perceived as the ultimate girl-next-door has achieved what already seems to be something of a legendary status. If she was killed by a stalker, she will be remembered as a feminist heroine; if she was killed by an underworld hit man, she will be remembered as a journalist heroine. Whatever happens, the bland blonde golden girl who always seemed so prematurely grown-up, already middle-aged, will never now grow old, while myself and a million other Toytown rebels will live quiet lives, grow fat and die in bed. ●

···

26 January 1999

Ian Mayes

Corrections and clarifications

The absence of corrections yesterday was due to a technical hitch rather than any sudden onset of accuracy. ●

The eclipse of the sun, August 11

Science and technology.com

. . . .

27 March 1999

Tim Radford
Hit and myths

The cosmos is a dangerous place: rogue asteroids stalk the solar system and planet Earth flies through cyclic barrages of cometary flak. Hits may be palpable but the bullet holes have to be inferred. Other planets stay pitted and pocked, but tectonic forces and eroding wind and water have wiped the Earth's scars clean away.

Even so, the arrival during historic times of, say, a comet 100 metres across, at 30 miles a second, or even a very near miss, would provide an unforgettable fireworks display, and probably a season of darkness at noon along with fire from heaven, partings of the waters, plagues, famine and seasons of wormwood. The question is: did anyone remember to write such things down, and how did they interpret what they saw? Asteroid scholars have had huge fun for the past two decades re-examining the ancient literature looking for written evidence of them. This has never been hard to find. It has, however, been hard to interpret. Is Moses a myth? Then surely Beowulf is even more of a myth, and the Arthuriad a nonsense? Why believe Byzantine scribes when they talk about showers of stones, and dry fog, and cometary portents, when what they say about emperors is patently propaganda? There are other explanations for the Dark Ages, or the fall of the Minoan civilisation, and their chroniclers may invoke the gods, but that does not mean the destruction was literally heaven-sent. Humans are terrific at causing human suffering, why pick on the environment?

Yet awful things did happen in the past, and there is a detailed record of it; quite literally, an annual register. The story of the world is written in wood. Think of an oak tree, or a pine, as so much solidified sunshine. Each summer it photosynthesises a fatter waistline, each winter it goes to sleep a little. There is a record of this in the annual growth rings in each cross-section of the trunk. Each of these growth rings tells a chapter of the story. Is the space between rings small? Then it was a cool summer, or a dry one. Is there a lot of new wood? Then it was wet and warm, or just possibly there was an extra supply of nutrients and more growing space after a forest fire.

Oaks can live for hundreds of years, bristlecone pines in Arizona can live for thousands. So trees are mute diarists of a past climate. Earlier this century, a new breed of scientists called dendrochronologists began trying to assemble a kind of 'wooden ruler' with which to measure the years. They realised that all trees from a particular species in a particular region at any particular time would hold, under their bark, the same sequence of tell-tale summers. A youngish tree and a gnarled neighbour would have histories that overlapped; find some shared pattern of years in each of them and you would extend the time-series. Unearth a waterlogged bog oak and look for yet another match, and the tree-ring chronology would be pushed further and further.

Why stop at trees? The castles and cathedrals of medieval Europe are supported with beams from oak forests that could push the story further back in time. Renaissance panels, and violins too, carry the countdown of the past. Individual trees in felicitous sites might tell an unrepresentative tale, so scientists logged – happy word – as many samples as they could, from as many sites as they could date. Sometimes the story gets complicated: a lot of medieval English oak, for instance, turned out to be carried from Poland by Hanseatic traders, so one national chronology was not enough. Dendrochronologists began comparing across borders, and then across continents.

Three years ago scientists from Britain, Germany and the US finished the Aegean 'Bronze Age' chronology: 1,503 years of precisely dated tree-ring sequences based on shipwrecks from the time of Egypt's Nefertiti to the time of King Midas in Phrygia. The adventure began as a study of vanished or sparsely recorded climate, a search for evidence of sunspots, of cycles of greater and less solar activity, and then extended to the peaks and troughs in climatic activity, with different patterns revealed from different national chronologies: seven fat years here balanced by seven lean years there.

There were, however, some odd things. The years around AD 540 were savagely cold both in North America and in northern Europe. There were years of famine in China and in Europe Anglo-Saxon chroniclers talked of 'eclipses' of the sun; Chinese astronomers noted that the star Canopus could not be seen and the plague of Justinian ravaged a continent.

Vulcanologists noted that Europe was in the grip, in those years, of a severe 'dry fog'. The Dark Ages followed. The tree chronologies also showed severe cold around 1628 BC, and again in 1159 BC and in 208 BC. Each of these episodes was marked by famine, epidemics, murrains of cattle, a darkening of the sun and the collapse of a civilisation or two.

Worldwide freezes require planetary-scale triggers. There is a case for volcanoes as troublemakers: the eruption of Santorini in the Aegean almost certainly pumped dust into the stratosphere and obscured sunlight, but not enough to last for years, Mike Baillie argues in *Exodus to Arthur: Catastrophic Encounters With Comets* (Batsford, £15.99). He likes the idea of a comet whacking into the skies now and again. That would be enough to explain darkness at noon, the blotting of the stars, and the failure of six harvests in a row. It would set off seiches and tsunamis that would part waters and produce legendary floods. Meanwhile, in such summer cold, the only thing that would flourish would be artemisia: yes, wormwood. Eat your heart out. Not only would all this shut down civilisation; it would be signalled by heavenly portents of change. Take that, King Minos. Moses, here's the pillar of fire you've been waiting for. Chinese dynasts, the Mandate of Heaven is withdrawn.

Mike Baillie is a dendrochronologist: a player in the tree-tale story. It gives him a chance to grab the literature of the past and – in an untidy telling, but huge fun to read – wring it for lurid evidence of visitors. He isn't the first to do so; fantasists have been at the same game for years. Some of the argument has to be right. Livy wasn't the only chronicler to talk of mysterious showers of stones from the sky around 208 BC. Babylonian astronomers in the seventeenth century BC recorded that they could not see the planet Venus for nine months and four days. That is not the stuff of myth. But Baillie takes the wooden evidence and fashions a kind of Procrustean bed on to which the human story must be laid. Yes, a cometary impact could just possibly produce the kind of phenomena reported in Exodus, if you believe Exodus is a real record of a historic event.

On the other hand, the conjectured date of Exodus doesn't fit the real date of the oak chronology. Does that mean Egyptologists and biblical scholars have been wrong for a century or two? Beowulf did battle with Grendel; was this tenth-century tale really a version of Comet Halley's arrival in AD 530? Was the search for the Grail, in the stricken landscape of the Fisher King, really a fictionalised description of a Britain in the first sunless grip of the Dark Ages? What separates this author from others on this murky path is that he knows – and ruefully admits – that he is on swampy ground. But the oaken evidence provides a sturdier stepway.

And Baillie isn't alone in believing in cometary impacts. Something huge certainly arrived 65 million years ago at the end of the age of the dinosaurs. The world watched 22 fragments of a comet slam into Jupiter in 1994.

Kiloton-scale explosions are detected from time to time in the upper atmosphere. At least one substantial heavenly visitor reached the ground this century, blasting the Tunguska forest of Siberia in 1908, killing no one but leaving distant witnesses with the distinct impression that they had been caught up in a rehearsal for the Apocalypse. Like the Terminator, this version of history will be back. ●

....

27 March 1999
Simon Rogers
Web witnesses put fresh spin on news

E-mail to the *Guardian* from a computer engineer in Belgrade: 'Last night two Nato airplanes came down not far from us. I spoke to my friends and they said: "Let's go hunt pilots."'

With Western journalists being expelled from Yugoslavia, e-mail and the Internet have become important sources of information from the war zone. This is the first large-scale war fought on the Internet. On the worldwide web you can now rub shoulders with the Kosovo Liberation Army, the Serbian government, Bill Clinton and Tony Blair.

Computers are reasonably common in the Balkans and there is no shortage of information. Nato governments have been developing their websites, and the US State Department is particularly active. Its website provides regular updates, transcripts of briefings, maps and background.

The Foreign Office site, regarded as the best in Whitehall, offers Robin Cook's speeches and latest updates below a grainy picture of a cruise missile.

On the other side, the Serbian information minister, Aleksander Vucic, is regarded as something of an Internet buff. On his department's website you can find stories on the West spreading 'phoney information' on the humanitarian crisis. Radio Yugoslavia broadcasts on the Internet in English.

The KLA response is a site telling the reader that it 'has always respected the international mechanisms, diplomats, military and humanitarians' and respects the 'war and peace conventions'.

But the search for news rather than propaganda is more difficult. Several sites in Kosovo and Belgrade itself provide accurate news from the ground, but not without risk. Mr Vucic recently expanded freedom of information legislation to cover the Internet. 'Verbal deceit' can mean fines and the site being shut down.

B92, the award-winning radio station closed down by the Serb authorities this week, views the Internet as a vital resource. When the station was closed for 52 hours during demonstrations against the Belgrade government in 1996, the web was the only place to hear independent news.

'It's essential,' said B92's UK spokesperson, Julia Glyn-Pickett. 'The people who have links print the information out and distribute it. People in Serbia are very aware of the sources of news and are very news-hungry.'

Operating from secret locations, the station was last night still broadcasting through its site, via the Netherlands. Other local stations Radio 21 and Koha Detore, both of which provided Internet services, have not been so lucky. Koha Detore was closed down by Serb police on Wednesday and Radio 21 on Thursday. A security guard was shot dead in a skirmish at Koha's offices. In a further blow, Serbian computer hackers have vowed to close down sites such as B92's.

At the moment the quickest way to get information out of Yugoslavia is by e-mail. This channel provides a conduit for news flooding to the chat boards that have sprung up to provide first-person accounts of the bombing.

'Last night's raid was civilised and decent,' said Srdjan on the board set up by Steve Clift, a US-based analyst. 'It all ended at midnight, so we could go to sleep in our beds instead of the shelters.'

Sava Jajic, a Serbian Orthodox monk, has been bombarding Western journalists with regular updates on the crisis from a twelfth-century monastery in Kosovo. His missives have become so frequent that Internet magazine *Salon* has nicknamed him the Cyber-Monk. He rises at 1 a.m. to take advantage of quiet traffic in cyberspace, prays and then gets online.

'It's giving people in the middle of the situation the chance to put their stories across,' said Mr Clift.

The Institute for War and Peace Reporting has been building up links with reporters in Kosovo for seven years. Following the exodus of Western journalists it has been taking news from reporters on the ground to put up on its site. 'The only way you can get the story out to the international media is through local people,' said the director of programmes, Alan Davis.

But that brings its own problems, said John Owen, the director of Internet campaign group the Freedom Forum. The more the war hits the lines of communication, the more likely it is that the only people getting news direct from Kosovo will be those in the West. Some campaign groups are considering using satellite technology in coordination with the Internet to broadcast information back into the war zone. 'The Net brings the information out,' said Mr Owen. 'The more important issue is bringing it back in.'

· ·

13 January 1999

Nick Gillett

Love bytes

I met Christy early on a Friday evening. It had been much like any other day in Arcadium, a chat room I liked, and I'd met and written to a few people before I got chatting to someone by the name of Brown Eyed Girl. She was nonchalant in her conversation, but had an intelligence and an understated intensity about her that charmed me completely.

When it was time for me to finish that night, instead of making my excuses and leaving, I suggested we exchange e-mail addresses so I could write to her again one day. Even as I typed the words, it felt somehow illicit, but at the same time thrilling, as though I'd crossed a barrier.

I wrote to her the following Monday from work. The first few days of our correspondence were sweet and exhilarating. In the same way as meeting somebody you instantly 'click' with in real life, it felt somehow as though we already knew each other, as if this were destiny knocking on our doors. In a world of billions of people, we had found each other on a crowded Internet. Well, she certainly gave good e-mail.

As the days became weeks, our writing became more intimate and we discovered that there was more to this than a simple early attraction. To my surprise I realised I was falling in love with a girl I'd never met. I would find myself eager to get back to my computer when I'd been away from it for a few hours, and reading her words filled me with the need to know everything about her.

It was several weeks before we first spoke on the phone. One problem with e-mail is that it introduces a world of potential fiction into events. Even though you may think you're getting to know a 5ft 9in red-haired girl from Alabama, you could in fact be pouring your heart out to a 6ft body builder from New York. It was with a measure of relief that I found out that at least elements of the story were true; she was a girl and she was definitely from the Southern States.

After those first faltering steps, our telephone relationship became a £150 a month telephone habit. E-mail was no longer enough.

It wasn't long before we decided we had to meet. She was at college and didn't have the money to come to England, so I flew out to meet her in New Orleans. It was incredibly romantic. Our eyes met across an emptying late-night departure lounge in the Big Easy, and even though we had never exchanged photographs we both just seemed to know. It felt perfectly right.

Far from being some geeky caricature or adipose leviathan, she was a pretty, willowy, all-American girl. She had freckles and thick red hair, and was feeling just as bewildered by the meeting as I was. We went out into the French Quarter and talked and just looked at each other. It was an amazing week.

When I returned to London, our relationship continued with renewed passion. Even though we had had slightly less to say to each other in the flesh than we had via international telecom, it didn't feel like a hindrance. The Atlantic was starting to, though, and we had to work out how we could be together.

I went back to America a few months later. After meeting, talking on the phone and writing longing e-mails wasn't enough. We both knew that if this was going to work, one of us would need to move, and to do that we would both have to be absolutely sure – about everything.

My second visit was to be a time when we decided whether this was something for which one of us would be prepared to switch continents. We needed to be absolutely certain, and we weren't. So we tearfully decided that this was not going to work and that we should end our relationship.

It's been nearly a year now and romance has turned into friendship. We still write and talk on the phone from time to time, and I count Christy as one of my dearest friends. Although ill-fated by geography, our Internet love affair was as wonderful and unspoiled as new love always is.

Arcadium, the chat room where we met, closed some time ago. ●

···

11 January 1999
Alan Rusbridger
How I fell in love with the Net

Confession (or boast): I am not an anorak. I do not know what http stands for, nor URL. I do not know the difference between http and www or why they seem forever destined to be separated by ://. I am the wrong person to ask about html, Boolean search engines, Javascript or cookies. I could no more build a website than build a cathedral. Whatever the opposite of an anorak is, I'm it.

But in my simple, untutored way I love the Internet. Indeed, I sometimes rather envy the life of an anorak. Nothing to do but surf all day long, the world literally at your fingertips. I could become a geek in no time at all.

I remember the early thrill of being let loose in the Cambridge University Library – one of the three copyright libraries in England and the only one with open access to most of the shelves. I went to the library every day for weeks on end, but I did virtually no academic work. I just ferreted my way through the stacks – miles and miles of them – like a dog in a rabbit warren. That, cubed, is the Internet. Except you never have to leave your seat, there's no closing time and there's three times as much fun to be had.

When I first used the Net I did what most Net virgins are said to do: typed my name into a search engine. I sat back and waited. After a minute or so one response popped up: For 'Rusbridger' try the Harry Ransom Humanities Research Center at the University of Texas at Austin.

It made no sense. I double-clicked and waited (this was the early 1990s: things were slow back then). 'Rusbridger' turned out to be in the index to the archive of Tom Stoppard's papers, which had been lodged with the university. This puzzled me, for I could not remember ever having written to Tom Stoppard. Then I recalled that I had once dropped him a postcard 10 years previously while editing a Christmas round-up of Books of the Year. This was presumably the precious document meticulously archived and indexed in Austin, Texas.

I was first dazzled, then disappointed. All that awesome computing power labouring to produce such a trifling mouse! How useless and how sad. The nerds could keep the Net.

Around the same time I met a couple of the first Net visionaries, both of whom spoke in plain English and neither of whom seemed to mind that I didn't know my browser from my server. They were Louis Rossetto, editor of a San Francisco-based magazine, *Wired*, and Nicholas Negroponte of MIT's Media Lab. We talked late into the night about how the Internet would change the world. I was hooked by the vision. And I was learning not to be scared of it all.

It was drugs that converted me from Netophobe to Netophile. My doctor had just told me I would have to take something called Losec to counter acid in my stomach which, thanks to a faulty valve, was leaking into my oesophagus and causing me some discomfort. If I started, he said, I might well have to take it for the rest of my life. The leaflet accompanying the drug was as useless as all such leaflets tend to be. Most people taking Losec tended to be just fine. But some suffered from (as it were) total hair loss, wracking coughs, scabid noses, purple teeth, dementia and death.

Before signing up to a lifetime of side effects I decided to check this Losec stuff out. The information on the Internet was awesome, and included full reports of clinical trials from all over the world. I was reassured enough to start taking Losec – another thing that changed my life. **www.druginfonet.com** After that there was no stopping me. The Internet became my first port of call for, well, more or less anything. Stuck for that Oasis lyric **www.oasisnet.com** or Emily Dickinson line **http://redfrog.norconnect.no/~poems/poets/emily—dickinson.html** that is needed for an editorial? It's there. What about trying to find my old schoolfriend Scot, who disappeared off to California 20 years ago, never to be heard of again? I find an astonishing database and search engine which, in five seconds flat, has located Scot in Chalcedony St, San Diego. In another 20 seconds I'm looking at a map of downtown San Diego and my computer is telling me his local pizza shop, his nearest gas station and where he goes shopping. **http://altavista.switchboard.com**

The next night I'm at home and my daughter's fretting because she's got to write about *Antigone* and she's left her text at school. It takes three minutes to find the complete text, with very useful footnotes. **www.uky.edu/ArtsSciences/Classics/ant/antig1.htm** Daughter hugely relieved. She never knew her father was such a nerd. A small, proud milestone.

Shortly afterwards I'm writing a speech about defamation and I've been told there's an important South African Supreme Court judgment which I ought to read. I find it at the South African Law reports. **www.butterworths.co.za** Later, writing about the Truth and Reconciliation Commission **www.truth.org.za** I am able to download the report before our South Africa correspondent has been able to stagger back to the office with his five volumes of paper.

There's a Weber CD I've been hunting for ages, and I can only half-remember the clarinettist. I find it at a site called CD Now **www.cdnow.com** and within a week it's been mailed to me. The same site helps me sleuth out a snatch of Brazilian music that's been haunting me. Now, once a week, I get an e-mail from CD Now telling me about new clarinet and Brazilian music.

And while we're on the clarinet I want to know where I can find a list of all the music written for clarinet, cello and piano for an amateur trio I'm playing in. There are, needless to say, numerous websites devoted to nothing but clarinets – buying them, selling them, playing them, repairing them. This is dangerous territory: hours could pass while I explore deeper and deeper. Eventually I come across one site in America with a section entirely given over to clarinet chamber music **www.luybenmusic.com/music/clarinet/clarinet.html** which mails stuff cheaply all over the world. My piano teacher has an Eames chair which, after his Steinway, is his pride and joy. After a few months of trying it out while listening to him playing as I can only dream of I decide I wouldn't mind one. You too? Do as I did. Go to **www.mancha.demon.co.uk/eames.html** and see if anything suits you. A nice man called Graham delivered mine two days later.

If you live near a giant Waterstones or a small, knowledgeable bookseller you may not need to use the Internet to buy your books. But the chances are that you'll find what you want quicker, and possibly cheaper, by searching electronically first. The best sites (Amazon is the obvious one, but others are catching up) will behave almost as a friendly bookseller would. Now they know you're interested in that author or this subject they'll guide you gently by the elbow towards other books you might be interested in. They'll even write to you in a rather old-fashioned way to let you know when something that might amuse you has come in.

I'm off to play golf at St Andrews. The BBC weather service has a four-day forecast for the Fife coast. **www.bbc.co.uk/weather/standrews.html** I check the times of the trains from the Railtrack information site. **www.railtrack.co.uk** I find an extremely thorough hole-by-hole guide to playing the Old Course, complete with maps and detailed contours for each green. **www.kingcrest.com/rivercup/oldcourse** The course still massacres me, but it has been a pleasant moment of fantasy. While searching I come across an Internet booking service for other great courses in the region. **www.linksnet.co.uk** I will try and plan my next golfing holiday on the Net.

And so on and so on. I now never read Hansard on paper: it's quicker and simpler (and searchable) on the Net. The full House of Lords Pinochet judgment was on my screen as fast as the Press Association newsflash. Ditto the Starr report and Reuters. I get my instant daily take on American news from Slate's catch-up summary of the US papers, e-mailed to me twice a day.

I am following the BSE inquiry through the *Guardian*'s reporting – but also through the official site, which has every witness statement as well as a full transcript of every day of the hearing. I have bookmarked newspapers all over the world, from the *Times of India* and the *New York Post* to *An Phoblacht* and the *London Review of Books*. The only thing that has defeated me so far is Tesco Online, which persistently rejects me for not living in a posh enough neighbourhood.

Just when you think you've exhausted present possibilities you bump into another surprise. One of my press-related interests is the great battles that raged around the time of George III between Parliament and press. I have two books on John Wilkes as well as a first edition of the letters of Junius, the anonymous essayist who caused so much trouble with his prose that he was charged with sedition. A minute or two searching for material on Wilkes led me to the fullest bibliography imaginable of literature to do with newspapers. **www.lib.siu.edu/ cni/index-w.html**

If anything is certain it is that this astonishing new medium will provoke further great battles over free speech and control to rival those of the late eighteenth century.

It's worth reading the full judgments of the district and Supreme Court in rejecting the Communications Decency Act (CDA) of 1996. **hhtp://pubweb. nwu.edu** They are more radical than anything you can easily imagine a British judge delivering.

Pennsylvania District Judge Steward Dalzell concluded his judgment in these unequivocal terms, which bear quoting in full:

> Cutting through the acronyms and argot that cluttered the hearing testimony, the Internet may fairly be regarded as a never-ending worldwide conversation. The government may not interrupt that conversation. As the most participatory form of mass speech yet developed, the Internet deserves the highest protection from governmental intrusion. True it is that many find some of the speech on the Internet to be offensive, and amid the din of cyberspace many hear discordant voices that they regard as indecent. The absence of governmental regulation of Internet content has unquestionably produced a kind of chaos, but as one of the plaintiff's experts put it with such resonance at the hearing: 'What achieved success was the very chaos that the Internet is. The strength of the Internet is that chaos.' Just as the strength of the Internet is chaos, so the strength of our liberty depends upon the chaos and cacophony of the unfettered speech the First Amendment protects. For these reasons I without hesitation hold that the CDA is unconstitutional on its face. ●

12 May 1999
Sarah Hall
God's e-mail address lands chaplain in row

Acambridge university chaplain has been accused of high-tech blasphemy after calling himself 'god' in his e-mail address. The Rev. Bruce Kinsey has come under fire from local clergy and Tory minister Ann Widdecombe for choosing the address 'god@dow.cam.ac.uk'.

'It's tactless, tacky, needlessly offensive and not funny,' said the Rev. Tom Ambrose, spokesman for the local diocese of Ely. 'If he wanted a funny e-mail address he should have chosen something else. This is just trivialising religion and we don't think that he was right to do it.'

'It is blasphemous and I might suggest he read the Third Commandment tonight,' added Miss Widdecombe, the shadow health minister.

But Mr Kinsey, chaplain and steward of Downing College and Director of Studies in Theology and Religious Studies, has insisted he has no deific aspirations and merely chose the address to make it easier for students to access him. 'Christians make heavy weather of everything in life. I am not calling myself God. It's just an easy way to reach me, and it's less dull than using the name chaplain. No one forgets it,' he told the student newspaper, *Varsity*.

Yesterday he said in a statement issued by the university: 'I have been using the letters g-o-d as an address for e-mail to be sent to, not as a user name. I am still listed as the Rev. Bruce Kinsey in the university address book. As a college chaplain, it's important that people are able to contact me easily. This new e-mail address has certainly proved to be memorable to both students and staff in the college.'

Former social security minister Frank Field, who famously intervened in the row between the organist and dean at Westminster Abbey, said: 'I think it's a rather neat thing to do. You might forget the chaplain's name, but even nowadays you wouldn't forget God.'

And being God online has amused some, with a major London firm e-mailing the chaplain for advice on a merger. 'It's nice to see that people can take a joke,' said Mr Kinsey. 'I really enjoy those sort of things, it makes the world a happier place.' •

. . . .

7 June 1999

Letters

Can GM feed the world?

As a member of the Nuffield Council on Bioethics working party on GM crops, may I respond to your letters (1 June)? Mr Paterson claims: 'People do not go hungry because of a lack of food in the world [but] because of the enormous inequalities of power and wealth.'

Unfortunately, for political reasons, these inequalities change only slowly. The world's 800 million clinically undernourished people need more food quickly and productive work to buy it with. The first Green Revolution of 1965–80 shows that higher food staples yields on small farms can contribute significantly to both. Absolute poverty, the proportion of people too poor to afford enough to eat, was halved between 1965 and 1988 where the high-yielding cereal varieties were widely planted: in the Indian and Pakistan Punjab, south-east China, central Luzon in the Philippines, Muda in Malaysia, most of South Korea and Taiwan, Java in Indonesia and north Mexico. The new cereals provided productive work and cheap food staples for small farmers and farmworkers. This helped them to live decently without relying on support from many children.

Research shows the high-yield cereals-fertiliser technology was 'scale-neutral', helping small and big farmers similarly – and, unlike tractors or herbicides, creating rather than destroying productive employment.

Unfortunately the Green Revolution did little for Africa and drylands areas, and has largely run its course. Since 1989, yields of main food staples in developing countries have grown at little above 1 per cent per year, half as fast as populations of working age will grow from now to 2020. Food farming is the only affordable way to employ most of these people; this extra work can be made economic only by yield growth. How is this, for food staples produced on small farms by labour rather than machines, to be revived and spread? Water and land are becoming increasingly scarce; agrochemicals carry risks.

Organic food is fine for those who can afford it. The world's poor need jobs and food staples from intensive, but safe and environmentally considerate, farming. GM crops should be an important part of the answer. Already millions of Chinese smallholders grow GM rice. Vitamin A-enriched rice is near release. Such GM staples can and will save millions of lives, unless stopped, either by failure to change the incentives and institutions now directing GM resources, or by blanket opposition.

Professor Michael Lipton
Poverty Research Unit
University of Sussex ●

Win McNamee

President Clinton at a National Prayer Breakfast during his impeachment

Over there

· ·

21 December 1998

Jonathan Freedland

History made with solemnity and farce

History, when it comes, does not always know how to behave. It doesn't always sit up straight; sometimes it forgets to bow its head in reverence for the moment. It fails to remember the future generations who will look back and judge.

So it was when the 435 members of the US House of Representatives cast the vote that will etch their own place in history. They did not give the chroniclers of the future the archive pictures they will expect – sombre rows of men and women, their shoulders heavy with responsibility, silently resolving to impeach the President of the United States for only the second time in that nation's history.

Instead they milled around, chatted and gossiped, leisurely running their swipe-cards through the electronic voting machines that tallied up their votes on two scoreboards. The House did not sit as one, on the edge of its seat, waiting for the fateful moment which would make Bill Clinton the first impeached president since Andrew Johnson in 1868, a figure more disgraced even than Richard Nixon. When that moment came, at 1.20 p.m. on Saturday, and the column marked 'Yea' reached the winning post of 218 votes, few on the floor were paying attention. It fell to the history-conscious press gallery to point at the board and to pause at what they had witnessed.

Maybe it was all too much. For Saturday was a day of drama overdose, coming at the end of a too-dramatic week. The Representatives were exhausted from five days of late-night debates, security briefings on the Gulf and the party caucuses which had rocked with dramas of their own. The result was an impeachment session that veered from the focused to the confused, from the solemn to the farcical. 'A disaster movie scripted by the Marx Brothers,' quipped Democrat Barney Frank.

Within minutes came a twist that threatened to overshadow even the monumental business before the House. Republican Bob Livingston of Louisiana, destined to be the new Speaker, stepped forward and called on President Clinton to resign.

'No, you resign!' bellowed a chorus of Democrats, shocking a chamber less prone to such parliamentary barracking than our own House of Commons. More swiftly than any of them could have anticipated, Mr Livingston obliged. First, he apologised for his own record of serial adultery, which he had been forced to confess on Thursday. Then, 'I must set the example that I hope President Clinton will follow. I will not stand for Speaker . . .'

Murdo Macleod

Monica Lewinsky, author

The oxygen sucked out of the chamber. A ghostly silence descended. Parliamentary resignations are rare, especially ones which come as a genuine surprise. There had been no leak, no speculation. Falteringly, the House recovered and continued the debate which had consumed 12 hours the previous day. The speeches were never longer than five minutes, some just 90 seconds, many of them repetitive and gratuitous, members addressing not the House but the TV audience in their own districts back home.

Republicans insisted that they were punishing not sex but perjury. At stake was the rule of law, the underpinning of the US Constitution. Democrats pleaded for proportionality, a punishment that fitted President Clinton's crime.

There were moments of grandeur. Dick Gephardt, the Democrats' leader in the House, delivered the best speech of his career. 'We are on the brink of the abyss,' he pleaded, begging for a last-minute reprieve. 'The only way to stop this insanity is through the force of our own will.' His own party leapt to their feet, offering a sustained ovation. Mr Gephardt waded through them, hugged by each in turn, his back slapped, his hand shaken – a display of that special brand of unity unique to the lost cause. He had fought the most valiant fight, but his own side knew they were beaten.

The contrast in that moment was clear. On one side of the House were the Democrats. If you blurred your eyes, it was an effusion of colour. Women dressed in purple, green and red; men with black or brown faces; some old, some young. The Republican side remained seated, an assembly of whey-faced, thin-lipped, blue-blazered men. They were sitting – in judgement. The Democrats staged a walkout, but, with only one exit open, got clogged up. Once out, they had to troop back in again seven and a half minutes later to vote against what they called a partisan *coup d'état*.

By then their fury had run out. Some slumped in their seats, forlornly watching the scoreboard. Republicans clustered, plotting the Livingston succession. The clock ticked away the 15 minutes of voting time. The Yeas mounted, the Nays trailed. Until the hammer came down and the acting Speaker announced the result: impeachment.

There were three more votes, for each of the remaining articles. As soon as they were done, there was a stampede for the doors, like thieves escaping the scene of the crime. But Henry Hyde, the Republican judiciary chairman who became Bill Clinton's chief prosecutor, stayed behind, charged with one more task. He had to walk the marbled halls to the office of the secretary of the Senate, to hand over formally the articles of impeachment, now in a leatherbound folder. 'Here,' the gesture seemed to say, 'you deal with it.' •

....

24 April 1999
David Sharrock
'Iraq is falling apart. We are ruined'

Taking a walk in this benighted city is a lesson in modern warfare. What may happen tomorrow in the Balkans was tested first in Iraq. You need only to take a few steps down any Baghdad street to feel the changes – feared by the majority and exploited by the profiteering few – creeping into every facet of life. It is clear that something sinister and irrevocable is under way. Beneath the outward calm, chaos is bubbling. 'Everything you see points to Iraq falling apart,' says a Baghdad veteran. 'This country is becoming a Third World Nation.'

Grubby street children sell bubble gum or beg at traffic lights, and prostitutes walk the major roads. This in a country which has undergone a religious revival. 'Iraq used to be a secular society with an educated population and a growing middle class,' says one Baghdad professional. 'It is simply impossible to believe what is happening. Tribalism and religion are asserting their old dominance. Urban society has been ruined, people are returning to the countryside to find food. We are utterly ruined.'

Go and ask the traders on Rashid Street, known as the 'thieves' market', what is going on. Or wait until they ask you — once they believe that the secret police are not listening to their small, brave acts of independence — to explain the 'Anglo-American plan' for their liberation.

You can find most things in this souk, from a video player to a corkscrew, everything that would have been commonplace in an average Baghdad household before the Gulf War. Now no item is too small for resale if it brings in a few US dollars.

Here I met Karim, a slight figure whose impeccable English betrayed his British university education — civil engineering at Birmingham. He was trying, without conviction, to sell black market cigarettes. 'Please, I would like to ask you a question if I may,' he said hesitantly. 'You are from England? It is a country I love. I made many good friends. I found they were gentle people. I want to know, do they know what is happening to Iraq? Do they know that our leaders are not getting hurt by the embargo, that it is only the ordinary people who you are harming?'

Quite simply, the West is conducting a monstrous social experiment on the people of Iraq. A once-prosperous nation is being driven into the pre-industrial dark ages. It will take years to fathom the harm being done to the lives of 21.7 million people here by a policy intended, according to its shapers in Washington and supporters in London, to bring Iraq back into the international community of nations by toppling Saddam Hussein.

Karim is typical of thousands of members of the Iraqi middle class. He studied in Britain and then returned home to pass on his knowledge. 'My professor begged me to stay. He said I reminded him of [his] own son and that I could make a better life in England,' he says. 'But I was young and idealistic. I wanted to fight to improve my country. I now know it was the worst mistake of my life.'

Karim married and found a job as a university professor with a salary of around £1,500 a month. That was plenty to raise his four children on before the war, when a quasi-socialist system and vast oil wealth gave Iraqis one of the highest standards of living in the Middle East.

As long as the oil flowed and you kept your nose clean, the excesses of President Saddam's regime — the all-enveloping security services and the war with Iran — could be managed with little discomfort. Nobody anticipated that President Saddam would invade Kuwait in August 1990, still less the consequences of his defeat. The West had long been an ally, arming Iraq for its proxy war with the Shi'ite fundamentalist regime in Iran. Even in 1988, when sarin and mustard gas were rained on the Kurds, killing 5,000 in a day at Halabja, Western protests were muted. But by challenging the regional order and threatening the status quo of the world's oil market, he was transformed overnight into public enemy number one.

United Nations security resolutions demanded that the Iraqi regime destroy its weapons of mass destruction, but Washington, with London's support, had bolder plans. Robert Gates, a deputy national security adviser under President George Bush, said that 'Iraqis will pay the price' while President Saddam was in power.

This presupposed that the Iraqi leader cared for his people. The economic blockade on Iraq was only partially relieved in 1996, when a UN oil-for-food programme was accepted after the World Health Organisation reported that most Iraqis had been on a 'semi-starvation diet for years'.

Within a year of the invasion of Kuwait food prices in Iraq increased by 2,000 per cent. Hyper-inflation turned Karim's comfortable salary into the equivalent of £3 a month and everything was sold, even his wedding ring. The experience has left him deeply suspicious of the US and Britain. 'Do they really want to get rid of our friend [the euphemism employed by Iraqis when they talk about their leader] by killing all of us first? Perhaps they are actually helping to keep him in power,' he says.

The strict rationing has certainly strengthened President Saddam's control over his people. On the eve of the 1995 referendum which asked 'Do you agree that Saddam Hussein should be president of Iraq?' security officers visited the 8 million eligible voters and asked two questions: 'Do you know how to vote?' and 'Are you receiving your food rations?' President Saddam won 99.96 per cent of the vote.

Off Saadoun Street is a pharmacy run by Dr Yussuf Kassab, who should have retired after a lifetime's work at the ministry of health. He is forced to work because his sons, one a dentist, the other an engineer, cannot afford to live independently. Many of his clients leave empty-handed, unable to obtain even such ordinary items as antihistamines and cough linctus. The situation has improved slightly over the last six months, but Dr Kassab says: 'There is a restricted amount of many of these products in circulation, so the patients . . . will just keep going round the city looking. Maybe they will be lucky.'

Ominously, a recent UN Security Council report notes that as of late January, £170 million of supplies and medicine purchased under the oil-for-food programme had accumulated in government warehouses – more than half of the supplies which have arrived in Iraq. Under the programme Iraq is in charge of distribution, not the UN. 'According to information provided by United Nations observers only 15 per cent of all medical equipment received by the warehouses had been distributed,' it says.

One officer in the relief field comments: 'Two months ago I would have said point blank that I did not believe that the Iraqi government was deliberately starving its people or depriving them of essential medicines, but I'm coming round to the view that, as part of their plan, someone somewhere is not rushing these things through as much as they might.'

Dennis Halliday, an Irish Quaker who was the UN humanitarian coordinator, resigned from his post last summer, bitterly observing that by his estimate sanctions have killed a million Iraqis, including 500,000 children. But when this statistic was put to the US Secretary of State Madeleine Albright in 1996, when she was US ambassador to the UN, she replied: 'I think this is a very hard choice but the price – we think the price is worth it.'

Today, 4,000–5,000 children are dying every month because of the poor water supplies, an inadequate diet and a lack of health care. Malnutrition among children under five, having fallen from 32 per cent since the introduction of the oil-for-food programme, is now stubbornly stuck at 23 per cent.

Pierrette Vu Thi, a planning officer for Unicef, has a different spin on one of the US military planners' favourite buzzwords, 'degradation'. While advocates of the military option talk about 'degrading' President Saddam's capacity to threaten his neighbours, Ms Vu Thi says that the real 'degradation' is occurring in Iraq's social fabric. Half of the country's schools are not fit for occupation, 10,000 teachers have given up their jobs because they cannot survive on the salary of £2–£6 a month and 30 per cent of children have dropped out of school. 'The oil-for-food programme has not addressed this degradation,' she says. Ms Vu Thi is careful to stop short of Mr Halliday's assessment of the merits of the sanctions campaign, merely stating 'Unicef's great concern'.

Crime is rising as Iraq's infrastructure crumbles. Electricity supplies are running at only 40 per cent of their pre-war levels. Up to £37 billion is needed to restore adequate supplies of water, electricity, education and health care.

Meanwhile, continuing bombing raids in the 'no-fly zones' in the north and south of Iraq are the heart of the latest phase in the US-British war on Iraq. A US assertion that around 200 bombs have been dropped in 'self-defence' on Iraqi military installations since Operation Desert Fox ended is 'far below reality', according to one independent observer. 'The Iraqi claim that 3,200 sorties have been flown by the Americans and British since Desert Fox is accurate. It is very nearly the same number as in the whole of the air campaign during the Gulf War. They are fighting a low-intensity, high-technology, undeclared war.'

Another Western source agrees, but doubts whether the Americans and British are any nearer to removing President Saddam from power. 'The Americans are gaining much more by chipping away every day at his military infrastructure than with a four-day intensive blitz as in December,' he says. 'The air strikes are happening on a daily basis but are going virtually unreported . . . I don't know if they have a strategy, it just looks like lashing out.'

The Iraqi people usually know what's going on, thanks to the Voice of America, the BBC World Service and the bush telegraph. They have just been told that the US is not at war with Iraq but rather, in the surreal phrase of Thomas Pickering, the US Undersecretary of State for Political Affairs, in a 'state of animosity' with Baghdad. Intriguingly, Mr Pickering also told a US Senate hearing that the UN oil-for-food programme is a linchpin for Washington's efforts to maintain sanctions. And according to the junior Foreign Office minister Tony Lloyd, the British government 'has decided to launch a new policy of better targeted, smarter sanctions' which will ensure that 'the people who are hit are the ones who should be hit'.

'Ah, your Mr Robin Cook,' said Karim, catching sight of the Foreign Secretary on an Iraqi news programme. 'He said he was going to give Britain an ethical foreign policy, didn't he? Can you ask him for me, what is there ethical about what he is doing to me or all the other ordinary Iraqis?'

At the Saddam Hospital for Children, there is ample opportunity to study the consequences of this ethical foreign policy. Ayat Abbad is a year old yet weighs just over 3kg, half her ideal weight. Like thousands of other babies, she is suffering from marasmus, a type of malnutrition which was unheard of in Iraq before the Gulf War and the sanctions, and has suffered gastroenteritis and pneumonia. The duty doctor holds out little hope for her survival. 'She will either die before the end of the year or she will live and grow up stunted and with low intelligence,' he says. 'It is not just the lack of medicines, they have created an entire culture of embargo . . . we are not receiving new-generation drugs, advances in medicine, science, food, anything.'

Besieged by US and British policy and by a government which treats its people as bargaining chips, the only real casualties of this unending war are those who can least afford to pay the price or raise their voices to be heard. What poses the greater danger to the West's 'vital regional interests' in the future? The survival of Saddam Hussein or a generation of Iraqis made bitter by the indifference of Western nations which are running daily raids in 'self-defence'? ●

· ·

10 February 1999
David Sharrock
Even in death, the peacemaker king brought sworn enemies together

Death gave King Hussein of Jordan one final victory as former foes of the Hashemite monarch and sworn enemies of other funeral guests rubbed shoulders on the steps of his palace on Monday and queued to pay their last respects in one of the last great gatherings of world leaders this century.

The funeral of the king, who died last Sunday of complications from cancer, held out the hope of a boost to the peaceful resolution of Middle Eastern enmities. Israel fielded a large contingent of politicians. The arrival of Syria's president, Hafez al-Assad, provided the biggest surprise of an occasion that combined pomp with high-grade funeral diplomacy.

President Boris Yeltsin of Russia roused himself from his sickbed to make his first public appearance in months, an act that clearly signalled the significance of the passing of a ruler whose poor, diminutive desert kingdom was eclipsed by his stature as an international peace-broker.

Mr Yeltsin, who had to be supported as he climbed the steps of the Raghadan palace, left early and was unable to attend the interment of Hussein's body in a simple Muslim ceremony at the royal cemetery. He spoke briefly with President Bill Clinton, who was accompanied by former presidents Jimmy Carter, Gerald Ford and George Bush. Mr Clinton, who had a private interview with Hussein's son and successor, King Abdullah, also exchanged words with the Syrian president as the world's leaders were obliged to mingle.

The day began with the departure of Hussein's coffin from his home at Bab el-Salam, where his widow, Queen Noor, and the other female members of the Hashemite family said their farewells. Prince Hassan, Hussein's younger brother, whom he deposed as his successor only two weeks earlier, shrugged his shoulders with finality as he was dismissed with a kiss from Queen Noor. Whatever family feuds may lurk behind the palace walls, the Hashemites were determined to put on an act of unity for the funeral.

Hundreds of thousands of mourners threw flowers and breached police lines in an attempt to touch the coffin as it was driven on a flower-decked open Jeep through the streets of the capital where Hussein ruled for 46 years. At times the cortège was slowed to almost a halt by the press of grieving Jordanians. Their pain was made all the more acute by the memory of Hussein's triumphant return from cancer treatment only three weeks earlier, when he braved driving rain to be cheered through the same streets, declaring himself cured of the disease.

Bells tolled from churches of the tiny Christian community, mingling with the cries of prayer broadcast from the city's mosques. By the time the cortège reached the Raghadan palace, Israel's representatives had already sneaked in through a side door.

More than 50 foreign leaders, many of them traditional rivals, filed past the flag-draped coffin. It was an extraordinary assembly.

President Assad of Syria, who once tried to shoot down Hussein's private jet, and who sent his tanks into northern Jordan on more than one occasion, provided the biggest shock. He paused before the king's coffin, turned his hands palm upwards and silently recited a prayer. The presence of the 70-year-old ruler, whose health is poor, underlined the generational change in the Middle East.

In the next few years the old faces will finally change and yesterday was the first step in this transition of power.

The crowd was so thick that at times the Circassian Guard – Muslim fugitives from tsarist pogroms in the Caucasus who settled here in the days of the Ottoman empire and who are among the Hashemites' most loyal followers – had to halt the flow of leaders squeezing through the palace doors.

The son of Colonel Muammar Gadafy, dressed in African robes; the Sudanese president, Omar Hassan al-Bashir; and the Iraqi vice-president, Taha Moheiddin Ma'arouf – all countries which have been the targets of US missiles – were just steps away from Mr Clinton and Tony Blair.

Yasser Arafat, who was expelled by Hussein from Jordan during a bloody struggle for power in 1970, and who fought with him over the right to represent the Palestinians, saluted twice and bowed before the coffin. He was preceded and followed by an array of Israeli figures. They included President Ezer Weizman; the Prime Minister, Binyamin Netanyahu; Foreign Minister Ariel Sharon; the Labour Party leader, Ehud Barak; the former prime minister and Oslo peace process architect, Shimon Peres; the new prime ministerial contender and former defence minister, Yitzhak Mordechai; and finally, to the amazement of most observers, the old war horse and unbending opponent of peace with the Palestinians, Yitzhak Shamir.

This was funeral diplomacy on a grand scale: Moscow eager to demonstrate that it has not given up on power-play ambitions in the Middle East, Syria sending a subtle message that it too wants to make peace, and Israel's opponents in the forthcoming elections showing off their credentials. The presence of Ephraim Halevi, the chief of the Israeli intelligence agency, Mossad, marked the fact of Israel and Jordan's close security relationship in a hostile region.

But it was a family funeral too and one conducted on the lines of British military tradition. A band of pipers played a Scottish military marching tune to lead Hussein's body, now transferred to a 90mm field artillery cannon, to its final resting place in the royal cemetery. Behind him followed Amr, his favourite white charger, whose stirrups were filled with Hussein's empty riding boots, pointing backwards in the old symbol of a fallen leader.

Hussein's sons lifted his body, wrapped in a white winding sheet, out of the coffin and placed it in the earth, next to his father, King Talal. A 15-gun salute was preceded by the traditional recitation, 11 times, of the Muslim prayer of the faithful.

It was an impressive farewell, one which outshone even that of the murdered Israeli prime minister Yitzhak Rabin, whose widow, Leah, was in Amman to console Queen Noor. Certainly one to compare with the funeral of Egypt's President Gamal Abdul Nasser, or even Winston Churchill. A final crowning achievement in a remarkable life, to have brought so many world powers together in a tiny, poor country, created by strokes of a pen on a desert map as a by-product of imperial designs, but yesterday a modern Arabic state with a new king.

And a day which seemed to answer the question Hussein had posed himself only a year ago: 'What does a man seek in this world? A position or a throne? ... All we hope for is that a day will come, when we have all gone, when people will say that this man tried, and his family tried. This is all there is to seek in this world.' •

21 August 1999

Ian Traynor
The land that is a tomb

On a road heaving with the human misery inflicted by the western world's worst natural disaster for almost a century, Cengiz Pulat came staggering along, desperate, in tears, seeking family survivors of the Izmit earthquake. Onlookers flinched at the sight of a grown man crying. 'Where's the shop selling Opel parts? Where is it? My cousins live next door to it,' he implored. 'Does anyone know where it is? Can anyone help me find it?' His shoulders burned by the merciless sun, his eyes mad with fear and worry, he harangued every passer-by on the chaotic approach to the town of Golcuk, a road that has become a repository of the human flotsam of the disaster, seething with victims, relatives, foreign aid workers, ambulances, soldiers, huge lorries, bulldozers and buses.

Travelling 15 hours by bus and on foot, Mr Pulat's quest brought him from eastern Turkey to the north-west, a region of millions of people who appeared to be in perpetual motion yesterday, vainly seeking respite from what is now shaping up to be the worst natural disaster to strike the western world since the 1908 Messina quake in southern Italy left more than 70,000 dead.

It was only yesterday, four days after the earthquake in the region around the city of Izmit, that the horrifying extent of this tragedy's death, destruction and chaos became clear. While the official death toll rose to just over 10,000, government officials told the United Nations that some 35,000 putrefying corpses remained entombed beneath the rubble of the stricken zone, meaning that the final death toll would almost certainly surpass the 33,000 killed in the Erzincan quake in Turkey in 1939. And at least 45,000 have injuries, many grave.

Huge ice-cream lorries tried to make their way along the gridlocked Galcuk road, ready to refrigerate the corpses in mobile mortuaries. Like everyone else on this hellish road, Mr Pulat wore an improvised mouth mask to guard against the risk of infection as rumours and warnings of cholera, typhoid, dysentery and hepatitis spread. In temperatures nearing 40C, the stench from the dead and the lack of sanitation and clean water became ever more nauseating and danger-ous. 'There is a problem with sanitary conditions and no running water, dead bodies and heat,' said Colonel Giora Martentanozits, member of an Israeli team of military paramedics operating in the town of Adapazari, east of Golcuk. 'We can't cope with this,' said a doctor there, Oguz Titiz. 'Vomiting and diarrhoea started showing up last night, especially among children and the elderly.'

The Prime Minister, Bulent Ecevit, described the earthquake yesterday as the worst in Turkey's history. 'Thousands of bulidings are in ruins. It is not possible to reach all of them,' he declared. At the crisis centre in the capital, Ankara, one official said: 'The figures are horrendous. Very many people are under the rubble. Many more than anticipated.'

At Friday prayers across the country, Muslim clerics called for national unity and fortitude. They relaxed rituals governing the disposal of the dead, allowing males and females to be buried alongside one another and easing traditional strictures on the washing of corpses.

In Adapazari, where almost 3,000 people were confirmed dead 84 hours after Tuesday's disaster, 963 victims were buried in a mass grave. More mass graves were being readied across the region, with earlier insistence on identification before burial being gradually abandoned because of the scale of the casualties and the risk of disease.

Medical teams began innoculating rescue workers against typhoid. In Istanbul, some rescuers collapsed of exhaustion as they hammered at the ruins, and had to be taken away on stretchers. Out of the mountains of debris, corpses were delicately manoeuvred. And a few people were rescued alive, though hopes for many more miracle survivors were fading.

One infant girl was brought out alive in Izmit by a team of Hungarian specialists and a teenager was saved in Golcuk by Russian paramedics. While he was being flown home from the same town of 60,000, a British man died of injuries he suffered there early on Tuesday. Another Briton had earlier died in Golcuk.

'We just go around all the buildings and look for signs of life. But there are no signs any more,' said Seyfettin Usta, a bus driver, in the village of Yaslik outside Golcuk. He peered through crevices in the debris with a child's purple torch while a mate held a pink and green parasol over him.

In the Avcilar suburb of Istanbul, where most of the city's confirmed 1,000 deaths occurred, soldiers excavating a huge mound of apartment rubble brought out the bodies of a local policeman, his wife and daughter. As ever, a crowd of onlookers mounted a vigil. The mood was one of quiet resignation and sullen hopelessness. 'I just want to go to those places to try to help the people. Just to touch them with your hand would be a help,' said an Istanbul schoolteacher. 'I've been arguing with my husband for two days, but he won't let me go.'

The clear-up operations from this earthquake will take months, the costs will be felt for years. Once the immediate devastation is cleared, hundreds more buildings in towns, villages and cities across the north-west will be uninhabitable and will need to be demolished.

The unrelenting suffering and the panic have produced a mood bordering on mass psychosis in the region. Millions slept on the streets and on open ground yesterday after CNN and Turkish television broadcast warnings of possible further tremors. 'It was not just a lot of people sleeping on the streets. It was everybody,' said one Istanbul man who set up camp with his wife and two children. In the fancy hotels overlooking the Bosporus, some wealthy westerners took their blankets and pillows into the gardens for the night.

'The problem here is everything is panic. We mistake rushing around for real action. We just can't organise anything properly,' said Bulent Yasargil, an unemployed casino croupier. 'There's plenty of help, but no professionals and people just get in the way. The politicians are all puffed up and important, but totally unqualified for what they should be doing. Many, many people are dead. But many could have been saved.'

In addition to the shock over the human losses, the colossal economic cost of the earthquake – which hit the country's industrial hub – is also just beginning to sink in. Estimates range from a conservative £15 billion from the head of the central bank, Gazi Ercel, up to tens of billions of pounds.

At petrol stations long queues of Istanbul taxi drivers formed amid panic buying after the huge three-day fire caused by the quake at the country's biggest oil refinery, the Tupras works outside Izmit. The blaze was finally tamed yesterday, but the damage to Turkey's biggest company is done. ●

· ·

3 May 1999

David Sharrock
Little Russia

'In Russia I was a Jew and now I'm in Israel they call me a Russian,' says Masha Shapira, pulling out the birth certificate of her four-month-old son Yochanan. Beneath the menorah, symbol of the state, the bureaucrats have inserted dashes in lieu of specifying religion and nationality. Officially, Yochanan, born in Jerusalem, is neither Jewish nor Israeli. Nor even Russian, as his mother is described in her ID. But Yochanan may be very significant to the Jewish state – he is possibly the millionth Russian citizen of Israel, newest member of what many here call 'the mini-state of Russia'.

Take a stroll in Ashkelon, a rapidly expanding Mediterranean city half an hour south of Tel Aviv on a Friday morning, as the weekend begins. There's a busker playing Russian melodies on his violin. At the pavement café tables, men are playing chess or reading Russian papers. The talk is Russian. The waitress is called Natasha and although she can speak Hebrew, she doesn't need to. The shops have Russian signs (Hebrew too, but smaller type); gift shops sell Russian kitsch; shelves of food stores groan with nostalgia – Russian tea, caviare, black bread, little plastic cups of vodka containing an individual hit for 20p. And pork. The city nearly went to war over pork last year; 32 stores were threatened with closure by the district magistrate unless they ceased selling it.

Most of the stores have opened since Ashkelon was settled by more than 30,000 Russians, following the huge waves of *aliyah* – return – from the former Soviet Union at the beginning of the 1990s. They have clung to the coast, with 45,000 in Haifa, 37,000 in Ashdod and 35,000 in Tel Aviv. Mikhail Gorbachev's decision to allow Jews to leave the Soviet Union has had an enormous impact on Israel, reshaping its cultural, social and economic landscape.

In their high professional and educational talent, the Russians are unlike any previous wave of immigrants. The unemployment rate among them is lower than that of other Israelis, around 7 per cent. Most have already bought their own homes; half have at least one car.

It sounds like the Israeli dream of the Jewish melting-pot come true. But it's not that simple, as the war of the sausages revealed. 'In Russia, they shut our mouths and didn't let us speak but here, in a democracy, they watch what we put in our mouths,' said Tamara, a customer at CMAK, a popular Russian delicatessen in Ashkelon.

It is run by Marina and Tatiana, who arrived four years ago from the Ukraine. Tatiana holds a masters degree in mining engineering, Marina is a qualified electrical engineer, but they both prefer selling sausages. Their Cyrillic list boasts of products in the style of Moscow and Odessa – all made in Israel, which does not permit their import. 'Very popular is pig's cheek,' says Tatiana in laboured Hebrew – she says she can speak good English, but only if we talk about rock density. 'Ukrainians like greasy sausage.' They had some problems with the Orthodox when they first set up shop: 'They used to come in and abuse us, but it doesn't happen any more. Maybe they got used to us.'

The pork dispute petered out as a basis for the city's older, mainly Sephardic population in their cultural battle with the Russians after a far graver incident last year. Jan Shefshovitz, a 21-year-old immigrant from Moldavia, wearing army uniform, was stabbed to death by a Moroccan at a city café. 'My son was murdered because he spoke Russian,' wept Jan's mother, Maya.

At the headquarters of Yisrael ba-Aliya, the Russian immigrants' party led by trade minister Nathan Sharansky, the killing still angers. Vladimir Indikt, the local party leader, rails against state prejudice: 'The killers were arrested but have been freed on bail pending trial and are supposed to be under home arrest. These murderers are walking around Ashkelon every day. It's outrageous, but what can we do? There are different standards of justice for Russians.'

He hopes Israel's general election, on 17 May, will change all that. The Russian sector has grown so large in a decade that no political leader can ignore its voice. Already the horse-trading has begun with both of Israel's largest parties, Prime Minister Binyamin Netanyahu's right-wing Likud and Ehud Barak's Labour, dangling the Interior Ministry before Sharansky as reward for the Russian vote.

The Interior Ministry, which supervises new immigrants, has been controlled by the ultra-Orthodox and Sephardic Shas Party for almost 15 years. Shas is anathema to the Russians, most of whom couldn't have told you what a barmitzvah was before they arrived in Israel; they are secular, and tend to be right-wing on the peace process. Foreign Minister Ariel Sharon revealed the reason behind his government's cynical – that's the US State Department view – and sudden courtship of Moscow when he told the *Washington Post*: 'The Russian vote will decide the outcome of the elections.'

For years, Netanyahu and Sharon had been urging the US to impose sanctions on Russia for assisting Iran's nuclear programme. Suddenly they wanted the IMF to extend loans to Russia. Israel's Russians, who get their news from their own-language newspapers and cable television, have backed this. Over Kosovo, Sharon and Netanyahu have been notably reluctant to support their strongest ally, the US, because most of Israel's Russians are pro-Serb.

In conversations with Russians, the same themes surface. Most say they will vote for Netanyahu, who has kept the lid on terrorism. Russians like a strong leader, they like the way Netanyahu spat in Washington's face and convinced President Clinton it was only raining. As for the Palestinians and land for peace, one Ashkelon chess-player said: 'Where I used to live, we had a huge country. And I came to Israel. If you look at it on the map, it's tiny. And they want to start giving bits of it away? Are they crazy?'

Most Russians (like most Israelis) have never been to the Occupied Territories of the West Bank and Gaza. They have no yearning for the Greater Land of Israel, which so inspires the Right. Yet they are contemptuous of Arabs, as they are disdainful of Israelis, whom they regard as vulgar and without culture.

'There is a double culture-shock at work,' explains journalist Sergei Makarov. 'Before we came here, most Russians had only preconceptions that Israel was like the West, and shared our values. We knew nothing at all about the Middle East. We found that Israel is not really like the West at all, so we were disappointed and we still don't understand the Middle East, which is alien.'

Israel once dreamed of a population of a nation united and confident. What happened? There is a rich and varied culture, but far more disunited than its founders imagined.

Larissa Gerstein is deputy mayor of the Jerusalem municipality and her husband edits *Vesty*, Israel's largest Russian newspaper. The more deeply involved she became in Israeli society the more she felt rejected. 'Russians don't care what the Israelis think of them, say about them and especially write about them. We now have cultural autonomy. Little Russia.' And they will vote for Netanyahu because he too is an outsider to the establishment and 'because they like seeing a Jew screwing the gentiles for a change'.

As Russia grows more unstable, so anti-Semitism there rises and the immigrants keep coming; 916,200 Jews still live in the former Soviet Union. Shas wants to make qualification for immigration more strict, so that Russians whose claim to Jewishness is only through a grandfather would no longer qualify.

It is thought that around a third of the Russian Israelis are not Jewish. A few are actively Christian. Ivan, who attends a Roman Catholic church in Jerusalem four times a week, recalls that when he attended the Israeli absorption centre in Russia: 'They told me to put down that I had no religious faith, but they knew and didn't care. They just wanted more citizens. Perhaps they believed that over time we will all be integrated into the Jewish character of Israel. That may be true, but they forgot that we will determine just what that character will be. Most of my countrymen and women don't care about religion at all. They don't care about being Jewish. That may create big problems some day.'

What about baby Yochanan Shapira? 'I think another big wave of Russians is coming soon,' says his mother. 'Ehud Barak says another million arriving here would be good for Israel, but I'm not sure he's right. I think the Israelis already have more Russians than they can cope with.' ●

....

12 June 1999
Larry Elliott
How did we get into this mess?

Imagine a family in the West having lower living standards now than it did in 1960 – before the Beatles, before compact discs, before mass ownership of fridges and dishwashers, before supermarkets stuffed full of ready-prepared Kenyan green beans. Unimaginable? In the West, certainly. Yet that is what has befallen 10 countries in Africa.

Imagine too that over the past 25 years, since the end of the golden age in 1970, per capita incomes in Britain had fallen by 20 per cent. Yet that is what the past quarter-century has brought the average African household. In 1960, per capita incomes in Africa were three times those in east Asia; now they are less than half as high.

Africa's slow economic development has meant that the average life expectancy and infant mortality lag behind the rest of the world, and the gap is growing ever wider. Whereas in developing countries across the globe, life expectancy has risen from 46 to 62 since the early 1960s, for sub-Saharan Africa it is 50.

As the millennium approaches, the impression is of Africa as the continent that progress forgot. While east Asia has been a model of rapid economic development over the past four decades, and even Latin America has managed to discover the benefits of democracy, Africa has lagged further and further behind, caught in a cycle of war, poverty and misery.

Like all stereotypes, this can be misleading. Botswana has enjoyed a faster rate of growth since 1960 than Hong Kong or Singapore; other countries have enjoyed rapid if unsustained economic expansion at various times since independence. The 1990s have seen democracy sweep sub-Saharan Africa in what the United Nations describes as 'an event just as dramatic as the political changes in the Soviet Union, though it has received much less attention from the world community. Nearly all countries in the region have undertaken democratic reforms and legalised opposition parties, changes often championed by students, labour unions and other civil society movements.'

In time, the reforms may bear fruit. But time is something that Africa does not have; in the new global economy, you do not get 150 years to catch up. The gap between rich and poor countries is accelerating. In 1960, 20 per cent of the world's wealthiest had 30 times the income of the poorest 20 per cent; by 1995, that figure had grown to 82 times. Democratic developments that took centuries to flower in the West are expected elsewhere to be successful overnight. The transition to market economies – long, irregular and often brutal in Britain, the US and Germany – must happen instantaneously. Africa has serious problems, and 10 big themes stand out:

1. The delicate balance of Africa's environment has been disrupted, with devastating consequences, particularly in semi-arid areas – for example, the cycle of drought and famine in the Horn of Africa.
2. The legacy of colonialism has cast a long shadow. The nation states created by Western cartographers owed more to the wheelings and dealings of European diplomats in the late nineteenth century than to any understanding of existing borders along tribal or geographical lines. Post-colonial independence meant fragmented states that were often too small to be economically viable, and cut off from the rest of the world.
3. The ramshackle way in which the colonial powers withdrew in the 1950s and 1960s intensified the birthpangs of independence. They bequeathed political systems without the civil institutions necessary to support them and after decades of undermining pre-existing social structures. The new nations were often unstable and many were caught in vicious civil wars.
4. Africa was an arena of the Cold War: the US and the Soviet Union propped up regimes favourable to them, and the US backed terrorist movements. So, for example, the strategic importance of the Horn of Africa saw the Soviet Union backing Somalia, while the United States stood behind Ethiopia in the 1960s. In the 1970s, following the Ethiopian revolution, Moscow changed sides and backed Ethiopia in the war against Somalia, which then became an important American strategic asset. In Angola, the civil war which followed independence in 1974 saw the South Africans, backed by Washington, supporting Unita, while the MPLA was provided with arms by the Soviet Union and 'advised' by thousands of Cubans. Moreover, the

impact of the Cold War spilled over into neighbouring states. Zaïre was used by the Americans as a base for operations in Angola, which meant billions of dollars were squandered propping up the Mobutu regime.

5. Apartheid was a major brake on development for the whole of southern Africa, affecting all the frontline states. Countries such as Mozambique and Angola were deliberately destabilised, and Namibia was illegally occupied.

6. The proxy Cold War struggle of the 1970s coincided with the onset of a severe economic downturn in the West. Recession brought collapsing commodity prices and economic retrenchment.

7. There has been economic mismanagement on a colossal scale. The temptation to use the power of the state to cut across racial and cultural divides coincided with the belief that large-scale interventionism was the way of the future, persuading the leaders of the new states and their Western advisers into many hugely expensive investment projects.

8. Such projects were financed with loans which are, in part, the origins of the current debt crisis – sub-Saharan Africa owes the West a staggering £225 billion. It takes two to party, and those Western lenders who extended lines of credit when it was obvious that the poor nations were in no state ever to repay were complicit in the build-up of unpayable debts.

9. Widespread corruption has ensured that much aid intended for Africa lined the pockets of officials and governments, and was used to build mansions and private jets, or diverted to private bank accounts.

10. What has made life for many Africans even harder in the last two decades has been the 'cruel to be kind strategy' of the International Monetary Fund. The structural adjustment programmes which it has forced on countries as a condition of loans or debt relief usually include draconian cuts in health, education and sanitation to meet Western targets for fiscal prudence.

The result of the interplay of these 10 points has been profound. Sub-Saharan Africa has a rapidly rising population of just over 600 million, but per capita incomes have been falling because growth has not been fast enough to match the forces of demography. The UN human development index, which looks at life expectancy, literacy and income, has only five African countries in the top 100 and 18 in the bottom 20. We cannot comfort ourselves that this gap will eventually narrow.

As David Landes sums it up in his book *The Wealth and Poverty of Nations*: 'Is the gap still growing today? At the extremes, clearly yes . . . Some countries are not only not gaining; they are growing poorer. Our [the rich countries'] task, in our own interest as well as theirs, is to help the poor become healthier and wealthier. If we do not, they will seek to take what they cannot make; and if they cannot earn by exporting commodities, they will export people.' ●

4 June 1999

Anthony Sampson

Out of the shadow of Mandela

How different will South Africa really be after this week's elections? Mandela's successor, Thabo Mbeki, is so opposite in style that the contrast with his predecessor seems dramatic: he is short, introverted, intellectual, preferring to deal behind the scenes rather than lead from the front as Mandela did – like Major after Thatcher.

More worrying to anxious white South Africans, he appears more like an African nationalist, favouring black consciousness aides and avoiding white advisers and journalists, whom he frequently blames for misreporting the ANC and neglecting the 'transformation' of South Africa.

But the outward contrast does not really reflect a contrast in policies. For the last two years, as Mandela never tired of explaining, Mbeki has been running the country – usually presiding over the cabinet, making much of foreign policy and strongly influencing economic policy.

Ever since Mandela came to power in 1994 the white-friendly economic programmes, including abandoning nationalisation and the conservative fiscal and monetary regime, were encouraged by Mbeki, who sometimes had to persuade Mandela. And behind the scenes Mbeki has been very close to white and Western influences.

Mbeki is in many ways much more deeply influenced by Britain than Mandela was. He relished his time at Sussex University – though at first he complained about not being at Oxford – and when he later went to Moscow for military training he wrote letters full of nostalgia for England. He imbibed Shakespeare, Yeats and a style of patient rational argument which made him a brilliant diplomat, able to charm and disarm the most hostile Western businessmen – as I often witnessed in London in the 1980s.

But many of his African colleagues saw him as too thoroughly English, with his sports coats and curved pipe. Even when convivial, he was bookish and serious; as Mandela said: 'He never played in his youth.' As one African-American unfairly complained: 'He's the only man in Africa who ain't got rhythm.'

And his time in exile was inevitably a political problem. He was not seen as a natural African leader, as Mandela always was. The fact that his father, Govan Mbeki, was a heroic freedom-fighter who spent over 20 years in jail was not altogether an asset, for Govan was an unreconstructed Marxist who was not very supportive of his pragmatic and cosmopolitan son.

More difficult, Mbeki had acquired the secretive traits of an exile beset by fears of betrayal: a preoccupation with close loyalties and a suspicion of outsiders. Returning to his home country, he surrounded himself with a few confidants and kept his cards very close to his chest. He became Mandela's successor without a painful power struggle, but he still appeared unnecessarily insecure.

He was not chosen by Mandela personally, as Mandela made clear to me. Mandela had some doubts, including the fact that Mbeki came from the same Xhosa tribe as himself; but he left it to the ANC leaders, including the influential Walter Sisulu, and to the Communist Party and trade union leaders, to decide his deputy, without (as he emphasised) 'indicating my own feelings'.

Mandela was still very supportive of his deputy, and by 1996 he was skilfully ensuring that Mbeki was accepted as his successor. But he gave occasional hints of worries. At the ANC congress in December 1997 he made a surprising, and little-reported speech, about the problems of being elected as an unopposed leader: 'He may use that powerful position to settle scores with his detractors, to marginalise or get rid of them (*applause*) and surround themselves with yes-men and women (*applause*).' He went on to explain that Mbeki understood those problems: 'He is not the man who is going to sideline anybody.' But his ANC audience saw it as a warning to his successor.

And Mandela had a fundamental clash with Mbeki when he tried to stop publication of the report of the Truth and Reconciliation Commission last December, which contained details of the ANC's own abuses of human rights. Mandela insisted it must be published in full. 'I am the president of the country,' he told me afterwards. 'I have set up the TRC. They have done not a perfect but a remarkable job and I approved everything they did.'

But Mbeki was then president of the ANC, subject to all the party pressures, and the key question remains: how far will his outlook widen, now that he is president of the country, no longer under the shadow of the great Mandela tree? Will he be an uncertain leader, like Eden after Churchill or Major after Thatcher, or a strong man liberated from an overwhelming boss, like Harry Truman after Roosevelt?

Mbeki certainly had a difficult time working with a mythological figure who could do no wrong. He took the blame for Mandela's mistakes and too little credit for his achievements, including making peace with the Zulu chief Buthelezi. He remains a superb negotiator and fixer; and South Africa still needs to be fixed.

The deeper question is whether his fixes will be at the cost of losing the moral high ground which was so crucial to Mandela's authority and influence. The immediate test is the issue of amnesty – which takes Mbeki back to the Truth Commission. For the Commission was based on the principle of granting amnesties only to individuals, after they had told the truth, while Mbeki is now clearly tempted to grant a blanket amnesty – not so much to protect the old apartheid governments as to make peace with Buthelezi, whose own Zulu forces have been accused of countless atrocities and murders, and whom he may now choose as his deputy-president.

Mandela has no doubt. 'There is no question as far as I am concerned of a general amnesty,' he said last November. 'And I will resist that with every power that I have.' Mbeki, who is more pragmatic, will be more inclined to bury hatchets for the sake of peace with the Zulus and right-wing Afrikaners.

But Mbeki is still likely to face some heckling from an old man of 80 in his country retreat in the Transkei. As an ordinary ANC member, Mandela has explained: 'I will have the privilege to be as critical as I can be.' If things go wrong, he has warned, he will interfere, unless he is stopped.

Many others too will interfere. For the fact is that South Africa is a democracy, with a strong constitution and careful counterweights; and the ANC's powerful national executive, re-elected in 1997, is strikingly multiracial – with only three Africans among the top 10. It is only when Mbeki chooses his new cabinet in the next few days that his true preferences and intentions will become clearer; but he will defy Mandela's legacy at his peril. •

17 June 1999
Leader
Mandela: a hero departs

The inauguration yesterday of Thabo Mbeki as the second president of a democratic South Africa has been characterised as the end of the Mandela era. But while that may be a convenient description of a historic period of time in South African politics, the phrase is inappropriate for a larger audience who, in an age not well populated with heroes, would also claim the great man as their own, and for whom the saga – the romance and the tragedy that is the life of Nelson Mandela – has still to run its course.

Part of the fascination of Nelson Mandela, which leads to worldwide identification with him, is his essential humanity. Though few would dissent from the judgement, to describe him as 'one of the great men of the twentieth century' is somehow to do him a disservice, because it tends to distance the man from the common experience, which is where his greatness lies. Some commentators have expressed puzzlement as to the 'greatness' of Nelson Mandela, particularly those closest to him in South Africa who are most aware of his shortcomings, both political and personal. But perhaps he is best understood less for his uniqueness than as a modern Everyman.

Mandela's personal life seems to have run almost the entire gamut of human experience, at least in terms of extremes. A felon convicted on capital charges, once subject to the judgment of judges, now flattered by their bows. An individual catapulted from the loneliness of penal confinement to become arguably – with apologies to the Beatles and other contemporary deities whom he has now surpassed – as popular a man as has walked the planet. A lover and husband consigned from the heights of passion born amidst the flames of revolution to the humiliation of public cuckoldry and worse.

But shared experience of however many extremes does not alone account for any man's greatness; it is in the way that he deals with it that his quality is gauged. And in the enduring popularity of Mandela there hopefully lies a message which will be heard by lesser politicians as well as diplomats in countries across the globe: that the future does not lie with cynicism posing as sophistication and the quackeries of spin doctoring, but with virtues of an ancient, enduring and simple kind, recognised as such by the public.

Yesterday's ceremony in front of Pretoria's Union Buildings provided yet another testament to Mandela's grasp of such virtues, in his appreciation that his presidential term of office was of importance more because of the limits he imposed than his enjoyment of it. His early, graceful and easy surrender of office offers a potentially lasting, symbolic lesson for South Africa's fledgling democracy on the desirability of the limitation of power (even if one probably lost on some of those from other parts of Africa who attended the inaugural ceremony). At the same time, he has shown the humility to make way for a younger man who is, at least technically, better equipped to deal with the problems now facing the country.

But if Mandela has shed the formal powers of high office, his moral authority remains undiminished. And as he takes up at least notional residence in his retirement home at Qunu – amidst the hills which remember him as a herd's boy in ragged trousers – he will surely now and then feel the temptation to return to centre stage. The manner in which he deals with such temptations will determine the final chapter in the rich and remarkable life and legend of Nelson Mandela. ●

Geoff Caddick

Mo Mowlam taking a break from Northern Ireland at an employment conference in London

So much to lose

· ·

17 March 1999

John Mullin

So much to lose

Tatty green, white and orange flags adorn each lamppost the grim length of the Garvaghy Road, Irish tricolours to symbolise residents' resistance to the Orangemen still overlooking them from the now notorious hill outside the Church of Ascension at Drumcree. Try pulling one of these down and there would be trouble.

Except that yesterday the Irish flags were being replaced with something more sombre: funereal black. The Portadown thoroughfare is quiet enough most lunch times, but locals gathered in odd groups yesterday. They felt they had lost a friend. They whispered that Rosemary Nelson, 40, mother of three, Northern Ireland's three thousand two hundred and ninety-third victim of the Troubles, had died for them, singled out for Loyalist execution simply because she gave legal advice to Nationalist residents of the Garvaghy Road.

They knew that, in their own terms, her murderers could find a host of justifications for blowing her apart in her silver BMW in a quiet estate in Lurgan, County Armagh. She was, for example, successful in defending Colin Duffy, 30, a leading Republican from nearby Lurgan, her home town. He was prosecuted four times for IRA offences and walked free each time, once after appeal. That one of those cases was the murder of two RUC constables in June 1997 provoked police as well as Loyalist ire.

She was also going for the RUC jugular by representing the family of Robert Hamill, 25, a Catholic who died in May 1997. He was assaulted by a Loyalist mob in Portadown as armed police allegedly sat in an armoured vehicle. Ms Nelson planned to sue the RUC over Mr Hamill's death. But her real aim was to mount private prosecutions against five other men originally accused as part of the mob and up to four police officers.

As well as that, she was a legal adviser to Sean McPhelimy. He produced a Channel 4 documentary, *The Committee*, in 1991, alleging widespread collusion between the security forces and loyalist murder gangs.

To those who knew the then Rosemary Magee at Queen's University in Belfast, her high-profile work in recent years came as a surprise. They remember her as quiet, hard-working and loyal to a close circle of friends. But none could remember her as political.

She was born in 1954 and attended St Michael's Grammar School, County Armagh. She did well in her A-levels and went on to study law. Her lecturers included David Trimble, now First Minister, and Mary McAleese, the Irish President.

Alex Attwood, an SDLP assembly member, studied with her. He said: 'It was a tumultuous time. Even at the height of the hunger strikes, she never seemed interested in expressing an opinion. She was very self-assured, though, and committed to the rule of law.'

Rosemary Magee graduated with a 2:2 in 1981 and set about finding a firm to take her on for apprenticeship. She soon ran into problems that had nothing to do with her legal abilities.

John Hagan, 56, a Portadown solicitor, explained: 'The left side of her face was quite badly disfigured, and many firms saw it as offputting. She had been to many, many people before coming to us. I took her on largely because I didn't want her denied the chance of qualifying.'

She rarely talked about how she got the scar. A friend said yesterday that it was a birthmark exacerbated by bungled surgery; others that she was in a fire as a toddler. While she was a legal apprentice an operation improved it. But she said that RUC officers still called her Half-Face Nelson and she was conscious enough of it to joke self-deprecatingly to photographers about her better side.

She married Paul Nelson, an accountant, while still an apprentice and then turned her back on a decent salary to set up an advice centre in Lurgan. Only in 1988, when introduced to solicitor Marie-Therese McKnight, did she opt to return to a more formal career.

McKnight, now 38, based in Lisburn, County Down, said: 'She had a fantastic way with people, and did her best for her clients whoever they were and whatever their background. We went together to the funeral of Pat Finucane in 1989 and soon after she left to set up on her own back in Lurgan. She was only with us eight months or so, but that was the deal when she joined.'

As she set up practice in William Street, Nelson was already a mother of two. But she set about building up her practice with gusto, and business was soon roaring. Much of it was civil work, and many of her clients were Protestants. Among them then were several police officers.

She also had a host of other interests. She was a governor of the primary school where she had been a pupil, which she sent her daughter to and outside which she was to die, and her love of classical music extended to putting her favourites on her telephone system at her modest office.

Ms Nelson's work appears to have begun to change after she was approached to represent Duffy nine years ago when he was accused of possessing 10 bullets. When he won bail with his two co-accused, a Loyalist hit squad was waiting. He and Tony McCaughey survived, but Sean Marshall was shot dead, and there were persistent allegations of security force collusion.

Charges were finally dropped and many Republicans flocked to her. Although her clients still included Protestants, one mid-Ulster lawyer said the balance of her business gradually changed as most decided to find themselves fresh legal representation.

She was the obvious choice when the Nationalists of the Garvaghy Road were looking around for someone to advise them as the Drumcree crisis began back in 1995. She was often on the streets in the early hours to gauge police harassment and the level of threat to the Nationalist community from the Orangemen.

Diane Hamill, 29, approached a Portadown solicitor first over her brother's murder. He said he would take the case, but never looked her straight in the eye. She decided to go elsewhere, and later discovered he was a golfing buddy of several police officers. Hamill said: 'Someone mentioned Rosemary's name. She was so on the ball immediately, so keen. She instilled me with this tremendous sense of confidence. There was never a time I couldn't phone her, even in hysterics, and she would patiently calm me down. I had invited her to my wedding in October. She kept offering me the use of the family caravan for a break in Donegal. I have lost a friend rather than a solicitor. She is a woman I would love to emulate, so strong and so committed to the rule of law.'

One former colleague said: 'It sounds dreadful to say but I think she was sucked in rather unwittingly. She went several miles further than the professional situation dictated. She became vigorous in pursuing a certain point of view.'

Loyalists already detested her, but Ms Nelson was soon alleging she was on the receiving end of RUC death threats as well. Many were passed to clients detained under the Prevention of Terrorism Act. Police officers were also alleged to ask inmates whether they were sleeping with her. They also accused her of being an IRA member.

Ms Nelson said she was hit with a riot shield as the RUC prepared to push the Orangemen down the Garvaghy Road in 1997. She claimed she was left with severe bruising. She detailed her allegations last year to Param Cumaraswamy, UN special investigator on the independence of judges and lawyers, when he was compiling a report on RUC intimidation. He said yesterday he had feared she would be killed. She told them too to a House of Representatives committee on human rights in Northern Ireland last September, when she pleaded for support for a judicial inquiry into Finucane's death. No lawyer in Northern Ireland could forget what happened to him, she said. She told them also to the Independent Commission for Police Complaints. It was so unhappy with the way the RUC was dealing with her allegations that it asked the Metropolitan Police to take over the inquiry, and is planning to publish its findings on Friday.

Ms Nelson's death will resonate for years. Sinn Fein claims collusion, though she was a soft target and little enough security force cover would have been needed for Loyalists to kill her. But her murder was a dirty choice, aimed at enticing the IRA back to war. RUC Chief Constable Ronnie Flanagan's decision to call in outside help in the investigation into her death will devastate police morale, though it may be pitched at heading off criticism in Friday's report. The RUC had never made such a move before, and there was an undefined sense that a turning point had been reached in Northern Ireland yesterday.

All of which matters nothing to three more grieving children. Horrific enough for Christopher, 13, and Gavin, 11, to learn of their mother's death on a school skiing trip to France. Imagine, though, Sarah Nelson, just eight, and a pupil at Tannaghmore Primary. She heard the blast that ended her mother's life. •

....

30 January 1999
Maggie O'Kane
Lonely and silent farewell

I t was just gone 1 p.m. when the door on the Barcroft estate opened and Bernie Collins, with her four children at her side, emerged to see more TV cameras and reporters than mourners. Aiofe, the youngest, was holding her mother's hand.

It wasn't much of a funeral for an Irish town, but as far as Republican Newry was concerned they were burying a traitor yesterday. The deceased, Eamon Collins, aged 47, was stabbed and bludgeoned to death. He was an IRA man who changed heart and wrote from the inside about the movement's brutality. He survived the outcry his book caused, but his continued criticism and willingness to testify against those he grew up with led to one of the most brutal murders ever in south Armagh – a county that has seen and bred much brutality, a land of hunger strikers, sacrifice and skies shadowed with British army observation posts.

Crumpled but proud, Bernie Collins and her children and 38 mourners followed the coffin down the street. Not one door opened, and the silence of their grief was wrapped in tension. Perhaps it was the brutality of Collins's murder, perhaps it was the arson attack on his home, or perhaps it was respect for the small parade of those who loved him, but they were allowed to pass with dignity.

On they went. Past a memorial that read: 'Erected in proud and loving memory to all those associated with the district who took part in Ireland's struggle for freedom.' Opposite, on a telegraph pole, was a notice with the shadow of a gun. 'Sniper at work,' it warned.

At a street corner a trio of women with shopping whispered, looking down as the coffin passed. As it neared St Catherine's in Newry, a man and two women muttered among themselves. 'Go on,' said one. 'No, you go on,' said another, and they slipped self-consciously in at the back of the cortège.

Eamon Collins expected to be murdered. Maybe it was he who chose the gentle haunting voice of a female soloist to sing 'Christ be beside me'. Or the words from the Letter of St Paul to the Corinthians: 'O death, where is thy sting? O grave, where is thy victory?'

The pews filled silently as the service moved on to bless his body. Aiofe used her long blonde hair to hide her face and her tears. Women with neat plaid skirts slipped into the congregation and the numbers swelled to perhaps 200.

A woman and her three children arrived late, defiantly walking up the aisle to say that she was there to mourn Eamon Collins.

In the graveyard overlooking the town, men in flat caps watched at a distance. As darkness drew in, Bernie Collins took a single red rose from the dozen in her hand and laid it on the grave of the man she had loved and stayed with through the years of death threats and shame. Then she and her children, thin, haunted and cold, climbed into a black limousine.

There were no final words of farewell. He had already written his epitaph in his book, *Killing Rage*: 'I've done some terrible things in my life. But worse, I had done those things in support of beliefs which I now knew to be deluded. I did not want to die knowing that nothing worthwhile had come from my actions. My hope is that someone, somewhere might learn something useful from the story of my life.' •

....

19 January 1999
John Mullin
What ceasefire?

The yellow tablets are for the phantom pains. He takes six of those. The eight red and green capsules are painkillers. The 10 white pills are sleeping tablets, which are often ineffective. The pink and grey one? That is to stop his stomach from rotting from his rainbow of medication, which stretches to 42 tablets every day. Plus, of course, the liquid antibiotic he swallows because his own body's resistance was shot to pieces when they blew off his legs.

Meet Andrew Peden, one of Northern Ireland's victims of peace. He was shot in a so-called punishment attack, paramilitary rough justice mushrooming in the wake of the Good Friday Agreement.

Peden, 35, was looking forward to the weekend. He and his wife Linda, 34, and three children – Gary, 15, Drew, 12, and five-year-old Shaunie – were going to his mother-in-law's caravan on the County Down coast at Newcastle. He drained his only pint in his local club in Belfast, ready to go home to pack.

Another drinker asked him for a lift. He agreed. His passenger, a top man in the Ulster Defence Association, was furious when they drew up at his house on the Shankill Road. Outside was the car of a leading figure in the rival Ulster Volunteer Force. He had stumbled on proof of long-suspected adultery. The UDA man immediately called in his troops. The UVF leader was severely beaten. He, in turn, ordered his revenge.

Peden had gone home immediately after dropping his passenger. Someone, though, had recognised his car, and he was grabbed early the next day and driven to a nearby flat.

'They beat me with poles,' says Peden. 'They said they were going to fill the bath. They made me write a last letter to my kids. My hands were tied, but I managed to lift the blindfold and saw the window. I ran for it, but I bounced off. I have never prayed as hard. I was drifting in and out. They finally took me outside. They shouted: "Lie down. Lie down." There was a bang and that's the last I remember.'

After 12 hours torturing him, his assailants resorted to a shotgun. A handgun is the usual tool for kneecapping – damage is localised and recovery, after expensive surgery, is often close to complete. As soon as the doctors at the Royal Victoria Hospital pumped blood into Peden, it was flooding out. They used up 200 units of blood during his first night. Peden's wife was asked to consider switching off his life support machine.

He died for 15 minutes. He later had two heart attacks and was on kidney dialysis for three months. He may yet need a transplant. He had a tracheotomy and was in a coma for six weeks. The doctors took off his left leg immediately. It is still like raw steak. They tried to keep his right leg, but removed it three months later. Both legs are amputated close to the groin.

The Pedens are upset at the lack of support from the state. The family's income is £109 a week in benefits and there has been no other financial help. They have to find £140 a month for the car and have had to borrow the money to have it adapted. There is still no wheelchair ramp at their housing executive home on the Glencairn estate. Nor is there a handrail.

They feel that Mo Mowlam, Northern Ireland Secretary, turns a blind eye to the escalating numbers of punishment attacks. They think she is afraid of upsetting the politicians linked to the terrorists.

'My two wee lads are growing up with so much anger,' says Peden. 'Gary can't look me in the eye. He just won't speak about it at all. I used to do everything with Drew, swimming and hunting and camping. He is struggling at school now. Linda had to bring him up to hospital one night because he was convinced I was going to die. He lay on the bed crying his heart out. He says he will get the men that did this to me one day. I tell him to wise up. They have to face God one day and he will judge.

'Wee Shaunie was my shadow. I never went anywhere without her. She thinks I fell down the stairs. She knows I'm getting fitted for legs, but she wants mine back. She kisses where they used to be. I just wish I could walk over to my daughter and pick her up.'

There were 34 Loyalist punishment shootings in 1998. A further 38 were committed by the IRA. Loyalists carried out 85 beatings; the IRA 80. The terrorists exiled almost 600 people, including partners and children of those ordered to leave Northern Ireland.

All such activity was meant to end under the agreement. But nine-tenths of those incidents were after 10 April, starting that very night when two men were shot, the first such victims in six weeks. Already this year, 19 people have been shot or assaulted as the Loyalist and Republican paramilitaries seek to maintain control. Attacks have risen fourfold since the IRA ceasefire in 1994.

Ex-IRA man Vincent McKenna, development officer with the human rights group Families Against Intimidation and Terror, says the violence is pitched less at petty crime or antisocial behaviour. It is used increasingly to settle personal vendettas. 'A senior IRA man once told me: "When people stop fearing us, they stop respecting us,"' McKenna says. 'This is all about power.'

Among IRA victims since voters overwhelmingly backed the agreement was Andrew Kearney, 33. His cousin served 20 years in jail for IRA crimes and an uncle was interned two decades back. His crime was to accuse a notorious IRA figure of bullying women and children, who complained about his use of punishment attacks, and then to embarrass him by thumping him when he called him out of the west Belfast pub. Two weeks later, Kearney was dead.

He was dragged from his eighth-floor flat in the Republican New Lodge area at midnight. He was wearing only his football shorts and was playing with his two-week-old daughter, Caitlin Rose, his fourth child. Left behind was his Coke and half a Toffee Crisp. Eight of them dragged him to the lift. They may have drugged him with chloroform and they tied his hands behind his back. They used a handgun, more powerful than usual, and shot him three times. An artery was severed and he bled to death. To make rescue impossible, they jammed the lift with a brush shaft. They had also ripped the phone in the flat apart.

His mother, Maureen, 65, until now a staunch Republican, says: 'Whenever a Sinn Fein person gets a clip round the ear from the RUC, they sue for tens of thousands. We were left to pay £2,200 for the funeral, money we had put away for our own burials. They have a cheek to lecture about human rights. There's not one blade of grass worth anyone's life. If a united Ireland means being ruled by this bunch of cowards, then no.'

The same IRA gang was responsible for kneecapping 79-year-old John Brown in the same New Lodge tower blocks, believing he was a paedophile. They got the wrong man.

At Christmas, one drunkard in a local club knocked drinks over the wife of an IRA man. He had both his hands smashed with breeze blocks.

At his home on the Glencairn estate, Peden says: 'The nightmares come every night. I just close my eyes and they come into my head. I dreamt last night they came for Linda and Shaunie.'

Mrs Peden, who carries her husband upstairs every time he needs the toilet, says: 'I lie beside Andrew in bed when he finally goes to sleep. It is like looking at a child. There is only half of him there, and all for what? Doing someone a favour.' •

. . . .

29 June 1999

Hugo Young
Artificial

Down at the wire, the word that fits the Trimble–Adams stand-off is a strange one. Artificial. That's the sense that screams from the positions taken by either side. Both are gripped by what they see as matters of inalienable substance: the substance of arms, of lifelong passion, of sanctified conviction, of justified mistrust, above all the substance of history. Could any two men on the face of the planet be deeper dug in behind impermeable rocks of actuality? But when you look at it, what their argument most seems is unreal.

Consider Mr Trimble and his party. They have already come a long way. They wanted the Good Friday deal, and their leader has taken some risks to keep it alive. They know also that the IRA will never give up all its weapons. They knew that all along. It is one of the givens they have learned to tolerate, as they contemplate sitting alongside former killers and torturers on the Northern Ireland executive.

They well understand, even if Sinn Fein–IRA were to hand over some weapons now, and make a pledge on decommissioning later, that arms will remain. The possibility of restarting hostilities will be there, moving out from arms dumps whose location the IRA has presumably mapped with greater exactness than it did the murder-graves of 20 years ago.

Knowing this, the Ulster Unionists none the less sat down with Sinn Fein–IRA and talked about a future that, as everyone silently understood, encompassed it. They did this because they believed the process would assist the outcome, saying, in effect, that politics should be allowed to take over, and that this experience in itself would begin to render the arms redundant. This was the point of Good Friday. With the growth of politics, battle would finally cease.

Yet, having swallowed all that, which required an impressive if long-delayed magnanimity on the Unionists' part, they are now balking. They can't make the final stride. They refuse to let the executive start functioning unless this is preceded by some tiny sign from the other side. The camel is digested, but the gnat sticks immovably in the throat.

Republicans too, however, are masters of the artificial point. By offering this tiny sign,

So much to lose

they would lose nothing. The scenario which the Unionists have privately conceded acknowledges that some weaponry would always, in the real world, remain. Certainly a great deal of it would still be there next week and next month if, this week, the IRA were to meet Mr Blair's deadline and launch a decommissioning process. For all that is asked of them to keep momentum going is a token, in effect a nullity, a symbolic act: a gesture of entirely artificial importance.

Yet they cannot do it. And people humour them in the not-doing of it. They established some time ago, especially among mainland opinion that is anywhere close to the government, that they could not be expected to do it. History entirely ruled it out. Those of us who wrote in the opposite sense – said that some little gesture of symbolic disarming was a *sine qua non* which Unionists were entitled to rely on – were given lectures about our regrettable insensitivity and our woeful lack of realism.

Sinn Fein–IRA has, like the Unionists, come quite far. It accepted the consent principle, protecting the democratic rights of the Ulster majority. It complied with the impulse in Dublin to redefine the constitutional objective of a united Ireland. It embarked on a process which implicitly conceded that its departed heroes had fought and died in a struggle that could no longer be won by military means.

But Mr Adams too, like Mr Trimble, goes to the wire quite willing, it would seem, to jeopardise all this by his resistance to a very small point. Actually, of the two, Sinn Fein's sabotage, if this is what it proves to be, is the more culpable. It has seized more, while offering less. It has got many of its killers out of prison early, but is not prepared even to urge that decommissioning should happen. While insisting on its separateness from the IRA, it will not expend so much as a single word telling the IRA what it thinks it should do.

Sinn Fein, in other words, will take hardly any risks. We assume that Mr Adams is desperate for Good Friday to survive, but he exhibits no equivalent public urgency. While goading Mr Trimble to take one more risk, he affects to believe that for his part it is not within his power to take the one everyone wants him to, because he continues to shelter behind the claim – the insulting fiction – that he carries no influence with the IRA. Judged by where it now stands, the negotiation has been one-sided in the concessions made, while sustaining the ridiculous pretence that any party close to a paramilitary group could not bring about sufficient decommissioning to allow the peace process to continue and the institutions to start work.

All the same, the points at issue remain definable by that word: artificial. Taking the process as a whole, their reality does not accord in any way with the scale of the prize that is otherwise available. Both sides have expended great effort, alongside the British and Irish governments, to achieve a change that has eluded these islands for 30 years – to name but the most recent fragment of time. It would now take only a small shift by either or both of them to enable the larger deal to make a measure of progress.

It is tempting to say this has to come from Sinn Fein. For while it is certainly easier to say what Mr Trimble should do – to tell him, with lofty disregard for his viability as leader of a functioning party, to move ahead without any decommissioning gesture from the other side – Sinn Fein's recalcitrance has been the more unyielding, and therefore the more culpably calamitous for the project its leaders want to see succeed.

What is more striking than the fault to be found on one side or the other, however, is the failure they share: their absence of perspective in the end-game. Must the gnats have another accursed victory? This is what today and tomorrow will have to be about. A venture that has seen, from all sides, a fair amount of largeness – reluctant and chippy and unadmitted, but also large – is in danger of collapsing round points that are not, in the broad scheme of things already accomplished, either large or real. Perhaps this is a definition of the Irish problem. But that is what seemed so close to being redefined. •

Miscellany

19 December 1998

Peter Lennon

The poet who won't rest in peace

When a gravestone weighing almost a ton was removed from the resting place of Irish poet Patrick Kavanagh this August and smashed 'into a hundred pieces', it seemed like something out of a badly written farce. Four 'burly men' had allegedly been recruited to wreck the gravestone in Inniskeen, County Monaghan. The parish priest blithely described the pulverised monument as un-Christian and un-Catholic. Kavanagh's own brother appeared unconcerned at the desecration. And, to top it all, this wasn't even the first time the grave had been disturbed.

Kavanagh, who died in 1967 at the age of 63, always had a gift for stirring the passions. He ranks alongside Yeats in the pantheon of Irish poetry, and had a powerful influence on both Heaney and the Welsh poet R. S. Thomas. But he was also a first-division hell-raiser. In the drab years after the war, he stalked the streets of Dublin with empty pockets but a full head, ready to give roaring delivery to any notion, tender or terrifying, that took his fancy. Most Dublin pubs knew they were not big enough for both him and his riotous friend Brendan Behan – and more than one issued an edict to that effect.

Kavanagh was the peasant to Behan's Dublin 'gurrier' (wideboy), but he was by far the greater talent. He proved his genius with the publication of his major poem, 'The Great Hunger', in 1942 and his novel of grim rural life, *Tarry Flynn*, in 1948. And he knew his worth. As well as describing most Irish writers as 'second-rate English literary journalists', he once said that the greatest mistake he ever made was to leave his potato patch in Mucker (the Place of the Pigs), Inniskeen, and go, in 1939, to live in 'malignant' Dublin.

He took revenge on the sophisticates for a few glorious months in 1952 with *Kavanagh's Weekly* – a comment magazine mostly written by himself, with practical and financial support from his brother, Peter. In it he laid into Ireland's sclerotic institutions. He declared that 'leaders whom Ireland has put on pedestals have in general been an unworthy lot – O'Connell, Parnell and de Valera (Prime Minister at the time) – empty, vainglorious featherers of their own little emotional nests'. Not surprisingly, this didn't go down well with the patriots.

Kavanagh finally became exasperated by the Dubliners' reluctance to purchase his scalding medicine and warned them that if they did not stump up £1,000 as 'a token of their intensity and enthusiasm' he would close down *Kavanagh's Weekly*. The wretches refused and it folded. As was the way with Dublin, the soul of the poet was acknowledged, but the only nourishment he was readily granted came in the form of booze – with the anticipation of a bit of malarkey.

Two years later, Kavanagh was responsible for one of the greatest literary spectacles in Irish history. He took exception to an anonymous profile in a magazine, *The Leader*, and sued for libel. *Le tout* Dublin flocked to the trial. Although already ill with the lung cancer that was to kill him, he spent three days in the witness box. It became a titanic struggle between the Artist and the Philistine – in this case, defence counsel John Costello, who that year fulfilled Kavanagh's claim that mediocrity ruled Ireland by becoming prime minister for the second time.

Even lung cancer could not quench his fiery breath and until 1967 Kavanagh could be seen coughing and hacking his way around Dublin, declaring that 'Irishness is a form of anti-art'. The destruction of the gravestone gives resonance to that assertion – and testifies to the strong feelings aroused by his marriage to the woman who now shares his grave.

During the last 10 years of his life, Kavanagh took up with Katherine Moloney, a boozy and loquacious book-keeper who accompanied him to the literary bars and the race track. The relationship reduced the influence of his family – and they obviously didn't like it. When, six months before his death, he finally married Katherine, they refused to recognise the union.

The strange affair of the vandalised gravestone is a variation of an incident in 1989, which turned Katherine's funeral into a pantomime. When her cortège arrived at Inniskeen graveyard, it became clear that the wrong grave had been opened, so that she would not lie with her husband. The ceremony was suspended and the grave-diggers took diplomatic leave, while two volunteers hurriedly grabbed shovels. The proper grave was opened and the ceremony proceeded. Shortly afterwards, the teak cross and simple stepping stones that had adorned Kavanagh's grave were removed and put on display at the Kavanagh farm at nearby Mucker.

The response of the Moloney family was to commission sculptor Tom Glendon to make a stone to replace the displaced cross. But when Glendon went down to reconnoitre the terrain for his new work, he says he found a strange notice. 'There were,' he says, 'words to the effect that this monument was removed on the day Patrick Kavanagh's grave was desecrated. The date of the removal was the date on which Katherine was interred.' Now, nine years later, Glendon's replacement lies in pieces.

'It's a family quarrel,' insists Father Peter McGuinness, the parish priest. 'No one, including myself, wants to get involved. You could be the meat in the sandwich. But the stone certainly wasn't Christian, you know,' he continues. 'There was no cross on it. It was standing there with a hole at the top of it. It wasn't Catholic.'

'I take umbrage at that statement,' said Glendon. 'My design was to carry through the Christian Celtic tradition of monument-making. The look-through circle is the symbol of eternity. The slab was commissioned by Helen Moloney, sister of Patrick Kavanagh's widow.'

On the pale, crinoidal Kilkenny limestone were traced lines from Kavanagh's 'The Hospital':

For we must never record love's mystery without claptrap,
Snatch out of time the passionate transitory.

'The bottom line in this affair is that there is a woman now lying in a grave which does not acknowledge her presence at all,' says Eunan O'Halpin, a nephew of Katherine and a member of the Katherine Kavanagh Trust, which controls the copyright in the poet's works. 'Whether she was the Queen of Sheba or the humblest whatever, it is just an outrage. It is in effect a denial that the marriage took place.'

The Garda are proceeding at a prudent pace with their inquiries. 'The affair was reported to us at the time and we carried out an investigation,' says Superintendent Flannery of the local Garda station at Carrickmacross. 'We did interview [Patrick's brother] Dr Peter Kavanagh. He was home from America at the time. Yes, the pieces of the gravestone were found in a bog adjacent to Peter Kavanagh's home. I don't know if he actually owns the land, but it was convenient to the house.'

Has the case been dropped? I ask.

'No, no, no.' Peter Kavanagh has lived in the US for many years, with frequent forays home. He is now 82. He spoke on the phone from his home in New York. 'That monument was put up in the dead of night by strangers without any permission,' he said. 'It is a vulgar thing which is pagan. Patrick is the only Catholic poet that Ireland ever produced. Pagan! No hint of a Christian symbol in it.'

So you condone this act?

'I was expecting someone would have knocked it down years ago.'

But it wasn't knocked down until you came to visit in August?

'That's correct.'

Are you admitting you knocked it down?

'I am not admitting anything, and certainly not over the phone to someone I don't know. But if you were around here in New York, I could give you a cloutin' article if you wanted it. They [the Katherine Kavanagh Trust] are the enemies of Patrick Kavanagh. They sent me a solicitor to tell me not to publish anything about him. I've been working constantly on him, but they have poisoned every well. I don't know why they hate him so much.'

All these shenanigans bring to mind one of the poet's comments on his fellow-countrymen: 'I could kick myself for all the people I did not kick.' •

. . . .

19 May 1999

Paul Evans
A country diary

Wenlock Edge

It began as a slit in the monochrome grey of the western sky which divided into two gashes of red light, eyes flaming with an intense fire. The eye gash split open like a wound and the bottom of a scarlet, burning disc began to slide out, dropping slowly to earth. Within a few minutes the whole disc appeared, deepening to a luminous blood red, haunted by slow-motion shadows as if they were huge grey birds. The clear, sharp edges of the red disc broke up in the branches of hawthorn trees, snowy with blossom, and as it sank into the west, the greyness thickened around the last calls of the cuckoo and the first hoots of the owl into the night of the new moon. Sunsets, eh? Even though they happen every day, it's usually when we're not looking.

Occasionally a sunset appears which is not just beautiful to watch but is so compelling that it drags us from our myopic, artificially lit worlds and fixes us into the phenomenon of the day's passing into night, as if it were a new experience. And of course, it always is.

The next morning there were frantic whirring sounds in the kitchen, like

Don McPhee

Buttermere and Crummock Water, the Lake District

tiny helicopters banging against glass. Drawn to the light through the window, perhaps because there was no moon for them to aim at, two fantastic nocturnal creatures struggled against the daylight – a pair of cockchafers. These large beetles, about 30mm long, have bronze wingcases, their hard bodies covered with a downy golden hair and with antennae like feathery amber combs. They are also called May bugs, because they emerge from their subterranean larval stage and take to the night skies in May to seek a mate. They were once so common that they were thought of as pests, but their numbers have greatly declined in recent years. Once they were clinging to my hand they calmed down and I took them out to a blackcurrant bush, where they stayed on the underside of leaves and began feeding, carving out moon shapes. The French say that a year of cockchafers is a year of apples – bright, burning red apples that vanish into the west perhaps. •

27 March 1999
Smallweed

Lord Lamont, I see, has described the government's handling of the Pinochet affair as 'an expensive fiasco', a sentiment echoed in much the same words by Margaret Thatcher. By happy coincidence, these denunciations emerged just as the judges were finalising the shortlist for the coveted Smallweed Awards for the outstanding British fiascos of the last quarter-century. The judges – Michael Portillo, Baby Spice, Robbie Fowler and Carol Vorderman, with a former suffragan Bishop of Beccles in the chair – had a fecund field to choose from. Rail privatisation came high on the list, especially when the train carrying judge number six, Richard Branson, took a wrong turning a couple of miles from Nuneaton and ended up in Nottingham. But by overwhelming consensus, the two contenders through to the final, I am proud to announce, are Norman's handling of the ERM crisis and Maggie's Poll Tax.

Which reminds me to pass on some valuable information gleaned from the *Daily Telegraph*'s small ads.

> *Baroness Thatcher*: Fine bone china limited edition (250) sculpture by Michael Sutty. Commissioned by Denis Thatcher, and depicted in her Garter robes. Each certificate of authenticity signed personally by Baroness Thatcher. £345. Tel 0181 467 1374.

I wouldn't want *Guardian* readers to miss out on such a dazzling opportunity.

As I expected, it did not take long to assemble an entire football team to destroy Hunter Davies's contention that no player exists whose name is a double place-name. Since the name he balked at was Brooklyn Peckham, I've felt free to use overseas names as well as British ones: my particular thanks to Gary, Indiana. My tentative nominations for what I intend to call a Hunter Davies Refutation XI sports in defence Warren Barton, Dean Blackwell, Lee Sandford and Dean Gordon. I've reluctantly omitted Rio Ferdinand, since I cannot find a Ferdinand anywhere, but only Fernandos. In midfield, Clayton Blackmore and Mark Pembridge would be joined by Kerry Mayo of Brighton. He may not be so well known, but he has to be in, since his name is made up of two Irish maritime counties. In attack, Dean Holdsworth and Lee Howey might play alongside Gary Penrice and Gary Crosby. This would still leave on the bench players as strong as Gary Kelly, though Leeds don't seem to have used him much this season. In goal, I might plump for the huge experience of the Sunderland, Hartlepool, Birmingham City, Walsall, Doncaster Rovers, Grimsby Town, Bristol City, Carlisle United, Darlington, Peterborough, York City and Stoke City sticksman Mark Prudhoe.

A Montrose supporter writes: I note you're not saying much about Cowdenbeath nowadays.

Smallweed soulfully murmurs: Too true. How long ago it now seems since I stood on the terraces at Central Park at the start of this season, watching Cowden put up a decent show against Livingston. True, they lost, but Livingston are having the sort of season which must bring a glow to the warm old heart of their local MP, Robin Cook. Within days of that clash, Cowden were top of the table; well, joint top anyway. And where are they now? Rock bottom, overtaken by even Montrose. I shall try to be there for one of their few remaining matches, but events – a summons to jury service, perhaps, or an invitation to climb Mount Ararat – seem doomed to intervene.

Gwyneth Paltrow may have to be cloned. The British-inspired but US-financed multiple Oscar-winner *Shakespeare in Love* only got off the ground, I heard it reported this week, because they found an American actress to play the lead. The producers weren't willing to tolerate a mere Brit. But not any American actress. The point about Paltrow is that while indisputably American she sounds more British than the real British. As I pointed out at the time, the accent she assumed for *Sliding Doors* caught to perfection the way that New Britain speaks: aggressively classless, with just enough estuarian to keep it from sounding posh; no hint of a childhood in great country houses, but with none of the aggressive down-market practices affected by some at Demos.

For *Shakespeare in Love*, she was pure English Rose. I hope she goes on to film something by Arnold Bennett, so she can learn to speak Potteries, or by Lawrence, to treat us all to her Nottinghamshire; after that, perhaps, she will give us her

Merseyside – modulated Merseyside, I would guess, rather than the kind of delivery that makes Beryl Bainbridge's teeth stand on end. US audiences will be happy, since they know that whatever accent she uses, deep down she is one of them. But we in Britain need at least two of Gwyneth to ensure we keep winning Oscars. I suggest they call the second one Gwyneth Wortlap.

Elsewhere in today's Smallweed:

Those Oscar gowns, p. 2.
Those Oscar shoes, p. 3.
Those Oscar socks, p. 4.
How I almost took the award for best clapper-boy, p. 7.
What Sly Stallone told me during a coffee break, p. 10.
Paul Johnson, p. 12.
Frank Johnson and Boris Johnson, p. 13.
Any number of other Johnsons, p. 22. ●

. . . .

29 June 1999
Matthew Norman
Diary

And so to our Book of the Month, *Prince Edward*, by Ingrid Seward, editor-in-chief of the revered *Majesty* magazine. We begin with a hint as to why, at his wedding, Wessex described the Queen as 'probably the most wonderful mother on earth'. One birthday morning, Miss Seward reveals, Edward joined his mum in her private dining room, even as her pipe major was playing beneath her window. 'If Edward was expecting something,' writes Ingrid, 'nothing was forthcoming. There was no card, no present, not even a birthday greeting. When Edward kissed his mother goodbye, still nothing was said.' Do not be fooled into imagining the sovereign is cold-hearted. When Edward told a member of the household that his mother appeared not to know it was his birthday, 'a hasty telephone call was put through to the Queen's page, to remind Her Majesty that it was her youngest son's birthday. By lunch time, Edward had his present.' Doesn't it make you swell with patriotic pride? Tomorrow, Prince Philip's moving thoughts on what the birth of his fourth child meant to him.

Inspired by the *Guardian* freedom of information campaign, a reader rang the Home Office to ask for Jack Straw's e-mail address, hoping to share his thoughts with the Home Secretary. 'It is not our policy to give out addresses,' a secretary in Jack's office said. 'They are highly confidential.' Oddly, this paranoia cannot be put down to some nonsensical Whitehall regulation. When the reader asked for the e-mail address of Richard Wilson, the Cabinet Secretary, he was given this immediately. The head of the Civil Service is more accessible, in other words, than the one-time student firebrand. The campaign would appear to have a little way to travel yet.

News that the Tories have reacted to Greg Dyke's appointment as director-general by hiring a firm of professional media monitors to seek out BBC political bias will astonish all regular 'Diary' readers. My old friend Dr Julian Lewis made his name, you will recall, as a uniquely officious seeker of bias, when he spent several years scouring the airwaves for it, as the radio ham of Central Office. Now that he is an MP it seems peculiar that his talents should be overlooked . . . especially as they would doubtless be offered for free. When we ring Central Office, however, a press officer points out that Dr Lewis might not make a truly independent monitor – though his observations will be met, he insists, with gratitude. Poor show.

Regardless of how emasculated the trade union movement may have become, our libraries remain a hotbed of militancy. An Oxford University student who requested a book from the Bodleian reports that she was handed a slip of paper informing her although the book was in stock, she couldn't have it. The reason, she was later told, was that it was stored high on the shelves and union regulations precluded staff from climbing that far. The book would be moved, she was assured, but in the meantime they would be happy to order a copy from a library outside Oxford.

Having wilfully refused to take the advice of the 'Diary' and appoint my friend David Yelland, the alopecian *Sun* editor, as the new editor of *Tatler*, Nicholas Coleridge heaps sloppiness upon impertinence. Writing amusingly in our Media section yesterday of his quest to fill the *Tatler* post, the Condé Nast boss mentions that one strong candidate was described to him as being 'one walnut short of a Caesar salad'. If the man in overall charge of *Tatler* doesn't know that walnuts belong not to a Caesar but a Waldorf salad (you will recall Basil Fawlty telling a bolshy American guest: 'I'm sorry but we're out of Waldorfs'), what chance do the rest of us plebs have of avoiding such embarrassing *faux pas*? For heaven's sake, Coleridge, buck up or ship out. ●

....

22 March 1999

Jonathan Glancey

Can Barcelona save the city?

The first time I went to Barcelona was, by happy chance, the week General Franco died. The city was spectacular then as now, but seedy in large parts and patrolled by Civil Guards who could have been mistaken for Nazi soldiers, or at least extras from *Where Eagles Dare*. Before the week was out, I watched some of the same soldiers helping students take down street signs on what was then the Avenida Generalissimo Franco and is now the Diagonal, the great retail avenue that slashes across the nineteenth-century grid of the part of town known as Eixample, in which you find Gaudí's eye-boggling Sagrada Familia.

I joined a party at the old Amaya restaurant on the Rambla Santa Monica. My hotel, the España – a wonderfully eccentric design by Gaudí's contemporary Domenech i Montaner – in the Barri Xines (Chinatown), was at the heart of all-night celebrations. Soldiers, students, dock workers, loudly painted whores. If it seemed that the capital of Catalunya was awakening from a long and dismal dream, it was because it was. The sense of liberation was extraordinary and something not to be experienced in a European city again until the fall of the Berlin Wall 14 years later.

Much has changed since. Barcelona has risen from the banality of Fascist repression into perhaps the most respected and best-loved city in Europe. The Hotel España, a romantic dive in my student days, is now quite expensive and the Barri Xines no longer the dark and dangerous quarter it was before the 1992 Olympics clean-up. The things that haven't changed are the plodding onwards-and-upwards construction of Gaudí's Sagrada Familia (there is no date set for the completion of this extraordinary stone vegetable patch) and the city's unswerving commitment to the very best in architecture and urban design.

So much so that last week the city was awarded the Royal Gold Medal for Architecture. A gift of the Queen from the hands of the Royal Institute of British Architects, the award remains the most prestigious of its kind worldwide.

In the past, the medal has been largely the preserve of heroic individuals – Frank Lloyd Wright, Le Corbusier, Mies, Lutyens, Foster, Piano, Niemeyer, Tadao Ando. It passed by Barcelona's Antonio Gaudí, but as this brilliant individualist is well on his way to becoming a saint, it is very unlikely that he is fretting in heaven as a result of the RIBA's dismissal, or ignorance, of his protean talent.

The award is an inspired one, for it is to Barcelona that so many of us look when thinking of how our own cities in Britain could develop. No one, least of all the Gold Medal committee judges (including Sir Norman Foster, whose communications tower is one of the most striking recent designs in the city), is pretending that Barcelona is a model of urban perfection. Except in the imagination, and at the end of *Pilgrim's Progress*, there is no such thing. Barcelona, for all its natural and man-made beauty, remains a hard-edged port and is still ringed around with dismal high-rise suburbs that are about as friendly as a member of Franco's Civil Guard. It is, rather, the strides that have been made in urban design and architecture over the past two decades that fired the judges' imagination.

In the first few years of liberation from Franco and day-to-day rule by Castilian Madrid, visitors to Barcelona thrilled to a shot of youthful exuberance represented in a new wave of supremely self-confident and beautifully designed cafés, bars and nightclubs. Barcelona was in party mood.

Remarkably, the results were not ephemeral: 1980s bars like Alicia Nuñez and Guillem Bonet's Zig Zag, Eduardo Samso's Nick Havanna, Alfredo Arribas and Samso's Network – as well as a later generation, including Xavier Mariscal and Arribas's Gambrinus and Arribas's homage to David Lynch, Velvet – have all stood the test of time.

The joy of Barcelona, unlike, say, London, is that the interiors of buildings built solely for pleasure are as well designed, well built and as well looked after as museums and art galleries. Old bars and cafés, ones where Picasso used to drink (Bar Pastis on Calle Santa Monica) or grand Art Nouveau joints like Bar London (Calle Nou de la Rambla) remain as they were. Their heyday has yet to pass. In the design and fate of these glorious bars, one gets a good-time feel of why Barcelona works so well as a city: it has allowed one layer of design and architectural excellence to overlay another without the one defacing or destroying the other.

In Britain we have a tendency to strip out interiors and to demolish buildings with wilful abandon. In the quest for the new, however transient, we try to pretend that the past is a foreign country, or else we cling to it as we do to a battered old teddy bear and pretend the present, let alone the future, doesn't exist.

Barcelona's multi-layered quality is evident at every turn. From the port and the old Gothic quarter, the city opens up like some gigantic flower, with petals of eighteenth-, nineteenth- and twentieth-century architecture, much of it neat and regular, some of it – Gaudí, of course – utterly fantastic.

Recent high points include plans for the redevelopment of the Sagrera-Sant Andreu district around the new international rail terminal (unlike us, the Spanish like their railways), and the reconstruction of the old docks and seafront that were realised in time for the opening of the 1992 Olympic Games.

There's the restored Liceu Opera House, the pristine and icy new Museum of Contemporary Arts (every city has to have one: this one was designed by the US architect Richard Meier), but, above all, the sheer quality of the revitalised public places and spaces that thread their way through the city down from the heights of Tibidabo to the seafront. These weave the centre of the city together in a delightful manner; they are a model of their kind.

They began under the aegis of Oriol Bohigas, the charming architect and urban planner who was the city's delegate for urban affairs from 1979 to 1983 and, more recently, councillor for culture. Bohigas's programme of urban revival was a work of quiet genius. Rather than begin with grand new plans after Franco's descent into hell, Bohigas recommended improvements at a very local level and on a small scale. Bit by bit, from tiny inner-suburban plazas to grandiloquent spaces such as the Placio dels Paisos Catalans, outside the city's main railway station, the public face of the city was imaginatively groomed. Only after this work (which continues) was well under way did the grand plans start.

Meanwhile, the urban infrastructure – roads, trams, buses, metro – was improved to a standard that equals the best in the world. Contrast this with London, where the transport network has been carved up, flogged off and slewed into an aesthetic and commercial gutter.

Here we enter the territory of city politics. The transformation of Barcelona that has encouraged RIBA to award its Gold Medal would have been impossible without an ambitious, intelligent and coordinated democratic local government. It would also have been impossible without such dynamic and popular local politicians as Pasquall Maragall or such effective urban planners as Oriol Bohigas.

The belief these politicians have in an integrated city – and you will be hard-pressed to find one ignorant of the fine details of architecture, design, art and urban planning – is one that we can only wonder at. Where we treat our cities as some sort of low-rent department store to be cut up, deregulated, privatised and trashed at will, the men and women who have raised Barcelona to new international heights over the past 24 years see their city as an organism to be nurtured and treated as a whole, not as a book of bits.

In awarding Barcelona their Gold Medal, the RIBA judges are expressing a political sentiment: Barcelona is a lead we might yet follow. This will not require the death of a dictator, although it will require a small revolution. Our cities will not be ripe for Gold Medal treatment until they elect politicians who truly believe in them, politicians who see them as places for people to live civilised lives and not as playpens in which to exercise the tired old dogmas of deregulation, privatisation at any cost and architecture on the cheap. Go to Barcelona, if you haven't, to see what we could do if we tried. •

21 May 1999

Letters
You're a good Eigg

Allow me, as trustee of the Isle of Eigg Trust, to record the profound gratitude that many Scots feel towards the *Guardian* for having success-fully stood up to the libel action of erstwhile laird, Mr Keith Schellenberg ('Millionaire's libel case against *Guardian* fails', 20 May).

Our seven-year campaign that finally brought the island into community ownership in 1997 was made possible only by the outstanding generosity of *Guardian* readers, one of whom gave £1 million and many of whom numbered amongst 10,000 donors. The resultant community purchase of Eigg thereby set a new paradigm in land tenure. Its residents are now secure tenants unto their own non-profit trust. This squares the opportunity for self-reliant entrepre-neurship with the virtues of democratic community accountability. It suggests that, henceforth, we need law and not fund-raising to protect people against despotic feudal remnants.

At various times, the Trust's work on Eigg was jeopardised by islanders' fear of speaking out to the media. Had Mr Schellenberg won his rich man's libel game, a suffocating curtain would have smothered the land reform debate, not just on little Scottish islands, but throughout the British Isles.

Thank you, so very much.

Alastair McIntosh
Edinburgh ●

10 April 1999

Matthew Engel
Beccles and Eccles

Private Eye recently showed a cartoon depicting a middle-aged and rather repulsive-looking man standing beside an open chest of drawers wearing a bra and panties. He was bellowing furiously to an unseen figure: 'Muriel, where are my bloody tights?' The caption read simply: 'Cross dresser'. The word you need to consider here is Muriel. There are hundreds of well-known women's names. But somehow that joke would not have worked with any of the others. Perhaps Marjorie would have done, but she would have become Marje, and that would have been quite wrong. Definitely not Kate or Jane; nor Anthea or Melinda; nor Cherie or Ffion.

I'm not sure I've ever met a Muriel, though there was a Muriel Young on TV in the 1950s. But there's something about the name that was perfect for that cartoon. Why? It's a bit like what Louis Armstrong said when asked what jazz was: 'Lady, if you have to ask, you'll never know.' The humour of names is deeply ingrained but hard to analyse. There is a running gag in *Shakespeare in Love* about an early draft of *Romeo and Ethel* (the gag runs too long if you ask me, but they won their Oscars without asking). Basil and Sybil would never have been funny as John and Mary. Can anyone imagine Eric and Ern as Simon and Gavin?

This goes, in spades, for place-names. Large chunks of our humour depend on getting them right. In *The Sunshine Boys*, Walter Matthau explains that it all depends on whether or not there is a hard C sound in the name. Thus Cleveland can be used in jokes, but Cincinnati can't. There is some evidence to back this up. In New York, the Bronx and Brooklyn are clearly funnier than Queens or Staten Island. In New Jersey, Hackensack makes it but Trenton doesn't. British geographical humour is infinitely more complex than this. All our best writers understand how to get a laugh from using a well-judged place-name; Northerners Peter Tinniswood, Victoria Wood, Alan Bennett are maestros. Every half-decent repertory panto script contains a couple of deft local references, simply based on inserting the right town at just the right moment.

Clackmannan, Kilmarnock and Killiecrankie all score highly. So do Doncaster, Castleford and Keighley. Beccles is funnier than Bungay (though you can't laugh in a cinema in either place, see below). Kettering was immortalised in the Monty Python travel agent sketch, and the great writer J. L. Carr carried the joke so far as to actually live there.

But *The Sunshine Boys'* theory has to be an over-simplification because Corby, up the road, isn't funny at all. South Wales is a mother lode of humorous place-names, but Cardiff is nothing like as funny as Abergavenny, Pontardawe or Llantwit Major. The first and most important consideration is euphony: three and four syllables are more effective than two. You can't go wrong with Budleigh Salterton; and Frankie Howerd once had a comic riff in which he reinvented himself as the theatrical knight Sir Melton Mowbray.

The second criterion is that the town must conjure up a clear image: perhaps of shabbiness or maybe gentility. Swinton works as well as Frinton, but very differently. Catterick has traditionally scored not because of the double K sound but because of its familiarity to generations of squaddies. A place-name mustn't be over-used. Scunthorpe and Wigan are hackneyed. Come to that, so is Hackney. Try Walthamstow or Stoke Newington instead. There is a counter-intuitive variation on this, as used by Steve Coogan, who skilfully based his Alan Partridge character in Norwich, on the face of it a very unfunny place indeed. There is a potential thesis for someone in which the entire country could be graded into funny towns, unfunny towns and potentially funny towns. Perhaps it is a project for the University of Luton. (If, by the way, it turns out that I do know a Muriel, then I make my apologies now, particularly if she lives in Swinton and is married to a bad-tempered transvestite.)

Don't think this is an exclusively English-language phenomenon. A few years back, I spent a fascinating evening in Tirana as a local friend explained the significance of each provincial town in Albania and the perceived characteristics of the inhabitants: one lot were sly, another boastful, another simple. We've suddenly reached a moment in history when this information might be useful, but I'm damned if I can remember which place was which. I'm pretty sure that when I asked about Kosovo, he just shrugged. There wasn't anything funny about Kosovo. Even then. Even if it does begin with K.

The Broadway Cinema in Bungay, Suffolk, featured here four weeks ago, has now flickered into darkness, apparently for ever. Bungay, I am told, has greeted the news with indifference. But Gill Shinton, in nearby and equally movie-less Beccles (pause for titter), shares my grief. She arrived at the Broadway with a companion one evening to watch a Robin Williams film, to be greeted by the owner, Gordon Chapman, asking if they minded coming back another night as they were the only two customers and he wanted to go home and watch the football. In the midst of the discussion, four others turned up and the show had to go on.

Various letter-writers have tried to convince me of the continued existence of other Broadway-like movie houses: the Electric Palace at Harwich; the Rex at Wareham in Dorset; the Art Deco Metropole at Welshpool; the Town at Wotton-under-Edge, run by fans like a preserved steam railway; and, back in Suffolk, the Aldeburgh Cinema. But frankly they all sound a bit too ritzy for me. RIP the Broadway. Perchance it is not dead, but sleepeth. ●

· ·

1 May 1999

Ian Mayes

Some very cross words

The Quick Crossword will be back in G2 from Monday, returning to the section which has housed it for the past six and a half years. I can't tell you how relieved I am. I am probably the only person who has read all, or very nearly all, the correspondence. We have kept it from more impressionable members of the staff.

We may quickly agree that in the present state of the world crossword deprivation (actually not even that) does not rank highly in the catalogue of suffering. However, in many *Guardian* households (many more than we thought) simultaneous engagement with the quick and cryptic crosswords has played an important part in the morning gathering of wits, the domestic ritual of preparing to meet the day.

I have not precisely counted the number of you who protested. My impression is of more than 300. We should be pleased to put right what was clearly a mistake, if only for the couple who wrote from Lancashire: 'We are in our nineties and are housebound, so one of our perks is to have a light breakfast at about 7.30 a.m. and afterwards return to our separate bedrooms' – she 'with a nice cup of tea and G2 to do the crossword', he with the main part of the paper and the Sports section.

One protester had been reading the [*Manchester*] *Guardian* for more than 70 years. Many readers made it clear that they felt they were asserting a right to have their views considered after years of allegiance. One, presumably younger, reader said the new *Guardian* was fine until, seated in a van on a building site enjoying his dinner, he tried to find the quick crossword. 'Can you imagine unfolding the broadsheet in such a confined space?' Put it back in G2, he pleaded, 'before I'm thrown out in the cold'.

We can do nothing but sympathise with those other readers who find inconvenient the placing of the main crossword in Sport on certain days. Particular apologies to the couple from West Sussex who last Monday sent off, as usual, the Sport section to their grandson in Aberdeen, to find that the cryptic crossword had gone with it. You will, I'm afraid, have to cut it out first. If you consider the placing of the crossword in Sport an irregularity, it will be a regular one, flagged by the index.

Many of the complaints about the crosswords, most of which should now be resolved, were accompanied by compliments for other changes, ranging from what some of you, happily, perceive as an improved layout and generally easier readability to the 'marvellous' illustrations now accompanying 'Country Diary' on the new 'Miscellany' page.

Apropos 'Miscellany', one reader complained that theatre reviews had been 'relegated' to this page. This is a perverse view. The 'Miscellany' page has, according to the arts editor, provided a much-valued increase in the amount of space available for reviews, which continue to appear in the Arts pages of G2.

There have been many complaints about some of the effects of the new edition arrangements for the 'Guide' on Saturdays. Where there were three regional editions there are now five. This has been done in response to requests for more local information. Among other things, it has meant that many readers just outside the present limit of the London edition are no longer told what is going on in the capital. Many of you affected in that way should find more West End information in today's 'Guide'. The editor of the 'Guide' says he will keep the situation under review.

Some of you are still in the process of refocusing on the new typefaces and type sizes. One reader complained: 'To have different type sizes for the leaders and the rest of the text is malfeasance of the highest order.' Surely not? One reader said he took an instant dislike to the redesign but couldn't work out why until he read my column last week, in which I pointed out that the text type size had been slightly increased. 'By my calculation,' he wrote, 'we are now paying the same price for 6 per cent less text.'

A column on a page in the main paper set in the new text type has lost about 16 lines. This has been done in the interest of readability. If quantity is the issue, there is more than adequate compensation in the form of extra pages. Some of you complain about that too, on ecological grounds.

Forgive me if I tell you that my favourite letter came from a reader in Worthing who said he continued to enjoy the *Guardian* after 40 years: 'You won't believe me when I say I had not noticed any changes.' •

1 June 1999
Matthew Norman
Diary of a hypochondriac

Tuesday

My run of good health concluded at 8.03 a.m. when, during the fortnightly cranial-oral examination, I discover something in the mouth – a hard, almost bony mass on the right hand side, parallel with the tongue.

'Ahmagodge, av foond uff chewmarrh,' I say to my wife.

'Try that again without half your arm inside your mouth,' Rebecca replies, gouging the stone from an avocado.

'I said, "O my God, I've found a tumour."'

'On second thoughts, put your hand back in,' she said. 'I prefer it when I can't understand a word you're saying.'

Wednesday

I have been vomiting almost hourly.

'Do you think it's spread to the stomach?' I ask my wife.

'I imagine so, yes,' she says. 'It can't have anything to do with you putting your hand halfway down your throat all the time like a bulimic, can it? Or the fact that you've been drinking whisky all day on an empty stomach?'

It's true, I have taken the odd drop, to calm myself.

'No, all in all,' says Rebecca judiciously, 'I'd say a stomach tumour was favourite.'

Thursday

Too scared of the inevitable confirmation until now to consult my excellent physician, Sarah Jarvis, tonight I can contain myself no longer. Finding Rebecca's address book (in a new and surprisingly obvious hiding place, buried beneath the phone directories), I dial the number.

'Hello?'

It is Simon, Dr Jarvis's husband. I introduce myself.

'It's 10.30,' he says, before fetching the doctor.

'It's 10.30,' she says.

Stifling an inquiry as to whether the Speaking Clock Family Training Course is residential or whether you can take it at home, I report my discovery.

'I'm at home tomorrow,' she says wearily. 'You'd better pop round at 12.30 p.m.'

Friday

Perched on Dr Jarvis's sofa with a cup of coffee, I experience a historic moment. The doctor's latex gloves are in the car, she says, and she cannot be bothered to fetch them, and so for the first time she embarks on an internal examination without them. The fingers root around.

'Is that it?'

'Nugghh.'

'Is that it?'

'Naaggghhhh.'

'That?'

'Nugh.'

'Is that it?'

'Yeuuth.'

'That's your hyoid, a kind of bone,' she announces, heading for the sink. 'Everyone has one. But how did you find it? How? How did you find it?'

How? I just looked.

Saturday

I awake feeling tired and tetchy, despite having passed a curiously untroubled night, and check the mouth . . . not this time the right side, but in search of the equivalent hyoid on the left. There is nothing there.

Sunday

For two days now, this perplexing absentee has preyed on my sanity. It is true that my waist is far plumper on the left side (albeit the right side is no Gandhi), the left shoulder is extremely hairy where its equivalent is smooth as a billiard ball . . . and yet, disturbing though they are, these asymmetries seem trivial next to the missing hyoid.

Although I am typically stoic and attempt to keep my concerns to myself, Rebecca suspects some private agony whether telepathically or because I do not speak for five hours – and calls the doctor to arrange an appointment in my usual slot, tomorrow at 6.20 p.m.

Monday

In Room 19, after explaining my doubts as to whether Dr Jarvis felt the correct bit on Friday, I sense a regression in our relationship when she dons the latex gloves she so blithely eschewed three days ago.

'It is definitely the hyoid, and the epiglottic cartilage,' she insists, and, fetching *Grant's Method of Anatomy*, points out a diagram.

'Yes, but why is there no hyoid on the left side?'

'Everyone is different,' she says. 'It's there but it's tucked away behind the skin so you can't feel it.'

'I'm sure you're right, but all the same I'd like a referral.'

'Well, you're not having one.'

'Please.'

'No.'

I ponder this for a second. 'Doctor, have you ever thought I sometimes tend to worry unduly about my health?'

This answer she delegates to her eyebrows.

'In that case, I'd like to be referred to a psychiatrist.'

'Nope.'

'Oh, go on.'

It is her turn to ponder. 'I'll think about it,' she says eventually.

The tantalising spectre of an entirely new chapter in my medical history elates me, and, almost skipping, I begin the journey home. ●

. . . .

10 September 1998

Maya Jaggi
The pleasure principle

Every discovery is arrogant, says Federico Andahazi, and possibly none more so than that charted in his remarkable novel *The Anatomist*. At its heart is a real Renaissance scientist from Padua who made the bizarre claim to have discovered the clitoris – or at least flagged it in European anatomy books for the first time.

That the man was called Mateo Colon and was a near contemporary (though no relation) of his more famous Genovese namesake Cristobal Colon – Christopher Columbus – was an irresistible call to likening the mapping of territories and bodies, the driving of proprietorial flagpoles into earth and flesh. Andahazi, a 34-year-old Buenos Aires psychoanalyst of Hungarian descent, was awarded Argentina's main literary prize, the Fortabat, for this, his first published novel. But while his anatomist is tried as a heretic and his work banned for unveiling that which should have remained hidden, Andahazi found his topic scarcely less of a taboo 400 years on. Tipped off about the book's contents, the 72-year-old 'Cement Queen' heiress Amalia Lacrose de Fortabat cancelled the prize ceremony. Her objection: the novel failed to 'contribute to the exaltation of the highest values of the human spirit'. The jury stood firm and the 10,000 pesos cheque was quietly slipped under the writer's door. The book became a bestseller across Latin America – more than 70,000 copies sold in Argentina alone – and the spat helped secure the unknown Argentinian a record $200,000 for English-language rights from Doubleday in the US. His novel now appears in English for the first time, with film-makers including *Amadeus* director Miloš Forman and Hector Babenco, who made *Kiss of the Spiderwoman*, knocking at his door.

While the scandal might seem laughable (Mrs Fortabat choicely denounced Andahazi as a 'communist porn artist'), the author is not amused. In London, after speaking at a writers' gathering on censorship in Spain, he points out that under Argentina's dictatorship of 1976–83, and its Dirty War in which 30,000 people 'disappeared', 'to call someone a communist or a pornographer was to sign their death warrant; any censorship today reverberates with the loss – through murder or suppression – of the previous generation of writers'.

Sex has always troubled the powerful, not least for its ability to vault socially constructed barriers – of wealth, class, race, even gender. And the subversive potential of female desire has evoked a particular dread. The kleitoris (from the Greek 'little hill') has doubtless been known of – and enjoyed – for centuries. The Latin poet Juvenal made reference to it as the 'cock's comb', while those in Africa and the Middle East enforcing the pre-Islamic, Pharaonic practice of female circumcision knew only too well the site of women's pleasure since they cut it out, the better to rule their wives and daughters (two million girls are still mutilated each year). Yet what was known in private was not named in public – and what women knew was not 'knowledge'. Even today, of 15 standard GCSE sex education textbooks, only five mention the clitoris or label it on diagrams.

'The clitoris is odd,' says Andahazi. 'It's perhaps the only bodily organ which has no other purpose than to afford pleasure. Its discovery – or invention – in the sixteenth century obviously had an impact on the representation of women as agents of pleasure, not just as a source of pleasure to others. Until then, sex for women was supposed to be a conduit to childbearing and nurturing, not enjoyment.' His interest was first piqued by an apparent historical blackout. Although Colon was a reputable scientist of his day who theorised about the circulation of blood 50 years before its English 'discoverer' William Harvey, little is known of him. 'How could someone of that stature pass unnoticed through history?' asks Andahazi, in whose novel identifying a diminutive 'female penis' ('It's a man,' cries the startled anatomist's aide) is as great a heresy as Galileo's remapping of the heavens.

Yet what emerges is not so much a clash between rational science and the obscurantist Church as a contest between men for control over women. The clerics, jealous of a man rumoured to leave women bearing 'a smile like the Mona Lisa', want the discovery locked up in forbidden books. If knowledge is power, then secrets are a means of keeping power out of others' hands. 'What would happen', they ask, 'if the daughters of Eve were to discover that, between their legs, they carried the keys to both Heaven and Hell?' But the anatomist is himself a conquistador of the female body, driven by thwarted love of Venice's most expensive prostitute and a timeless male quest for the font of female pleasure. His first experiments are with poisonous love elixirs smeared on his penis and lethally ingested by fellating prostitutes. Far from being a liberator in naming his America, the Amor Veneris, Colon imagines he has found the 'anatomical cause of love' and hence the 'instrument that subjugates the volatile female will'. For him the goal is not to pleasure a woman but to possess her.

'Every act of discovery brings with it an act of appropriation; that's the only reason you discover things, to patent them,' Andahazi says. 'The most brutal example is the discovery of the New World, which became the property of the Old. But it's a metaphor for what happens to women; male power is about appropriating them body and soul.' According to Aristotle's theory of conception, a father's semen conferred a soul (on male offspring) while the mother furnished mere flesh and blood – a curiously circular apologia for Greek laws of male inheritance. Yet in Andahazi's comic burlesque, the valiant explorer gets lost in his own rib – as the biblical origin of woman would have it. Both his women (Ines de Torremolinos and Mona Sofia, the madonna and the whore) opt to own their bodies and be mistress of their hearts – the saint turned 'witch' by slicing off her own clitoris.

'It's recreating two male versions of women – the saint and the whore,' says Andahazi. 'Inevitably, the distinction isn't so absolute; it dissolves the more you look at them. They each take a different route to rebelling against being colonised. So it's the story of a failure: Mateo Colon thinks he's possessing his body and soul of a woman but he fails utterly because there's no way force can appropriate another person's will.' Andahazi, who describes himself as 'a man of the left', declines to label himself a feminist, since 'feminism for me is not an all-explaining theory; the struggle is much wider than the battle of sexes'.

He may want his critique of power understood as more than a history of female anatomy, but an evident thirst for the subject may frustrate him. A New York Times survey in Buenos Aires found women were buying the novel in droves to give to their husbands and boyfriends – hinting they might learn something. As one woman put it: 'It's apt that the book is set in the Middle Ages because that's exactly the level of knowledge most men have when it comes to female anatomy.' Andahazi laughs that the response of women in other countries is unlikely to be different, since 'It's not just macho Latin American men who are preoccupied with their own pleasure – though there may be some truth in the stereotype.' But he is alarmed to find his novel of ideas approached as a sex manual.

Ironically, it may itself be flawed as such. The book describes the clitoris as 'barely exceeding the size of the head of a nail'. According to Australian research reported in *New Scientist* last month, the clitoris is '10 times bigger than the average person thinks', encompassing erectile tissue that extends far into the body. Scientists may be catching up with what women's studies – Shere Hite, the Boston-based Our Bodies, Ourselves – have insisted since the early 1970s: that there is indeed far more to the clitoris than meets the eye. Perhaps the most obvious thrust of that discovery is that men and women might not be so different after all. Now there's a heresy. •

....

25 June 1999
Linda Grant
Almighty gamble

Every few months someone knocks at my door or stops me on the street and asks me if I would like to go to their church. There are inestimable benefits. I will receive a warm and friendly reception. I'll make new friends. If I'm troubled in my spirit, if I have problems at home or at work, I'll have someone to talk to, who understands and may even be a trained counsellor. It might even be possible to arrange a retreat where I can contemplate the problems of my existence in tranquillity. And I'll have the satisfaction of knowing that I will be making a contribution to social justice through the many outreach programmes, whether it's ending hunger in Africa or providing shelter for the homeless in London.

What else can offer all this? Nothing I can think of, not the bars and restaurants I frequent where people look you up and down when you walk in. Not the hectic talk of war and its ills and the scramble to be on the morally right side. Not the holiday I'm planning, nor the supermarket that's open on Sunday, nor Thomas Harris's *Hannibal* that I read last weekend with its perplexing account of the battle of evil against evil. What a lot the churches have to offer and yet their membership wanes rather than waxes. Why are people not flooding in to take advantage of the benefits? What's stopping me from accepting those sincere invitations?

What's stopping me is that I don't believe in God. Not in an agnostic sense but in the spirit of pure atheism which asserts that man invented divinities to account for the temporarily inexplicable. So some of Britain's finest historic buildings stand empty and God's non-existence is the line drawn in the sand which prevents us entering. But this weekend representatives of Britain's 350,000 members of Methodist churches are to think the unthinkable. At their annual conference in Southport they will debate a new report which proposes that lack of faith should not preclude membership of the church. It will become possible to have a religion without believing in God.

Now the Methodists, of course, are not on the verge of turning into humanists. Rather they hope that the person who approaches the church, whether it's through a mother and toddler group, or having been brought along by a friend, will wind up arriving at faith within a reasonable period of time. 'Traditionally churches have linked membership to a public declaration of faith,' says Rev. Dr Stephen Mosedale, coordinating secretary for the Unit for Church Life and the author of the report. 'But people initially attend for a whole range of possible reasons. Maybe a minister has helped them through a personal crisis or they want to arrange a religious funeral but hardly ever because they've had a startling conversion experience. We're prepared to welcome as members all those who love Jesus or who seek to love him.'

In doing this the Methodists may well be returning to what was probably the role of religion for centuries. Churchgoing 150 years ago offered a social life, a dating service (see the novels of Jane Austen, in which many chapters are devoted to the question of what to wear to church), the opportunity to hear live music at a time when nothing could be recorded, respectability and a chance to make contacts in the community. For the Methodists and other nonconformists with a system of lay-preaching, church membership was a means by which working-class men could acquire upward social mobility or skills (like literacy, which they needed to study the Bible) which they could use in other walks of life. Most of the Tolpuddle Martyrs were Methodists and the term father (or mother) of chapel in the National Union of Journalists reflects the religious origins of the trade union movement.

I rang round a number of religious groups to ask them if non-belief in God would be any barrier to attendance. 'By law established we could not turn you away,' a Church of England spokesperson told me. 'You have a right at law to attend your parish church, to be married there and be buried. The church belongs to the people; it's your parish church and you have a legal right to insist that you can participate. However, if a set of atheists turned up and asked, "Could I have my baby baptised?", we would have to tell them a baby is not baptised into a church but into a faith and the baptism could be delayed for the purpose of a course of instruction. But there's no central diktat.'

Jews were just as welcoming, as long as you're Jewish by birth or conversion. Would I, as an avowed atheist, be turned away, I asked Rabbi Pini Dunner, of the Orthodox Saatchi Synagogue, which opened its doors in St John's Wood last October to cater for Jews under the age of 45? 'Absolutely not. Judaism doesn't require belief in God and synagogue membership isn't mentioned in the Torah. It's a community organisation. I have never seen on any synagogue membership form a question about belief in God. There are synagogues where you are asked if you are *shoma shabbat* [strictly observe the rules of the Sabbath], but they don't ask if you believe in God. Our members' parents went to the synagogue by default but their children just don't go and so they've opted out of organised Jewish life. What they want from us is some affirmation of their Jewish identity. We're not shoving religion down their throats.'

If you're a Christian and you really want the beef in the burger, you need to go to the Catholics. 'If you just want to turn up for the music, then fine, you can go to any Catholic mass, but, except in exceptional circumstances, you can't take communion and you might find it a little difficult to articulate the words of the creed,' said the Catholic Media Service spokeswoman, Patricia Hardcastle. Reaching for her missal, she then read me the baptismal promise, which started off with the relatively easy demand that I rejected Satan and all his works and then quickly demanded that I accept that Jesus Christ was God's only son, born of the Virgin Mary, was crucified, died, rose from the dead and is now seated on the right hand of the Father. With no evidence of any of these matters, I had to beg off. 'That's the Apostles' Creed,' she said. 'It's the absolute minimum you can get away with.' If I wanted a Catholic wedding, I would have to marry a Catholic and would have to have a Catholic understanding of marriage, which would include its positions on contraception and divorce. There is, she conceded, a degree of culture involved in being a Catholic, citing Clare Short, who has apparently referred to herself as an 'ethnic Catholic'.

Finally, there are Muslims. 'I would assume that nobody goes to the mosque who doesn't believe. It's an oxymoron in Islamic society,' said Zia Sardar, a Muslim writer. 'You could be a secular Muslim, but that means that you differentiate between the mosque and politics. But if you don't believe in God you're not a Muslim, you're a Pakistani or an Iranian or a Saudi. All morals for us have religious origins.' Yet it is the mosques and to some extent the synagogues that most closely resemble the churches of previous centuries, as centres of communal life.

'The mosque plays a very strong role in organising the community. One of the quickest ways of getting help is to go to the mosque and ask for *zakat*. Muslims pay a minimum of 2.5 per cent of their income to the mosque to help people in need. The mullahs act as a switchboard connecting people. Mosques have never just been a worshipping place, which is why they are perpetually open, so anyone can go in at any time for anything. Worship is only one component in the role they play.' This fact has been noted by some recent converts, who, according to Sardar, are more interested in the *zakat* than the Koran. It leads me to wonder whether there may be rather more non-believing Muslims attending mosques than the mullahs know.

The curious thing about religion in this country is that it is beginning to diverge along two quite separate pathways. I asked Rev. Dr Mosedale why he thought membership of the Methodists was declining. 'It's clearly very complex. I suspect that it's materialism more than anything else, but there may be other things such as the individualism of society in general. Posh Spice said that while her wedding would be religious, her own religion was private, between her and God. People don't want others to take control. They don't want what they see as organised religion getting in the way of that relationship.'

So we may wind up with a very curious state of affairs whereby there is a large number of people outside of any religious institution feeling that they have some kind of spiritual sense of things, and a large number of people attending church who do not. 'One could see this as the measure of a church quite desperate about its declining membership or as a sensible sign of realising that religious commitment is not just about assenting to a proposition,' says David Boulton, editor of *Sea of Faith Quarterly*, the religious humanist network set up 15 years ago which sees faith as a human creation.

The movement claims as active members 40 or 50 Church of England vicars and some Catholic priests. Hypocrites? 'These words that we mouth are imaginative poetry,' Boulton asserts. 'They are the way in which previous generations of one faith community have expressed their faith. We're happy to express our solidarity with our faith community.'

I have often wondered why religion has taken such a strong hold in America and why it has declined here. We say that people are losing their belief in God because of materialism, but you don't get more materialist than the US. Travelling round America, where people assume that you have a church of your own to belong to, wherever you come from, one senses that loneliness of the self in the vastness of the landscape. The individual feels small and diminished. Government is far away and only patriotism provides the old ties of ethnicity that form the sense of belonging that people take for granted in Europe.

I suspect that everyone needs to feel that there is something bigger than ourselves of which we are a part, whether it's Socialism or God or being a Serb.

Will Posh Spice's very own personal God, like a personal stereo, sustain her if the marriage to David Beckham doesn't work out as she expected? And if not, what will she turn to then? •

....

24 October 1998
Catherine Bennett
Changing Charlie

Lucky us. Deep down, the Prince of Wales is a gem. Just as the Albert Memorial, long misunderstood to be a useless pile of clapped-out kitsch, is now recognised to be a superb, exuberant flowering of the Victorian imagination, so Prince Charles, long considered to be a boring, whining nincompoop, has finally been acknowledged as a selfless, witty high-achiever, a doer of good works of the type we no longer have enough moral refinement to appreciate. If Charles does not, quite yet, deserve to be covered in two coats of 23-carat gold leaf and seated in state beneath a glittery canopy where he can dazzle all posterity, he does, his restorers insist, merit the respect and fond birthday wishes of his future subjects.

On 14 November the Prince will be 50 years old. His new, thrusting people's PR outfit has clearly been working overtime to ensure that everything is made of this great, reputation-repairing opportunity. Two newspapers have already featured protracted birthday tributes, swooning over the mind and body of the man who will, whether we like it or not, be king. In the *Mail*, Ann Leslie had been granted 'unprecedented access to the Prince's inner circle', and even to the Prince himself. She discovered a man who is 'misunderstood and deeply caring', 'extremely funny', 'very modest'. From Fatty Soames, Patty Palmer-What's-her-name – the usual suspects – she heard how he has performed 'countless acts of kindness to people in all walks of life' that no one will ever know about. All the same, he 'longs to be appreciated for all the pioneering – and often ridiculed – work he's done for inner-city youth, his initially lonely crusades against genetically modified foods and brutalist architecture . . .'

The *Telegraph*'s Graham Turner was also invited to Highgrove, where he discovered a gifted performer – 'Gielgud could not have done better' – of 'great physical courage', 'talented in all kinds of ways', who is also a 'superb host' and a 'fantastically good shoulder to cry on', with a surpassing gift for talking to black people. Turner does mention that the Prince is also renowned for his bad temper and bottomless self-pity – only to point out, in mitigation, that his life has been an 'epic of suffering, an epic of courage, an epic of duty'.

The Prince's hope, having shared his feelings with representatives of a press he is known to abominate, is that we should like him as a person. He is continuing a project he began in 1992, after Andrew Morton brought out *Diana:*

Her True Story. In a memo to the Queen's private secretary, Charles suggested cooperating with the media, instead of always snubbing it. 'I do hope we can make as much use as possible of television,' he wrote. 'As the medium which carries the greatest weight of authority with the public, it should be a real asset in countering tabloid excesses.'

As good as his word, the Prince decided to collaborate with Jonathan Dimbleby on a 600-page biography and a television documentary. If, for many people, Charles's name summons up a picture of a great inarticulate, petulant child, it is largely thanks to these elephantine attempts to ingratiate himself. How do we know, for sure, that the Prince, at an age when most people have invoked a personal statute of limitations on family grievances, still blames his parents for his troubles? Because he told us. How do we know he's a world-class whinger? From that bit in the film when he tried to wriggle out of some minor royal duty. That he married Diana for cold, dynastic purposes? He admits it. And this emerged in a book by his own creature. A creature who humbly suggests that 'future generations will judge that in the latter half of the twentieth century Britain was blessed to have as heir to the throne an individual of singular distinction'. Though Dimbleby was clearly prince-struck, a similar conclusion from normally reliable writers is enough to make one pause. The latest charm offensive almost works. Maybe he really is misunderstood. Maybe, on reflection, he's not such a bad sort. And that Prince's Trust does awfully good things.

But so what? If you're against the royals, the main objection is the same as towards hereditary peers – that they inherit office no matter what they're like. It's nice, of course, if Charles is courteous to old ladies – but he'd still become king if he beat them off with an umbrella. The Prince's Trust is not going to convert any republicans. Equally, monarchists defend the institution on principle, not on the quality of passing personalities. They know that for every Prince Albert, there is a Philip, or an Anne, or an Edward, or a Sarah . . .

Will Charles never learn to keep his mouth shut? He doesn't need to read all the Bagehoty bores about daylight and magic simply to observe his mother. She has, as everyone suspected, and Woodrow Wyatt's diaries more or less confirm, never said an interesting word in her life. She is not particularly nice, or particularly nasty. She's just the Queen, and most people seem to prefer that to her anguished, crowd-pleasing son.

Perhaps Charles feels threatened by the recent Demos proposal that succession to the throne should be a beauty contest, decided by the electorate, not by blood. Right now, with the *Mail* and *Telegraph* behind him, he might just win. But what happens when he tries to marry Camilla? Or decides, fatally, 'to make as much use of television as possible'. ●

11 January 1999

Sabine Durrant

Frances Partridge looks back on a century of art, gossip and loss

The last surviving member of the Bloomsbury Group lives in a flat in a quiet street in Belgravia. Here, among such signals of advanced age as a giant magnifying glass on wheels and a surfeit of carefully placed side-lights, is a mini-shrine to a movement dedicated, among other things, to 'the enjoyment of beautiful objects'. The windows are huge, the walls are pink, the bookshelves (Byron, Virginia Woolf's *Letters*, *A Guide to the Flowering Plants of Great Britain*) pale green. There is a mosaic of a cat in the fireplace and paintings by Vanessa Bell, Duncan Grant and Dora Carrington, including her famous portrait of Lytton Strachey. And there is Strachey's furniture: an armoire (now stuffed with diaries and letters), a chest of drawers (appropriated for personal items) and his favourite wing-backed armchair. 'He would sit like this,' said the Oldest Member, throwing her arms up so that her hands clasped the wings in a gesture between insecurity and abandonment. 'Isn't the light nice here? The sunlight comes in until lunch time. And all the books shine up. I've just had the leather ones cleaned. I don't know why Lytton sat like this. Perhaps he was showing off his hands. Perhaps he didn't know what to do with them. They were so very extraordinarily long.'

Frances Partridge was born a Victorian, in March 1900. Her father, an architect who played in the first final at Wimbledon, knew Darwin. Her mother was a suffragette. Partridge, then Marshall, went to Cambridge, before getting a job at the bookshop owned by the writer David Garnett, a lover of Duncan Grant. Garnett married Frances's sister Ray, and then later Angelica Bell, supposedly the daughter of Vanessa and Clive Bell, but actually of Vanessa and Garnett's former lover, Grant. The daughter of Garnett and Angelica was later to marry Burgo, the son of Frances. Already committed to Bloomsbury tenets such as atheism, socialism, pacifism and rationalism, Frances was soon to be tangled up in the social and romantic intricacies that were the true passport to the clique. She became a Bloomsberry.

There were dinner invitations from Woolf: 'a formal little letter: "Dear Miss Marshall" . . . I went with hands trembling.' And heart-to-hearts with E.M. Forster: 'very gentle and friendly and homosexual. Had a laugh like a sneeze, a sort of neigh.' And parties thrown by Maynard Keynes: 'It doesn't make sense to say he was a homosexual. He adored his wife. He was bisexual.' And weekends at Charleston with Vanessa Bell and Clive Bell, her husband, and Duncan Grant,

Eamonn McCabe

Frances Partridge, last of the Bloomsbury set

her lover: 'I wasn't socially confident at first. But I do remember saying these are the people I want to spend my life with, these are the people I want to know.'

And so to Ham Spray, the Wiltshire farmhouse, the scene of a second Bloomsbury ménage. Strachey was living here with Carrington and her husband Ralph Partridge, a vaguely literary figure, in a strangulated triangle – Carrington loved Strachey, who loved Partridge, who loved Carrington – when Frances turned up. 'I was a spanner in the works.' Before Strachey's death in 1932 and Carrington's suicide soon after, Ralph left and set up home with Frances in a London flat. They were asleep together when the gardener rang to tell them that Carrington had shot herself. Later, Ralph and Frances married.

Was Strachey jealous of their relationship? 'No. He was realistic. I'm an accepted fact. He was a civilised man. Though I had this famous interview with him, when he threatened to leave Carrington if I took Ralph from him.' And Carrington? Quentin Bell once said her Sapphic interest in Frances softened the blow. 'Well . . .' mused Partridge. 'I think she had leanings that way, but I didn't. I preferred male company when I was young, but we got on perfectly well. She wasn't like anyone else. You couldn't describe her. She describes herself in her letters, which are awfully good. She was very funny . . . one seems to want funniness in this dreary life.'

She had moved chairs – 'my legs are not very long' – and was perched in the corner of a threadbare green sofa, a glass of Evian trembling between bruised hands ('it does make a difference, doesn't it, water?'), but otherwise, in tartan trousers, pink shirt and a red silk scarf, as striking to look at at the end of her life as at the beginning. Elements in her looks have become accentuated by age: the strong lower jaw, the brown beady eyes, and the wrinkles like a crumpled piece of paper which someone has tried to stretch out. She is a Navajo Indian chief, in a diamanté brooch. She lives on her own, with the help of 'my dear Vera' who comes in at 10 a.m. and does her cooking and shopping. 'I used to cook, you know how people of my sort did mostly cook oneself, but I got rather hysterical. I set fire to a frying pan . . . On the whole I invite people to tea or drinks.' She goes for a walk every day, unless it's wet or windy: 'I've been blown over a few times.' Her sight is still fine (though she says her eyes seem to crave more and more light) and her hearing tiptop. Only her voice, she says, has gone. 'I used to talk at a screech, but it breaks up as you get older. And I have done rather a lot of talking over Christmas.' She has done a lot of talking over the last 100 years. She has published six volumes of diaries, from the servant problems of her 'pacifist's war', through the loss of her husband in 1960 and her only son Burgo in 1963, to the comfort of friends in the early 1990s. There is much about life and death in them, of art, love and suffering, and gossip. One extract of 1945 reads: 'To lunch with Clive Bell at the Ivy: conversation fast and furious . . . About what did we talk? I hardly remember. Politics, Flaubert, Anthony and Kitty West.' At Ham Spray, where she lived with Ralph until his death, they instituted the Charleston regime of spending the morning independently, 'otherwise the constant talk would finish us off'. She and Ralph 'had lots to say to each other'.

As she perched on her sofa, with the morning sunlight slowly disappearing over the rooftops, her voice one minute strong, the next a birdlike croak, her conversation followed a similar pattern. There were general musings about life: 'It's the relation of one generation to another that's always changing. The young are very nice to one. I expect to be seated by the samovar like in a Tolstoy novel, but they treat one like an equal.' And she dipped her toe (clad in smart leather slippers) into politics: 'Unlike my friends, many of whom have got more right wing with age, I'm still a socialist, but I think politics is a murky business. I followed New Labour at the election, but I was fed up by the way they didn't carry out things and when they asked for money as usual, I wrote: 'Please note that I am no longer a member of the Labour Party', but they paid no attention.' When she talks about people, she sometimes seems to forget who's alive, who's dead. Cyril Connolly, she once wrote, looks like a china pug on a mantelpiece. 'Yes, it's true. He does.' Did she agree that Virginia Woolf wasn't very nice to women? 'Oh, you thought she wasn't?' Partridge replied, with cocktail party tact. 'I thought she didn't much like girls. I was a girl when I got to know her and she didn't like girls to be educated. I was pretty well read, too much her world. Virginia liked to make a picture.' Leonard, who 'rowed horribly' with Ralph when they worked together at Hogarth Press, 'was a dear'.

'Everyone is dead now,' she said suddenly. Her mother died 'some time in the 70s. Or was it when she was in her seventies?' Her five siblings? 'They all came rather in a rush.' Her granddaughter, Sophie and her great-granddaughters want her to see out the millennium: 'Everyone wants me to get the Queen's telegram, but I don't care a button whether I do.'

She still feels the sharpness of the death of her husband and son. 'Very much so. I feel more lonely,' she said. 'I don't like life as an old person. But I don't groan when I wake up. I still enjoy the stuff that life is made of. I love nature, the countryside. I enjoyed both my Christmas holidays.' She divided the time between her granddaughter in Devon and Patrick Leigh Fermor's house in the Cotswolds. 'And at New Year we had a very nice lunch at Cyril Connolly's married daughter's. Cressida. Husband was called Charles. I can't remember the surname. Awfully nice people.' She had said her voice would last an hour, but she still insisted after that on giving a guided tour of her bedroom, where we gazed on a Vanessa Bell still life and a frosty Carrington landscape of the view from Ham Spray. A picture of a New York skyline caught her eye.

'That,' she said, 'was painted by Angelica (Bell). It's the result of a curious episode when she went to America and had a passing affair – which nearly broke up her marriage to Bunny (David Garnett) – with a painter, whom Duncan Grant had once been in love with. And Duncan was her father . . .' And the last Bloomsberry gazed into the middle distance with a half smile on her face. ●

17 April 1999

Letters

Larry Adler kicks Pinter's ass

I wouldn't try to match my use of English against Harold Pinter ('Letters', 8 April). But when it comes to American, I can teach him something. 'Kiss my arse or I'll kick your head in' – no 'damyankee' ever says 'arse'. Hasn't Pinter ever heard one of John McEnroe's tirades: 'Why don't you just kiss my ass?' Can you imagine McEnroe or, for that matter, me using 'arse'?

Larry Adler
London ●

11 August 1999

Roger McGough

Everyday eclipses

The hamburger flipped across the face of the bun
The frisbee winning the race against its own shadow
The cricket ball dropping for six in front of the church clock
On a golden plate, a host of communion wafers
The brown contact lens sliding across the blue iris
The palming of small change
Everyday eclipses

Out of the frying pan, the tossed pancake orbits the Chinese lampshade
The water bucket echoing into the *well, well, well*
The lifebelt spinning past the open porthole
The black, snookering the cue ball against the green baize
The winning putt on the eighteenth
The tiddlywink twinking toward the tiddly cup
Everyday eclipses

Neck and neck in the hot air balloon race
Holding up her sign, the lollipop lady blots out the belisha beacon
The foaming tankard thumped on to the beer mat
The plug into the plughole
Two thin slices; first salami, then mortadella
In the fruit bowl, the orange rolls in front of the peach.
Everyday eclipses another day

Goodbye bald patch, hello yarmulke
A sombrero tossed into the bullring
Leading the parade, the big bass drum,
We hear cymbals but cannot see them
One eclipse eclipses another eclipse
To the cold, white face, the oxygen mask.
But too late

One death eclipses another death
The baby's head, the mother's breast
The open O of the mouth seeking the warm O of the nipple
One birth eclipses another birth
Everyday eclipses.

Tom Jenkins

Uncle Cricket, the fanatical Pakistan fan, with his fellow supporters at the Pakistan vs. New Zealand World Cup semifinal

Sporting moments

14 December 1998

Matthew Engel

Self-respect gone to Ashes

Just after lunch yesterday, there was a loud whoop and then a groan from a group of Australians gathered round the TV at the back of the Adelaide Oval media lounge. At last something had gone wrong for them: Fizzi Lizzi had got caught on the line and short-headed out of first place in the two o'clock. Shortly afterwards, one of Australia's best-known cricket writers emerged from the same corner and said excitedly: 'Did you see that putt?'

Meanwhile, out in the middle, Australia were in the process of ensuring that they will retain the Ashes into the next millennium. But they had stopped worrying about that. This is a new development. In a country where victory usually has 15 million parents and defeat is always an orphan, another win over England is ceasing to be a matter of import. Even the Aussies are getting fed up with this.

On a mild, overcast Sunday morning England lost seven wickets in 70 minutes and their vestiges of self-respect.

Since the day also contained revelations casting doubt on the validity of England's one-day triumph in Sharjah last winter – regarded at the time as a blazing new dawn – it was about as bad a day as the country's cricketers have ever experienced. Which is saying something.

Sir Donald Bradman, aged 90, now refuses to leave his home in the suburbs even for Adelaide test matches. But the sage has been telling worshippers who come to kneel before him that England's trouble is that their batsmen refuse to dominate the bowlers.

England are about to fail for the sixth successive Ashes series, partly because Australia just happen to have a far more skilful generation of cricketers. No amount of tinkering with personnel, management, pitches or the structure of county cricket will change that.

The gap had started to narrow because – after several years of managerial incompetence – England started to make the most of the resources they did have. Now it is starting to widen again. And the key seems to be that they are losing any sense of self-belief.

The team is constantly being told how rotten it is. Newspapers, English and Australian, shout it in banner headlines. The crowd shout it from the boundary. 'Hey, Al,' someone called to the Aussie-bred Alan Mullally, 'you must feel pretty stupid turning into a Pom.'

Lord MacLaurin, chairman of the England and Wales Cricket Board, has himself become one of the worst offenders in his public pronouncements.

If you think you're going to get out, you get out. If you think you're going to drop a catch, you drop it. If a spin bowler doesn't really believe he can turn the ball, how is he going to get the batsman worried?

It was a rotten performance all round: even Nasser Hussain, the batting star, was negligent in failing to protect the tail. England have been competitive in this series for days at a time, but then everything goes wrong at once. Horribly wrong.

Their best efforts in the series have come in moments of counter-attacking exuberance. And – with hindsight – the decision to play Dean Headley ahead of Alex Tudor here now seems over-conservative, which is what the Aussies thought at the time.

It remains true that England have had no luck whatever. As predicted, the weather cooled down as soon as they were about to finish in the field. And marginal decisions have gone against them, shamefully so in a couple of cases.

Australia has an umpiring crisis just as England is in crisis in just about every other aspect of the game. Steve Davis, in his second test, gave Mark Butcher and Headley no benefit of the doubt whatever. And third umpire, Paul Angley – who has only ever stood in two first-class matches – gave his only decision, against Michael Atherton, in what was probably blind panic.

Steve Bucknor, the master of the slow death, has taken more time over some of his decisions on the field than Angley took looking at the TV replay of Mark Taylor's slip catch.

Of Australia's two top umpires, Steve Randell is suspended while under indictment for alleged sexual offences, and Darrell Hair has had to pull out of the forthcoming matches with Sri Lanka because of his views on Muralitharan's bowling actions. Below them the standard seems very poor.

Maybe England should do what players do when middle age kicks in: retire from the battle and concentrate on what they do best. We should become a nation of umpires, benignly supervising a game everyone else now plays much better than us. ●

· ·

6 March 1999

Mark Lawson
Blind prejudice

As if in some great ethical census, the public has been asked in the last fortnight to examine its levels of prejudice. Sir William Macpherson, examining the killing of Stephen Lawrence, suggested that we test ourselves for unwitting racisms. This week, we learned that an England footballer – Graeme Le Saux – is suffering abuse because of a belief that he is homosexual.

The player is not gay but made the mistake of reading books, visiting the theatre and collecting antiques. The *Daily Mail* suggested, in what seemed intended as a compliment to both sides, that he was the only footballer who could be envisaged appearing on the BBC2's *Late Review*.

Two comments have been widely made about the Le Saux business. The first is that football – a profession in which men are expected to share showers and a trophy blonde is as vital an accessory as a fast car – is the last bastion of homophobia in society. The second, which has been attributed to Le Saux, is that if players made equivalent racist remarks, they wouldn't get away with it.

Both of these assumptions are worth exploring. The discussion of relative prejudices is rather like that game in which you have to choose which of the senses you would lose: blind or deaf, insensate or tasteless? In either case, the best choice would be not to have to make one. But, though it could never approach the gravity of the Stephen Lawrence case – the Le Saux incident usefully encourages people to take measure of their attitudes.

Although racism is often based on a suspicion of strength (particularly, when aimed at black men, of sexual strength) and homophobia is frequently rooted in an assumption of weakness (effeminacy), both result from distrust of a change in the national make-up. The blacks will take our jobs, the bigots think, the gays will take our sons. Parents worry that, in schools, a minority culture will be promoted at the expense of a majority one: I don't want him celebrating Diwali/ I don't want her reading Janet and Janet books.

The mechanics of prejudice clearly differ. While a black person may be psychologically in denial about their colour (several celebrities in Britain and America have been accused of this), they cannot convincingly adopt a physical disguise. There can be no skin equivalent of the 'beard' marriage or insistence to the press that your sexuality is a private matter. To risk personalising this, in Hollywood Denzel Washington has never had the Jodie Foster option.

But, even without considering the consequences of being required to deny in public a significant part of your nature, the comparison becomes complicated here. Because homosexuality can be invisible – for the older gay generation, had to be on pain of jail – it is easier for homophobia to be opaque. Even racist people are now relatively careful around other races, whatever the graffiti they secrete in their minds. But the employee who is gay but not known to be must endure the George Michael gags and turkey-basting baby jokes which are still unthinkingly delivered in most offices with the assumption of a consensus.

Sometimes, it is true, this invisibility might be an advantage. There has been much liberal self-congratulation about the fact that four admitted or assumed homosexuals have reached Blair Cabinets. In contrast, there is hand-wringing over the fact that all Cabinet ministers are white. But only one of those politicians was known to be gay at the time they were elected. Racists on constituency selection committees can effect their prejudices through a simple glance as the applicant arrives. The homophobe on the same committee always runs a risk of being surprised in the future.

None of this, written by a double-outsider, is to suggest that either form of prejudice is lesser than the other and certainly not that non-whites in Britain have it easy. What interests me is the double-standard to which Le Saux referred. It even, for example, frequently operates in the media world, a place where, in the popular stereotype, homosexuality is not just tolerated but virtually obligatory. When contributors are discussed, there are tolerated codes (and I have used them myself before a dark afternoon of the soul in a meeting a few years ago) such as, 'I always feel that X has a bit of an agenda' or 'Doesn't Y have an odd manner?' (sometimes, explicitly, 'a bit camp') or, even, 'What was he wearing?' Similar innuendo aimed at the race of a participant would invite a tribunal.

Audience reaction is similarly steered towards two different in-trays. It seems to be generally accepted within the BBC that letters from viewers or listeners which object to the use of black contributors or the discussion of black issues may be thrown away unanswered or, in extreme cases, passed to the police. This is an unchallenged (and, in my view, correct) position. Yet, in contrast, letters which express outrage at the presence of gay people or subjects must be agonised over and answered. Might the discussion not have benefited from the presence of someone who was opposed to homosexuality? Should the presenter not have at least acknowledged that some feel these activities should not be presented on the screen at all? These questions will eventually be answered in the negative, but the fact that they are even raised reveals the surprisingly durable residue of homosexuality's illegality and the Thatcher government's move against promotion of homosexuality by local government in the 1980s.

The BBC is not homophobic but suffers tremors over same-sex relationships which are surprising in a broadly liberal institution and challenges the widespread view that football is, in the matter of tolerance, some little Jurassic bit of England. Without even starting on the army and the police, there is the entertainment industry in which it is still frequently thought to be wiser to keep quiet, despite the prosperity of the careers of Sir Ian McKellen, Sir Nigel Hawthorne and Anthony Sher. Even in America — where, according to the British right-wing press, a gay lobby is more or less in control of culture — Sir Ian will attend the Oscars as the only male movie star who admits to being gay. There will be many black actors taking a rightful pride in who they are.

The late Justin Fashanu — who committed suicide last year after a career in which he had the misfortune to attract two kinds of bigotry — was eventually accepted in the game for being black but never for being gay. Football has been presented this week as being the one weak link in an ever-lengthening chain of tolerance. Perhaps, though, the game's double-standard on the permissibility of bigotry is on a level with other playing fields. ●

··

14 July 1999

Jonathan Freedland

Move over, lads. Soccer is kicking feminism into a whole new league

Few things appear to unite Bill and Hillary Clinton these days, but this week there came one. Husband and wife were brought together by their shared desire to meet 11 fit and beautiful young women. President and First Lady alike were desperate to meet Mia, touch Brandi and chat up Cindy. They wanted to be linked to the newest, hottest, sisterhood in American life: the women who won the World Cup.

For America's women have done what the men never could; they have made their country fall in love with soccer. By winning the Women's World Cup final on Sunday – an event all but ignored in Britain but which became a countrywide obsession over there – the US national team has brought football in from America's sporting cold.

In the process, they have made stars of themselves and given soccer its best chance of winning over a nation hitherto immune to the soccer bug. But Americans insist they have done something more; they have won a victory in the battle for sexual equality, one whose impact will be felt for decades.

Such talk may seem hyperbolic, but something extraordinary did seem to happen at this tournament. Anyone travelling across the US these past two weeks, as I did, couldn't fail to notice the attention lavished on the cup, generating a buzz unprecedented for an all-female contest.

Sunday's final was played before a Rosebowl crowd of more than 90,000 – the largest audience for a women's sporting event anywhere, ever. The tournament opener, at Giants' Stadium in New Jersey, pulled in 80,000 – the largest gate since the Pope came to town.

The footballing women have been on the front pages of America's leading papers, cheered along as they racked up wins against Germany, Brazil and finally China.

Big league sponsors gave the event a helpful kick. Nike, Adidas and traditionally male products like Chevrolet cars and Budweiser beer, ran TV ads showing off the team, while little girls painted their faces in the red, white and blue of the national team. In a reference to baseball's greatest team, the 11 were hailed as the Girls of Summer.

How did this happen? Even football-mad countries – such as Britain – have little time for the women's game. Yet America has next to no soccer culture.

The World Cup of 1994, hosted in the US, barely registered. How did the women of '99 turn that around?

Part of the answer lies in America's fondness for winners. Team USA never lost. Glamour played a part too. The media fell for the photogenic, ponytailed stars – taking a particular liking to captain Mia Hamm, goalie Briana Scurry and defender Brandi Chastain, who celebrated her match-winning penalty on Sunday by whipping her top off.

But the deeper fact is that football – the ultimate laddish activity in Britain – has been reinvented as a women's game in America. Pollsters talk of 'soccer moms', the suburban, thirty-somethings who ferry their daughters to football practice and enjoy a kick-around among themselves. The soccer mums say they like the teamwork essential to football, a welcome contrast to the pressure on individual performance inherent in more traditional women's sports like tennis or gymnastics.

But that's not the only reason why 7.5 million American girls are registered in soccer leagues and why most weekend parks in the country include a mixed-sex game of footie. America's culture of equal rights has been a factor too. A 1972 law, Title IX, requires all government-funded schools to spend as much on girls' sport as boys'. While women's football here has been starved of cash – ensuring that no British teams made it to this summer's tournament – the American game has been nurtured.

The result is a hat trick for American women, with the first goal the victory on Sunday. The second is a remaking of the American ideal of female beauty, now expanded to include strength and athleticism. Gone is the dyke-like stereotype of sportswomen past, replaced by an ideal which sees no contradiction between muscle and femininity. Hence the role for Team USA in TV ads for Always tampons and the birth of – wait for it – Soccer Barbie.

One American paper caught the mood with a perfect cartoon of a football crowd. 'You play like a girl!' screams one banner, while a bemused male onlooker mumbles to his buddy: 'Remember when that was an insult?'

The final winner for America's women is the three-week long showcase the World Cup has offered for female success. One commentator suggests that the first woman US president will cite the victory of 1999 as the moment that inspired her. If that's true, it is no wonder America's women are feeling over the moon, Brian. Make that Briana. ●

· ·

5 July 1999

Frank Keating
High as the sky

H istory was up for grabs on a blustery, pewtery midsummer afternoon in London yesterday and the American champion Pete Sampras reached up and grabbed it by playing one of the most mercilessly ravishing and faultless Wimbledon finals in anyone's memory.

It was a momentous Wimbledon day and, if the audacious Sampras italicised it for posterity with his blazing three-set win against his compatriot Andre Agassi, so earlier did Steffi Graf, seven times women's champion here, who announced her retirement from Wimbledon after her two-sets defeat by another American, Lindsay Davenport. She will continue playing on the Tour but may well retire this year.

For the Americans, all is as high as the sky on the Fourth of July. Agassi may have been overwhelmed but he was generous to a fault: 'Pete played probably the perfect match. His was impeccable tennis. I ran into a buzzsaw. I maintained focus and intensity, I had some chances, but there was simply nothing I could do to stop him.'

Sampras is as modest and gallant as any champion has ever been, but he also shook his head in disbelief, as if he had been on a plane outside himself or up with us in the press box watching his other self in action. 'I truly don't know how I do it, to be honest with you, I really don't. I'm still in a spin, my mind's still racing, because I was detached from myself out there and I was on fire. I was in a zone on a different level. It must have been as well as I can play, but quite why it happened today, I'm like you, none the wiser.'

A quarter of a century ago they began to write off Björn Borg's five successive titles as 'boring'. Same now with Sampras's six in seven years. Boring?

When his impregnable Liverpool football side was labelled boring, Bill Shankly used to beam and say: 'Laddie, that was the general idea. I want us to be as boring as the great Joe Louis' – the unbeaten world heavyweight champion for a dozen years and Shankly's hero.

Only the Wimbledon greybeard William Renshaw elbows Sampras off the topmost plinth in the pantheon – from 1881 to 1889 he collected seven titles – but those were different days, and last night the whole litany of saints would have been acclaiming Sampras as almost certainly the best ever to perform on their ancient patch: Doherty, Tilden, Budge, Hoad and Laver, McEnroe and Becker, all lined up to give best . . .

The utter operatic nervelessness of Sampras's show yesterday can be collected in miniature with his stroke for game, set, match, championship. It was 40–30. He netted his first service. Agassi settled himself once again beyond the distant baseline. Sampras pulled the second ball from his pocket, bounced it once, twice, then swayed and coiled into his unadorned service action.

Crack! Straight down the centre line, millimetre perfect at 120 m.p.h. An ace! With his second serve. Wow! Has a Wimbledon championship ever been won before with an ace on a second serve? Sampras tried to describe it: 'All of a sudden I realised the whole title was on my racket. One shot for the title. I missed the first serve. You breathe heavier then. I suppose I kind of went for it, no rhyme or reason. It was a great shot and, yep, I surprised myself by doing it, I suppose. But by then it's about instinct.'

It was probably the most savage, complete and wonderful Wimbledon win in a final of all time. It was by no means a capitulation by the loser, or a surrender. Agassi was bold and brave, always thinking, always highly skilful. 'Pete came at me in storms, and one after the other they just blew me away.'

It had, anyway, been a special Wimbledon. Record crowds, and the weather compressed the second week's programme but helped, in so doing, to make Saturday and yesterday so terrifically rich with delight and challenge.

Yesterday was also garlanded by all the finals being so chivalrously won and graciously lost. And Davenport's day was made complete when she added the doubles title in the gloaming. She's a big-hitting sports girl, with a bonny smile and nature.

'An American Hunter-Dunn,' said someone, quoting Betjeman. More an all-American long-legged smiler whom Gatsby would have been delighted to invite to one of his garden parties. The unbounded joy of her victory began to seep in after the buzz went around that Graf would play no more at Wimbledon.

The German was the out-and-out tennis athlete until injuries in recent years restricted her mobility, but this year her innate tennis nous gave her a famous victory in Paris and allowed her to come here confident of dictating most affairs magisterially from the back court.

She was found out at the very last. The American pretender boldly leapt at the favourite, her strong and accurate serving first ensnaring the German and then caging her. By the game, sometimes it seemed by the point, Davenport was looking stronger, more daring, more believing of herself as Graf pouted. Most importantly, she stopped Graf running round her backhand to set up the famous rifle-shot forehand.

Graf kissed the American on both cheeks. She did not even wave goodbye to the Wimbledon throng as they farewelled her to the echo. 'I didn't want them to think I was trying to take anything away from Lindsay. It was her day.' ●

....

31 May 1999

Mike Selvey

Goodbye to all that

It was all done and dusted shortly after one o'clock yesterday afternoon. A match that England had to win if their own bash was not to continue without them was brought to the most emphatic of conclusions when India's ace pace bowler Javagal Srinath caused the stumps of England's last man, Alan Mullally, to erupt from the Edgbaston turf as if they had been dynamited. The lone stick left standing as the ground was engulfed by whooping, hollering Indian fans seemed a fitting epitaph to a World Cup campaign that promised much and delivered precious little. Cue the Seekers: for Alec Stewart and his men the carnival was well and truly over.

The outfield became a sea of orange, white and green flags (and, incongruously, one stars and stripes) with not a cross of St George to be seen. In the England dressing room, the mood, according to the England coach, David Lloyd, was sombre, one of desolation. Tears were shed unashamedly; not Paltrow tears, but genuine ones of frustration, deep disappointment and the knowledge that when the biggest questions had been asked during the past fortnight the team had been unable to provide even the semblance of an answer.

Zimbabwe had thrown the most gigantic of spanners into the World Cup works with their fine win over South Africa (in whose interest it was, incidentally, that England rather than their next-door neighbours qualified) and, had they not done so, England would still have snuck through even with a defeat yesterday.

But the hard fact is that, in two successive World Cups, England have beaten only the United Arab Emirates, Holland, Kenya, Zimbabwe and Sri Lanka. Meanwhile, they have lost to South Africa twice, Pakistan, India, New Zealand and a rampant Sri Lankan side en route to their 1996 triumph.

When the going gets tough, England, it seems, barely turn the engine over. In this competition they progressed no further than Scotland.

This is the saddest of endings for Lloyd's three-year tenure and tears would have been shed for the man who has done his utmost to ensure that England teams of the modern era never take the field without the best possible preparation. He has brought innovation and organisation, together with limitless enthusiasm and optimism, to a previously inept system and can leave his post satisfied that the infrastructure, anyway, is in a vastly better state than when he took over. The players have no excuses other than their own shortcomings.

Lloyd will go with the team to Buckingham Palace on Wednesday to fulfil an official tournament function and then he will pick up his new career in television and pen his memoirs, while the team will disperse to their counties to ponder and dream of what might have been.

England's departure has blown out of the water the ambitions of this country's governing bodies to use the competition, staged on its home turf, as a magnet to attract the nation's youth to the game. When Radio 5 Live, as it did on Saturday evening, can judge Scunthorpe's win over Leyton Orient in the Third Division play-offs to be of more significance than that of Zimbabwe over South Africa, with all its implications, then the game really is up against it.

A strong run in this tournament was fundamental to the perception of England as a global force in the game and therefore as an attraction for the players of tomorrow. Now they will not get the chance to contest the World Cup on these shores for at least another two decades. The shop window has fallen victim to a ram-raid.

David Graveney attempted damage-limitation yesterday, saying that the chance to watch any world-class players should inspire youngsters to take up the game. But in reality he knows that the only kids who will draw succour and inspiration from the rest of the tournament will be those from India, Pakistan, South Africa, Zimbabwe and the rest of the qualifiers. And England will fall further behind.

For Stewart, it will almost certainly prove to be the end of the line for both his captaincy and, in one-day cricket, his playing ambitions. He wanted this tournament desperately, but his leathery features as he faced the media yesterday afternoon were pained with the realisation that his side were just not good enough. The captain, and for that matter the likes of Graeme Hick, Angus Fraser, Neil Fairbrother and others, will surely not be part of the plans four years hence and the break should be swift and clean now. It is time to move on.

The dust would need to settle before decisions are made, Graveney said, but he knows that the planning for South Africa in four years' time must begin now, not least with scheduling that will allow England to play as many matches in as many different conditions as possible. To the purists this may be anathema, but experience is all. Sachin Tendulkar, for example, was in his seventy-ninth one-day international match before he managed the first of his 22 centuries, more games than any of the England squad bar Stewart and Hick have played in total. Mohammed Azharuddin has spent 10½ months of his relatively young life playing his 320 limited-over internationals and eight of India's team in this match have more than 100 games to their name. It is little wonder that they are better.

Although the hosts have been eliminated, the tournament will continue to gain momentum. Though interest from England supporters may wane, there is scant evidence that there was a great deal there in the first place. Other supporters have provided what carnival feel there has been. Few England fans bothered to make the trip to Edgbaston yesterday to take up the seats to which their tickets entitled them, but the switchboard had been deluged with Indians wanting to buy tickets for the day. The place would have been full had they been allowed in, just as all the grounds will be throughout the rest of this tournament.

Today in Northampton, for example, Pakistan play Bangladesh in their final group match on an occasion the like of which has never before been seen at Wantage Road. And hang on to your hats when Pakistan and India meet in their Super Six match at Old Trafford on 8 June.

Ticket sales, as the tournament marketeers have been so keen to tell us, have been enormous, with not only group matches sold out but the second phase of the tournament as well. Any tickets that have remained unsold will be snapped up well before the first of the nine matches begins on Friday at the Oval, where India will probably play Australia. The following day Trent Bridge sees what many will regard as a dress rehearsal for the final when the South African machine comes up against Pakistan's flair. There is some stuff to be played yet. Gone England may be, but the party is only just warming up. ●

. . . .

16 April 1999

Martin Thorpe

Is this the greatest goal of all time?

It started in his own half and finished up in folklore. Ryan Giggs dazzled a defence and then a nation with Manchester United's winning goal at Villa Park on Wednesday night, capping an evening of spinning emotions with a whirling-shirt celebration which revealed not only one of the hairiest chests in football but the footballing heart that beats beneath it.

There is already talk of this being one of the greatest goals of all time. The yardsticks have been measured: Ricky Villa at Wembley in '81, John Barnes in the Maracaná in '84, Maradona against England in '86, even David Ginola against Barnsley in the previous round of this season's FA Cup.

But subjectivity plays such a large part in these comparisons. One could say that the run of the ball helped Villa, that Barnes's goal came in a friendly, that the memory of his first strike soured the glory of Maradona's second, and that Ginola waltzed through a First Division defence.

In that context Giggs, refreshed after coming off the bench, settled this semifinal replay by beating a tiring defence. But that would be nit-picking. In terms of skill and context his was a goal in a millennium.

Skill first. The key was speed. From the moment he picked up the ball 10 yards inside United's half to the moment he unleashed a shot high into the Arsenal net, Giggs ran 61.5 yards in 10 seconds. Not bad for someone with the ball at his feet and various Arsenal players at his elbows.

The move starts innocuously enough. Three minutes into the second period of extra time, with the score locked at 1–1, Giggs gathers the ball in the inside-left channel and begins an unbroken sprint that will ultimately take him deep into the Arsenal area. Ahead of him he spots four sentries in scarlet, but his pace will prove decisive, for it will keep the quartet on the back foot, constantly trying to assess the right time to tackle this weaving, speeding foe and never certain enough of their judgement to act.

Giggs reaches the halfway line and two things happen. Patrick Vieira comes across to challenge but Giggs jinks left to avoid the half-hearted lunge of a player who has learned the penalty of impetuous tackles. Also, Dwight Yorke starts a diversionary run from the middle of the pitch to the left wing. This will prove crucial.

Now the Welshman is in Arsenal territory and, next, Lee Dixon comes across to confront the threat. Instinctively Giggs feints right and goes left, wrong-footing the full-back, who seems to console himself with the thought that, anyway, there are covering players behind. It proves a false reassurance.

Giggs approaches Martin Keown, and this is where Yorke's positioning comes into play. It catches the England defender in two minds whether to cover a possible pass to the Tobagan striker out wide or to challenge Giggs's continuing run down that inside-left channel. Taking full advantage, the United winger cuts right to leave Keown off balance and capable only of hanging out a hopeful leg.

As Giggs skips by, Dixon reappears to his right. Now, though, Giggs is inside the area and the full-back, wary of conceding a penalty, risks only a soft shoulder-charge. Unconcerned, Giggs employs his right foot for the first time in this merry dance to push the ball forward. It rolls to the left of the box six yards out, and without breaking stride the 25-year-old fires for goal. With Tony Adams attempting a late, desperate covering tackle, the shot could, of course, have flown way over the bar and sullied perfection. But with an impeccable sense of occasion, Giggs's left foot propels United's winner into the top of the net.

David Seaman would have done better had he stood up longer. But Arsenal were too stunned to care, United too elated. Now Newcastle await in the final.

That was the skill. So what of the context? This was the second high-pressured semifinal these heavyweights had slugged out toe to toe in four days and going into extra time with the scores level the tension was mounting. Two goals already, another disallowed, a sending-off, a missed penalty. It needed a dauntless heart to break the deadlock. Enter Giggs.

Let us also not forget that this was not just any old defence but the much-lauded Dad's Army of Arsenal, the most parsimonious rearguard in the Premiership, with only 13 goals conceded in 32 games and none in their previous seven in all competitions. But though age has not withered them, Giggs's run certainly did.

And the upshot of his moment of magic? Universal applause and another ankle injury that leaves him doubtful for next week's more important semifinal in Turin. Given United's yearning to lift the European Cup, it might have been sensible for Ferguson and his aides to leave Giggs on the bench on Wednesday. Thank goodness they did not. •

....

13 March 1999

David Lacey
The cult of villainy

It is safe to assume that the passing of Joe DiMaggio attracted more coverage in the British media than did the retirement of Vinnie Jones in the American press. Yet just as the end of DiMaggio's baseball career left a void in the game he had graced with such distinction, so may football regard the absence of Jones as a vacancy which will be filled only with the utmost difficulty.

Heroes need villains and this applies as much to sport as it does to films or the theatre. In fact, so successful has Jones been in developing a cult of villainy that his transition from pitch to screen has been relatively seamless.

The acclaim which greeted his performance as a debt collector in the film *Lock, Stock and Two Smoking Barrels* has helped persuade Jones to give up playing at 34, after more than 12 years in the game, in order to concentrate on acting. One film critic described him as 'appealingly whimsical', which was not a thought that sprang to the minds of those he tackled.

Altogether Jones was sent off 13 times, yet he was never just another ill-disciplined footballer. There was always more to Vinnie than, say, the much-dismissed Mark Dennis or the now-reformed Julian Dicks.

While Jones did not exactly trade on his rough reputation, he did not pass up opportunities to profit from it. In 1992 this brought him a £20,000 fine and a suspended six-month ban for his contribution to an unpleasant video, *Soccer's Hard Men*, in which he gave a graphic description of foul play in the modern game. Reports of Jones biting a journalist's nose during some horseplay in a bar in Dublin suggested an image more loutish than laddish. Yet the media became increasingly fascinated by a character whose menacing appearance belonged to a baddie straight out of central casting but on closer acquaintance revealed a better and more profound side to his nature.

Invitations to address Etonians or the Oxford Union are not in themselves seals of public approval, but numerous interviews have revealed Jones to be a thoughtful personality as well as a caring husband to a wife with serious health problems. True, he did end up in court after a dispute with a neighbour, but so did Sir Bernard Ingham. Football will miss Vinnie just as the game's critics will miss the numerous excuses he gave them to knock him. Precisely at what point he ceased to be a rough diamond and became a gilt-edged security as a cult figure is hard to say, but it was Jones's good fortune to be around when the game started to boom and a high-profile player with a bad disciplinary record was likely to attract as much interest as the saintly Gary Lineker.

Jones, like Lineker, is a hard act to follow. The increasingly strict interpretation of the law on fouls and misconduct will make it difficult for any hod-carrying wannabe to take up where Vinnie left off. The tackle which takes the man as well as the ball is virtually outlawed and the destroyer will soon be obsolete.

A large part of Jones's value to a team undoubtedly lay in his strong physical presence and an ability to goad opponents and team-mates alike. But his tongue got him into as much trouble with referees as actual fouls and during his career he probably inflicted less pain on fellow professionals than, say, Bobby Collins or Graeme Souness.

As a footballer Jones was not in the class of this Scottish pair but he was not that bad a player either. In addition to his famous long throws he had an alert eye for a quick, perceptive pass and never forgot that the simple ball was often the most effective way to set up an attack.

These qualities persuaded Leeds United, Sheffield United, Chelsea and Wimbledon the second time around to pay a total of £2.6 million for his services; chicken feed compared to today's inflated transfer fees but still a recogniton of what Jones had to offer in terms of strength and commitment.

Would English football have been better or worse without the presence of Vincent Peter Jones? Arguably the career of Tottenham's Gary Stevens might have pursued a healthier course after November 1988, when a tackle by Jones put him out for the rest of that season, after which he made only a handful of appearances for Spurs before ending his playing days at Portsmouth.

Not that Jones was penalised that day, the referee ruling that he had played the ball first. Nevertheless, contact or no contact, a similar lunge today would bring Jones a yellow card or even a red.

He was not one of the game's subtler cloggers. At the beginning of 1993 a foul off the ball on Aston Villa's Garry Parker was described as 'stupid' even by Jones's own manager, Joe Kinnear.

Jones, however, is clearly far from stupid and has proved as much by making the most of his limited natural footballing talent. For a midfield player his biggest handicap was lack of speed and during the course of the average match he often made surprisingly few tackles. With more pace Jones might have been a better player. Then again he might have courted more trouble with more physical contact.

In Italy or Spain, where the most villainous footballers – Romeo Benetti, for example, or Andoni Goicochea – can also play rather well, he would have spent more time with his hod. Never let it be said that English football does not give the bad guy an even break, and in terms of success and failure Jones just about broke even. •

· ·

27 May 1999

Jim White

Drama at the death

How do you begin to describe this football match? How, in the crazy last few seconds, can it be comprehended? How, when every certainty is overturned, every paragraph about German superiority made suddenly redundant, can you quantify the incredible drama that sport alone can throw up?

The bald facts are these: last night Manchester United became the first English side in history to win the treble, beating Bayern Munich 2–1 in Barcelona to win the European Champions' League. But the manner of their victory was such that no one, not their manager, Alex Ferguson, not the thousands of delirious English supporters, not even the scriptwriters of *Roy of the Rovers* would dare to suggest. With the stadium clock showing 90 minutes, United scored not once but twice to wipe out an early goal scored by Bayern Munich and take home the European Cup, the largest piece of silverware in world football.

For most of the match they had been behind after Bayern scored from a free-kick and outclassed United, hitting the woodwork twice. It was not until injury time that substitute Teddy Sheringham scored the equaliser after a scramble following a corner. Another corner led to the winner from Ole Gunnar Solskjaer, with virtually the last kick of the match. Alex Ferguson said: 'We never gave in. It's fantastic. I'm so proud of my players.'

It was an astonishing setting to host the astonishing climax to an astonishing season. Barcelona's Nou Camp, its stand steepling up into the gloaming, oozed the kind of atmosphere that can reduce the most resolute of spines to jelly. And that was before the kick-off.

History was in the air all right: Bayern Munich and Manchester United were both striving to become the first football club from their countries to win the treble of domestic league and cup and the senior European trophy. But to walk through Barcelona before the game was to assume only one team was in it. All day the city had been turned into a suburb of Manchester. Tens of thousands of English fans had descended on the place, many without tickets, just wanting to be there, to marinate in the sun and beer, to be close to history.

Everywhere in the Spanish city Bayern Munich were outnumbered, out-sung, out-enthused by their English counterparts. Except, that is, on the pitch. There it was the German players who made the first claim for history, Mario Basler scoring with a free kick in the fifth minute. Despite the setback, United, being the team they are, never stopped trying: David Beckham's long legs galloped through the midfield, Ryan Giggs jinked and dashed, Andy Cole gave his all.

But German football teams are made of sterner stuff than the sides United

Tom Jenkins

Manchester United beat Bayern Munich in the European Cup Final, Barcelona

are used to playing in England. Bayern's steel-grey shirts seemed to reflect their determination. Until that is Ferguson sent on Teddy Sheringham and Ole Gunnar Solskjaer to provide the climax no one could believe.

So where does this leave United? Ferguson has always believed that a club's standing is measured solely by the accumulation of trophies. By that measure, his team found a unique place in Catalonia. But those who have been privileged to see Ferguson's side this season, who witnessed their European triumphs in Italy, believe they have been watching the greatest English team ever. Perhaps not the greatest individual players, but a group of men enthused with a spirit that lifts them beyond the ordinary, a team infected by their manager with a drive which will never say die.

And there is something else about them too. Back in 1968, when United last won the European Cup, it was the culmination of their manager Matt Busby's dream, it was about exorcising the ghosts of a team that died in the pursuit of the trophy, about completing a task curtailed 10 years previously at Munich airport. They all went home after that triumph sensing it was over, the job done.

But for their successors this victory is just the start. Ferguson has not strived for over a decade to stop here. So for poor Colin Shindler, who had a bestseller telling the world that Manchester United ruined his life, there is more misery to come. For the thousands who loathe United, the future will consist of nothing but standing up and hating Man U.

While he will have loved riding round the Nou Camp on the shoulders of his players, next season it will be back to the old routine for Ferguson. ●

. . . .

6 January 1999
Paul Weaver
Supermacs always have it so good

There are famous phobias. Sigmund Freud was afraid of trains. The composer Robert Schumann was frightened by metal, especially keys, while the problem with the novelist Wilkie Collins was taphophobia – a fear of premature burial. He even carried a letter with him, imploring anyone finding him 'dead' to contact the nearest doctor for a second opinion.

The author Karl Shaw has written a book listing these irrational fears, but his tome would carry more authority if he had included the English batsman's desperate aversion to leg-spin bowling.

Stuart MacGill's 12 wickets in Sydney made him the heaviest wicket taker in the Ashes series, with 27 at 17.7 – and he didn't even play on the bounciest pitch of them all in Perth. So much for all that autumn optimism that Shane Warne's shoulder injury might make the series more open.

We should not be too critical of England's batsmen at Sydney, which was such a 'Bunsen' that even Mark Ramprakash's gentle off-spinners were turning square on day one. England's biggest mistake there was losing the toss – perhaps, like Australians, they should work on their technique by playing two-up, in which two coins are thrown and bets laid as to how they will fall.

But by the time the players reached the magnificent Sydney Cricket Ground, the leg-spin damage had already been done. England's failure to dominate MacGill earlier in the series had helped the tyro develop into an ogre.

Almost as irritating as England's Ashes failure was the infamous Digger Ian Chappell's carping about England's incompetence against the Chinese torture of wrist-spin. His fellow commentator Mark Nicholas countered Chappell's jibes with English phlegm and much common sense. But whatever did he mean when he said, repeatedly: 'We're not very good because we don't come up against them in county cricket.'

Pardon? Pakistan's Mushtaq Ahmed has been playing for Somerset since 1993; Zimbabwe's Paul Strang played for Nottinghamshire last summer and for Kent the season before; India's Anil Kumble almost won Northamptonshire the championship single-wristed in 1995; and there is our very own Ian Salisbury.

Overseas leg-spinners, such as Intikhab Alam and Mushtaq Mohammad, were represented when county cricket was flooded with the world's leading players in 1968. Even before that, in the 1950s, Australian test leggies Bruce Dooland (Notts) and Colin McCool (Somerset) were playing county cricket, as was the left-arm wrist-spinner George Tribe (Northants). We just haven't learned anything.

Recently two former Australian leg-spinners, Terry Jenner and Peter Philpott, have been employed to teach English players all about the dark art, but to no avail. It seems part of the game's lore now, the sepia-toned image of a bewildered Englishman prodding hopelessly at a treacherous tweaker, usually Australian. When Captain Cook sailed to Australia he probably encountered an Aborigine with an implacable wrong 'un.

In the 1920s and 1930s Bill O'Reilly and Clarrie Grimmett tormented English batsmen. And remember old ET lookalike Richie Benaud? On his last tour of England, in 1961, England were heading for victory in Manchester, needing 100 with nine wickets in hand. Then Benaud, despite a sore shoulder, bowled round the wicket into the rough to take six for 70, including Ted Dexter, Peter May, Brian Close and Raman Subba Row, as England slid from 150 for one to 201 all out.

My favourite Aussie leg-spinner is Arthur Mailey. In his first series (against England) in 1920–21 he took 36 wickets. On two England tours he took 146 and 141 wickets including 10 for 66 against Gloucestershire. He found Australian batsmen more difficult, taking four for 362 when Victoria scored 1,107. 'If that chap in the brown derby at the back of the grandstand had held his catches I'd have had them out days ago,' he muttered. 'It was a pity Ellis got out at 1,107. I was just striking a length.' He became a journalist, then a butcher. 'I used to bowl tripe, then I wrote it, now I sell it,' he quipped. ●

Bryan Mosley and colleagues filming outside Buckingham Palace for Coronation Street

Passing through

....

9 June 1999

Ian Aitken
Victor Sassie

Victor Sassie, who has died aged 83, was proprietor of the Gay Hussar restaurant in Soho for 34 years. He was a one-off character – and not surprisingly, considering his origins. He was the son of a Swiss shipwright who came ashore in Cardiff to marry a Welsh girl, then moved to the shipyards of Barrow-in-Furness. That is where Victor was born, making him probably the only Northerner to become virtually an honorary Hungarian on account of his cooking.

He learned about Hungarian cuisine in Budapest and Vienna before the Second World War, most notably at the famous Three Hussars restaurant. After army service, he started up his own establishment, naming it the Gay Hussar in acknowledgement of his old academy. At that time, the word 'gay' had not been hijacked by the homosexual community.

Appropriately, it was a notorious homosexual, the left-wing Labour MP Tom Driberg, who set Victor on course to become the restaurateur of the Bevanite left. He took a fancy to the place, and to its extraordinary proprietor, and gave it a mention in his column in the now defunct Co-op newspaper, *Reynolds News*. Before long the place had become the rendezvous for Labour's left, and many a fiendish (but unsuccessful) anti-Gaitskellite plot was hatched in its upstairs room. Oddly, Nye Bevan himself wasn't a regular; perhaps he didn't like Hungarian food. But virtually all the rest of the Bevanites – Michael Foot, Barbara Castle, Ian Mikardo *et al*. – ate there regularly.

It was also the canteen for *Tribune*, and before long the Fleet Street political and industrial correspondents got wind of the fact that the Gay Hussar was where it was all happening. They, in turn, brought new guests, including top trade unionists and even the odd Tory MP. The Fourteenth Earl of Home was among them.

One man who might easily have become a regular was Robert Maxwell, whom Sassie had met in the army. Maxwell too had started up a business, Pergamon Press, after his demob, and he offered Sassie a deal: he would send his staff to Sassie if he would provide them with cheap lunches. But Maxwell began as he intended to continue and he didn't pay his bills. So Victor banned him, and stuck to it.

He also had the further claim to fame that he ordered a British foreign secretary out for groping a female customer at the next table. True, it was George Brown, which makes it less remarkable than it might seem. Moreover, the tables were – and still are – very close together, but chucking out a foreign secretary, even Brown, is still quite something. He didn't go quietly either.

As the years went by, more and more journalists patronised Victor's cold cherry soup, Bulgar salata, smoked goose and liptauer cheese. The upstairs room, with its big round table, became the venue for other things besides Bevanite plots. The *Daily Mirror* used (and still uses) it for farewell parties and the like. The *Guardian* used it more than once in the 1970s to thrash out its leader line in successive general elections, and perhaps the ambience helped to ensure that we usually ended up recommending our readers to vote Labour, albeit after a bit of havering.

Even the late Lord Rothermere dined (with *Tribune*, actually) in that same room – though not, it must be said, in Victor's time. He had to make do with the likes of Henry Kissinger and Kenneth Clarke, who was surely born for Victor's cookery.

The menu, though appealingly long, never varied. Moreover, the number of items on it was irrelevant because Victor did not allow his clients much choice in what they ate. If you were lucky enough to get your order in before he had spotted you, he would be over moments later to find out what you'd asked for. 'Don't eat that rubbish,' he would snap. 'It's tourist stuff. What you're going to have is the roast goose.' And you did.

But success brought its problems. Thus, when the shop workers' union entertained a Soviet distributive workers' delegation, the *Daily Mail* managed to get hold of the bill. They put it on the front page, and it was very large indeed. Instantly, most of the political diners vanished, judging that the place was no longer secure. Poor Sassie had to build up a new clientele, and he was reduced to getting in a gypsy fiddler. He suffered.

But not for long. The yearning for the Gay Hussar's unique mix of goulash and gossip proved too strong and soon the usual crowd were back, browsing and sluicing as before. But if goulash and gossip were the draw, the greatest of these was gossip. It was a commonplace that if you wanted to spread something round all your friends quickly, the surest way to do it was to tell Victor.

His technique never varied. He would greet you, sit you down, fillet your mind of everything repeatable and then trundle off to regurgitate it at all the other tables. By teatime your tittle-tattle would have reached every Fleet Street newsroom, Transport House and Tory Central Office. And, I strongly suspect, MI5 and the KGB.

When Victor finally retired in 1988, he walked out of the place he had created and never returned. His other interest was horseracing, and he actually owned a racehorse. We assumed he had gone away to indulge his fancy and perhaps he did. But if so, ill-health eventually put a stop to it. To the profound regret of his friends and admirers, we never saw him again.

But his wonderful creation still flourishes in Greek Street. The clientele is much the same, the chef is the same and the menu is the same. The biggest praise one can give it is that it is almost as good as ever. Almost, but not quite. It couldn't be, not without Victor.

He leaves his wife, Elizabeth, and daughter Liz.

Roy Hattersley writes
My first book, a biography of Horatio Nelson, was savagely reviewed in the *Daily Telegraph* and my publisher suggested a consoling lunch at the Gay Hussar. Victor Sassie was out when we telephoned to book a table, and when I later complained that he was absent from his post, he said: 'I was out buying your book.' I told him that I could only assume that he had not read the *Daily Telegraph*.

'That's all I have read,' he replied. 'It seemed a good day for your friends to buy a copy.' I believed then – and I believe now – that he was telling the exact truth.

One of the attractions of the Gay Hussar, in the days when Victor hovered behind the bead curtains, was his habit of joining his favourite customers for lunch and expressing his artless opinions on anything that interested him. He had a fund of stories about old Labour heroes who had eaten at his tables, and he wanted the restaurant to be part of history.

On the day in 1978 when Jim Callaghan decided not to call an election, I took my permanent secretary and political advisers to the private room at the top of the Gay Hussar and told them the news in absolute confidence. As we left, Victor shook his head and whispered in my ear: 'It's a big mistake.' I assumed that my frustrated expression had given me away.

A Hungarian deputy foreign minister told me that when he served in his country's London embassy he discovered that the Gay Hussar's food was as good as anything in Budapest. 'But the proprietor talked so much.'

Victor Sassie talked about everything – particularly the decline of the Labour Party in the 1980s, which he attributed to extremism and the emergence of politicians who did not eat in the Gay Hussar. He made his restaurant famous without being flash because the food was good and the owner was absolutely unique.
Victor Sassie, restaurateur, born 28 August 1915; died 7 June 1999 ●

CORRECTIONS AND CLARIFICATIONS

In our obituary of Victor Sassie, page 22, yesterday, we mistakenly described him as the son of a Swiss father and Welsh mother. In fact, both his parents were Italian, from Colorno, near Parma. The principal restaurant in Budapest, at which he learned about Hungarian cuisine, was Gundel's, after the chef, Karoly Gundel. The first London restaurant in which he was involved was the Budapest in Dean Street. He did not own that, but he was the owner of its successor, the Budapest in Greek Street, which preceded the Gay Hussar.

19 June 1999

Mark Lawson

The god who failed a holy man

In the sentimental days immediately after the death of Diana, Princess of Wales, Cardinal Hume stood out as the one public figure prepared to talk about her as a flawed human being rather than a saint or goddess. His own death has brought no equivalent sense of proportion.

Most newspapers attribute to him the unfashionable quality of holiness and even saintliness. Publications which hounded Glenn Hoddle out of office for his belief in reincarnation seemed humbled and impressed before the equally bold and challenging certainty of this other public figure that he was going from his cancer ward to eternal life.

Although the personal qualities of the cardinal attested to in these columns and elsewhere – kindness, intelligence, a charisma which took the paradoxical form of bashfulness – are not in doubt, the widespread adulation for this man of God is in many ways strange.

In statistical terms, the cardinal's record in office was, frankly, Majoresque. Congregations have almost halved. The church to which he gave his life is in a perilous state, short of clergy to minister even to those diminishing parishes which remain. The obvious solution of married priests and women priests is blocked by the Pope in Rome, although Hume himself would have accepted some liberalisation of the qualifications, just as he favoured greater kindness towards divorced Catholics. Several of the existing clergy have been implicated in sexual scandals which have diminished the church's claim to moral authority. In a profession in which the successor inherits actual chalices, the metaphorical one is poisoned.

In most businesses, this record would have wrecked a reputation. But the cardinal has received the kindest English obituaries of anyone since the princess he refused to call a saint. This was largely the result of a confidence trick, and I do not mean that nastily. Hume inspired confidence in both his own religion and the concept in general.

Whoever first had the idea of moving him from his monastery to Westminster in 1976 is revealed in retrospect as a genius of PR, a Vatican Mandelson. For – like Pope John Paul II, for all the difference in their views – he had the gift, vital in a televisual age, of being able to dramatise his faith facially. Strikingly reminiscent of Paul Scofield as Thomas More, he looked like a holy man was expected to.

And yet – as can be seen from the general decline of the faith he represented so charismatically in public – his holiness was more honoured in admiration than imitation. It is striking that the tributes from both the Prime Minister and the Archbishop of Canterbury mentioned the cardinal's appeal to both non-Catholics and even many non-believers. This was presumably meant as a compliment – suggesting that the cardinal had what is known in the entertainment industry as 'cross-over' appeal – but, on reflection, it reveals the extent of the problem which organised religion has. It indicates that the cardinal was admired as a diligent representative of an exotic but essentially irrelevant profession: much as miners, horse-and-carriage drivers and calligraphers are today.

What Hume had was an 'aura', a key word in the vague New Age spirituality which is the favourite faith in the contemporary West. Just as hundreds of thousands of people find the Dalai Lama personally impressive without believing for one moment that he is a reincarnation, so Cardinal Hume stood as the embodiment of holiness and goodness even for many who had no understanding or acceptance of his claim to eternal life. (There is a lot of this about. Tony Blair and Bill Clinton are politicians for people who don't really believe in politics.)

Despite the conversion of some famous Anglicans who disliked women priests, Hume's brilliance was not evangelism – look at those declining congregations – but what might be called surrogatism. He believed for those who could not. It was a strength, but one which rose from the church's increasing weakness.

Now the institution left behind by this man commonly acclaimed for his holiness faces a very secular problem in replacing him. Hume was appointed cardinal as an unknown who was able to develop his profile over a number of years. His successor will be subject to a level of immediate media scrutiny which is quite new to Catholic ecclesiastical appointments. After those many recent sexual scandals – bishops with women, priests with boys – any candidate with even the smallest secret in their past, an ambiguous friendship, an unwise remark, will suffer journalism's version of crucifixion.

It is not a very appealing job description: a man of absolute personal purity who can radiate a sense of what a secular age regards as holiness but will not be permitted to make any of the changes he might consider necessary in the church unless the present Pope should die and be replaced by a crusading liberal. Whether or not Hume becomes a saint, his patience must certainly have been severely tested.

Basil Hume, clergyman, born March 1923; died 6 June 1999 ●

20 May 1999

Martin Wainwright

Peter Jaconelli

P eter Jaconelli, who has died aged 73, was the outsize ice-cream king of Scarborough who also weighed into local politics to lasting effect. Initially trained as an opera singer – his 21 stones and 50-inch waist would have matched Pavarotti or Placido Domingo – he loyally took over the family business after his father's death and built it into a national wholesale empire.

Unshakeably jovial, Jaconelli was born into a classic Italian ice-cream dynasty founded by a great-great-grandfather, who emigrated to Scotland in 1833. Among the earliest of tingalary men, named after their ice-cream carts with bells to summon trade, he established himself in Glasgow, where the family flourished for a century.

Competition increased, however, and in 1933 Peter's father decided to move to Scarborough in search of the lucrative seaside trade. At the age of seven, Peter helped dispense ice cream, a skill he practised until well after his official retirement.

His outstanding voice persuaded his father to send him for operatic training to the Royal College of Music and later to Naples. But he had learned enough of the ice-cream trade as a teenager to be well prepared when the family businesses needed him.

As chairman, he combined a hands-on approach with canny expansion into restaurants and the national distribution of ice cream and fancy desserts. He particularly enjoyed being a walking advertisement for his products and the joys of eating generally. As Mayor of Scarborough in 1970, he entered the *Guinness Book of Records* (and remains there) for downing 512 oysters in 48 minutes and 42 seconds.

Jaconelli's council career stemmed from the amount of advice he got used to giving while serving dollops of ice cream, and a natural interest – personal as well as commercial – in the town. He was prime mover behind the successful turnaround of Scarborough's small 750-year-old port from semi-dereliction to profit. He also worked with his wife, Anna, to get a drinks ban introduced on the sometimes rowdy seafront streets.

Jaconelli was chairman of North Yorkshire County Council Planning Committee for many years and of the economic development, planning, land and harbour committees of Scarborough district council. He was sometimes accused of being an over-mighty local personality, but avoided pomposity and gave as good as he got.

He retired through ill-health in 1991 but was invariably to be found about the town. The best possible memorial for him would be a Jaconelli play by Scarborough's other most-famous face, Sir Alan Ayckbourn.

Peter Jaconelli, ice-cream magnate and councillor, born 25 November 1925; died 15 May 1999 •

....

22 March 1999

Michael McNay
The colour of genius

Patrick Heron, who has died at the age of 79, was one of the half-dozen important British painters of the twentieth century. Many things contributed to this country's late awakening to the power and importance of modern art after the Second World War, but among them Heron's work as painter, critic and polemicist was a key factor.

When Heron began his professional life, the great modern French masters were relatively unregarded here. His painting and writing were seminal in ending an English tradition of narrative, inward-looking figurative painting. He regarded Matisse as the greatest master of the century and would dearly have loved to elevate Bonnard to second place. These were the two painters from whom he drew most.

It was sometimes remarked that Heron got by on his colour, that he was no draughtsman. This was untrue. His drawing was as incisively accurate as that of Ben Nicholson, the friend from whom he inherited the studio overlooking Porthmeor beach at St Ives. But his portraits of the late 1940s and early 1950s, such as the one of Herbert Read, were not successful, and the big compositions, like *Christmas Eve* and *Harbour Window with Two Figures*, were only doubtfully so, though it is unlikely that Heron himself, a great protagonist for his own achievements as well as those of the other painters he admired (Matthew Smith, William Scott, Peter Lanyon and Roger Hilton foremost amongst the British) ever thought so.

These linear paintings were attempts to combine the rigour of Braque's shallow space with Bonnard's tapestry-like 'all-overness', to use Heron's inelegant but accurate phrase. But the over-complicated line on the flattened picture plane worked against them, reducing them to an illustrative mode of Cubism. Still, the 1998 Tate retrospective of his work ('20 years too late,' Heron remarked), arranged so that the last gallery with the late paintings adjoined the first gallery with pre-war and early post-war work, showed that the elements on which his career would be founded were already in place.

When the mesh of lines dropped away, he was free to concentrate on his abiding commitment, the non-figurative exploration of colour and the effect on the retina of the juxtaposition of pure colours (he insisted on the term 'non-figurative': all art, he would say, was abstract).

Patrick Heron was born in Headingley, the son of Tom Heron, an entrepreneur who moved to Cornwall when Patrick was five to set up a garment factory in three converted fishermen's cottages overlooking Newlyn harbour. This was to blossom into Cresta Silks at Welwyn Garden City, with McKnight Kauffer designing the stationery and packaging and Wells Coates the exemplary modernist shops. Patrick, still a schoolboy, made some remarkably successful designs for the fabrics. If not a prodigy, he certainly had a high talent that dated back to the age of three, as an extant drawing of *Coniston Old Man* testifies. Before the war, he had a year at the Slade School of Art, but never felt it gave him very much.

Tom Heron was a pacifist; Patrick likewise. His chronic asthma would have excluded him from military service, but he insisted on registering as a conscientious objector and worked as an agricultural labourer for three years until doctors ordered him to desist. He returned to Cornwall and worked for Bernard Leach for the final 14 months of the war. One of his friends was the *Guardian* journalist Mark Arnold-Forster, who, a few years later, sold him Eagle's Nest, a house with a famous garden high above the Atlantic at Zennor, near St Ives, where Heron had spent childhood holidays.

Heron's move to Eagle's Nest coincided with his move into non-figurative painting, and among his first works of the period were the garden paintings, opalescent meshes of colour streaked and dribbled vertically on to the canvases.

Painting, as he found it in the late 1940s, was sunk in insularity. The Tate Gallery's modern collection, from Impressionism to Fauvism and Cubism, was thin and inferior. It was during this time that Heron was also an art critic for *Arts* magazine of New York, for the *New English Weekly* and then the *New Statesman*. He deplored the criticism of John Berger, not because it was Marxist but because it was prescriptive, and he coined the phrase 'Art is Autonomous' for an article he wrote in rebuttal of Berger's arguments.

He stuck to this phrase throughout his life, meaning not that art is uninfluenced by society, but that it cannot be used as a tool within society, that once an artist begins to play to the gallery his work descends to propaganda or pot-boiling. His best criticism was collected in *The Changing Forms of Art*, long out of print when the Tate published another collection, *Painter As Critic*, to make available again some of the most perceptive and trenchant English criticisms of twentieth-century modernism.

Heron saved his own propaganda for his later writing, sometimes in ferocious defences of the landscape of the Penwith peninsula against would-be developers or the Ministry of Defence. His most notable piece was the almost 14,000-word article spread over three days in the *Guardian* in 1974 in which he attacked the marketing of the New York school of painters by galleries and critics, principally the critic Clement Greenberg, who at this stage was actually dictating to painters and sculptors their disposition of forms and colours.

Partly because he had been the first champion in England of the Abstract Expressionists, Heron's word now carried great weight and checked a tendency even, or especially, in English art circles to discount the achievement of the St Ives group of painters. But it also confused the issue. In spelling out in dates and paintings how he personally had by several years got in ahead of, say, Morris Louis, with his vertical stripe paintings, Heron seemed to suggest that St Ives and New York were doing the same kind of thing. Certainly there were cross-influences between the two, and the Americans looked at the work of the St Ives group as well as vice versa, but the roots of the Americans lay in European Symbolism and Expressionism, whereas the St Ives group were closer to the English landscape tradition, or, in Heron's case, to the school of Paris.

For a colourist of Heron's generation, the great challenge and exemplar was the Matisse of the *papiers decoupés*, the abstracts cut and pasted out of sheets of gouache-soaked paper, like the wonderful *L'Escargot* that Heron saw many times during his visits as a trustee of the Tate. Heron himself made hundreds of small gouaches, deploying a range of colours brushed on with tiny Chinese watercolour brushes – even on the 15ft canvases – originally in adjacent colour areas pushing up to a fuzzy separating edge, though later the edge became a clean break (Heron called himself at this period a 'wobbly, hard-edge painter').

The aim, as it had been since Gauguin, Cézanne and, of course, Heron's beloved Bonnard, was to make all areas of the painting of equal importance; there was to be no such thing as an image laid on a ground – the sum of several images made up the totality of the main image, the finished painting. The variations seemed infinite, but then in 1979 Heron's wife, Delia, his childhood sweetheart, died quite unexpectedly. For a time he did not paint at all; then he began afresh a series of paintings which retained the images of his later work but returned to the misty effect of the garden paintings of the early 1950s. Delia had been mainly responsible for restoring and giving new life to the Eagle's Nest garden. Maybe this new approach to painting was the only way left for Patrick to commune with her.

A few years ago, Heron asked me my age. Fifty-six, I told him. 'Lucky bugger,' he said. He himself had turned 70, but he still had productive years ahead, including the late garden paintings carried right through until his Tate retrospective, the window at the St Ives Tate, and Big Painting Sculpture, the project at Stag Place, Victoria, carried through with the help of his son-in-law Julian Feary.

Heron accepted a CBE but rejected a knighthood, for what Downing Street apparently took to be the utterly frivolous reason that it would make him look silly to other serious artists. There has been talk in the family of turning Eagle's Nest into a permanent gallery for Heron's art, something about which he was untypically diffident. But a Heron museum above the Atlantic would certainly be a beacon shining from a great period of British painting.

Patrick Heron is survived by his daughters, Katerine, an architect, and Susanna, also an artist.

Ravishing beauty born out of chaos: Adrian Searle remembers Patrick Heron
Patrick Heron, dressed in clashing shades of acrylic knitwear, a lurid purple scarf slung rakishly about his neck, stood on a chair in my art school studio and berated me about colour. I never asked why he stood on the chair. His voice was a bit wheezy, reedy and almost camp. 'As I wrote in 1954,' he said, 'colour is the only direction for painting.'

This was 1973, the chair was his soapbox and I, a cowering student, was his only audience. He reminded me then of a psychedelic Lord Soper. Heron really believed in colour, he was evangelical about colour, he was a walking advertisement for colour and painting.

He was, I thought then, a bit bonkers. He believed, for instance, that cars were nowadays brightly coloured on account of paintings like his, which had attuned the public consciousness to the pleasures of colour, and that the influence of painters like Bonnard and Matisse had dragged British culture out of its grey and umber post-war dinge.

Walking with him around his Tate Gallery retrospective last year, he gave me a running commentary on his recent work, punctuated with hilarious impersonations (he was a great mimic) and gossip. But he was most at home amongst the painted stripes, the fuzzy singing lozenges and blobs and his huge 'wobbly, hard-edge' canvases.

His last paintings were full-on, risky, filled with bright squiggles, painterly flurries and cartoon doodles. They should have been chaotic and absurd, but they were instead open and vital, eye-rocking and beautiful. Heron's retrospective was ravishing, and had the vitality of a much younger artist.

As a painter, Heron got younger as he got older, and couldn't care less for distinctions between abstraction and figuration. The paintings were, instead, filled with life. He briefly returned to portraiture in 1997, with a portrait of A. S. Byatt, now in the National Portrait Gallery. It looked as if it took just a moment to paint. His last paintings were, I think, very much about capturing the vitality of the moment, and were a celebration of it. He was a passionate and civilising influence on the culture of the past 50 years.

Patrick Heron, artist, born 30 January 1920; died 20 March 1999 ●

8 *March* 1999

Derek Malcolm

The genius who outdid Hollywood

Stanley Kubrick was one of the greatest of post-war film-makers and one of the most controversial. He was also one of the most reclusive, living in a mansion in Hertfordshire and never leaving it except to make films.

For at least half of his career he fought and beat Hollywood, getting its money to make his expensive films but only on condition that no one interfered with him or them in any way. His power thus became greater than any of his contemporaries and most of the great film-makers of the past.

His latest film is a case in point. In his contract for *Eyes Wide Shut*, which has cost $60 million, he had the option that it would never be released if he did not like it.

He had spent the last two years making the film with Tom Cruise and Nicole Kidman. It is said to be still incomplete, though there has been almost total secrecy surrounding its subject matter and its making.

The secrecy was part and parcel of the almost magical appeal of Kubrick, who lived in a house full of information about the world, with a mass of cable channels and access to all types of media, and then stepped outside to film his often bilious comments upon it.

It is likely that *Eyes Wide Shut* will be one of the most controversial he has ever made, with copious sex scenes, including an orgy sequence in a private West End club. It is said to be about two psychiatrists with some of the sexual problems of those they treat.

Kubrick, of course, was no stranger to controversy, having made *A Clockwork Orange* in Britain in 1971. That film, based on an Anthony Burgess novel about the endemic violence running underneath so-called civilised society, was passed by the censor but hooked out of release by Kubrick himself because he thought the British, and particularly the British press, had mistaken its pessimistic message and proclaimed it as glamorising violence.

There is no doubt that Kubrick had a misanthropic vision of the world and many of his films prised out the worm in the bud. But he had more to say than that the world was askew.

Many of his films are already on the lists of cinema classics, not just because they are brilliantly made but because they had something pertinent to say. *Paths of Glory* was one of the finest ever made about the waste and essential hypocrisy of war. *Dr Strangelove* was an unbeatable satire about the absurdities of the Cold War, and *2001: A Space Odyssey* was an ultimately hopeful epic about the way technology might in the end be defeated by human rather than mechanical values.

Kubrick vowed that he would never make films without total control after the experience of taking over *Spartacus* from Anthony Mann and dealing with the demands of Kirk Douglas, star and executive producer.

His next film after that was an adaptation of Nabokov's *Lolita*, which he made into something of a tragi-comedy largely because there was no way, in the early 1960s, that he could get its openly sexual subject matter on to the screen.

Kubrick was one of the very few serious film-makers who could still manufacture a hit with the public all over the world – witness *The Shining*, which gave Jack Nicholson one of his most famous parts. His films could thus be considered art movies and commercial prospects at the same time.

His detractors have complained that his search for perfection led him into artistic culs-de-sac of his own making, that he was an essentially cold film-maker, brilliant but unable to stir the emotions.

There is some point to that. How can anyone see the world clearly from a St Albans mansion? Yet he knew the business of film-making from the ground up, and could argue with technicians, actors and even the suits of Hollywood on their own terms. He was, in fact, unique, and, though it's a cliché to say so, we will almost certainly never see his like again.

Stanley Kubrick, film-maker, born 26 July 1928; died 7 March 1999 ●

. . . .

11 February 1999
Nancy Banks-Smith
Bryan Mosley

Bryan Mosley's death is a stern reminder that pipsqueak producers must not, sometimes just for the hell and headlines of it, kill off characters who have appeared in a soap since it began. Soap opera stars are not like other actors. They are famous but hardly known by their own names at all. They are absorbed by soapy osmosis into the character they play and, the better they play it, the less they have any other identity. After a while, the character is their life support system and they cannot breathe without it.

Bryan Mosley first played Alf, the corner-shop keeper in *Coronation Street*, in 1961. He was a living tribute to something of value which still survived, and now can hardly be found at all. He was, for instance, the last man alive to be called Alf. The last to wear a trilby. Indeed, if you saw a hat at all in the Rovers, you knew Alf was under it. He belonged to a time when advertisements, not commercials, said If You Want to Get Ahead Get a Hat and Let Burton Dress

You. The same Monty Burton who now means no clothes at all. The starched white overall he wore like a uniform was the pure sign of a blameless life. Alf had such faith in his produce that once, when coarse aspersions were cast on his Christmas pudding, he ate a whole pudding to prove its wholesomeness. It put him in hospital, of course.

Corner shops were so important that *Coronation Street* began with the first customer. It was Ena Sharples. Having efficiently extracted every drop of relevant information about the new owner, she ordered: 'Half a dozen fancies and *no eclairs*.' Why no eclairs still puzzles me, unless she thought there was a whiff of impropriety about them.

Alf so loved little shops that he regularly married or tried to marry women who owned them. The three wise monkeys who, leaning on the Rovers bar, spoke his obituary remembered that.

Fred: 'That's how he came by the corner shop, you know. Oh yes. Belonged to his second lady wife. What were her name, Renee.'

Vera: 'I'll tell you summat now. He proposed to the woman that had the shop before Renee.'

Jack: 'Sounds to me like he wanted to marry the shop.'

Fred: 'Oh aye, he did love that shop.'

A shop was an aphrodisiac to Alf. He had the same name, Alderman Alf Roberts, as Mrs Thatcher's father, who was also a grocer and taught her all he knew about self reliance, thrift, industry, pig-headedness and believing passionately in your own Christmas pudding. *Coronation Street*'s corner shop has now appropriately passed into the hands of Ravi Desai, an Asian who owns a chain of small shops. But something solid and dependable has gone with Alf. It seems wholly proper that the sophisticated computer system is down again, and I am writing this on an old typewriter. Which works.

Bryan Mosley, actor, born 25 August 1931; died 9 February 1999 ●

. . . .

9 February 1999

John Ezard and Amelia Gentleman
A shining light even in the darkest years

The death of Iris Murdoch yesterday closed an old age clouded by Alzheimer's disease, a sadness her readers and admirers had shared in close, unprecedented detail through the account published by her husband, John Bayley.

His book *Iris: A Memoir*, published last year, broke new ground by blending a vivid and tender recollection of their first meeting, courtship and 43 years of marriage with an unflinching portrait of the effect of the condition on her mind and memory and daily behaviour.

He wrote:

Alzheimer's sufferers are not always gentle: I know that. But Iris remains her old self in many ways. The power of concentration has gone, along with the ability to form coherent sentences, and to remember where she is, or has been. She does not know that she has written 27 remarkable novels, as well as her books on philosophy; received honorary doctorates from the major universities; became a Dame of the British Empire.

If an admirer or friend asks her to sign a copy of one of her novels, she looks at it with pleasure and surprise before laboriously writing her name and, if she can, theirs. 'For Georgina Smith. For dear Reggie . . .' It takes her some time, but the letters are still formed with care, and resemble, in a surreal way, her old handwriting. She is always anxious to oblige. And the old gentleness remains.

For some years, the illness had ended but not dimmed admiration for the prolific output of a woman who was widely seen as perhaps the most luminous, intelligent and inventive novelist to emerge during the post-war years. Her last book, a study in religion and philsophy, *Existentialists and Mystics*, was not published until 1997.

When her first novels, *Under the Net*, *Flight from the Enchanter* and *The Sandcastle*, burst into print from her untypical background as an Oxford philosophy lecturer in the mid-1950s, she was seen as a writer who might become a major modern classic, a new George Eliot with touches of the passionate imagination of a Brontë.

This wild hope receded as the years passed. But she was always in the front rank of unpredictable, original, serious writers exploring the deeper themes of ancient as well as contemporary experience.

Last night her fellow novelist Malcolm Bradbury paid tribute: 'If one was to compile a list of the best five English writers since the war, she would be up there. She was the most charming and delightful and rather magical person. She managed to convey this in her own life and in what she wrote. Something of the impish magic which was her character sprang off the pages of what she wrote.'

A. N. Wilson, who is writing a book about her, said he was very distressed at the news: 'The novels were successful because they spoke to a generation of people which was trying to rediscover its moral sense after the war, and were about a generation trying to come to terms with a new morality. The novels are all about people who are making up their lives as they go along and finding that it doesn't work; they describe lives of emotional and intellectual chaos. She wrote about six very good novels which will still be being read in 50 years' time. Almost more remarkable was her determination in a very arid period of British philosophy to go back and rediscover Plato, which was a very strange and original thing to do. The books contain wonderful things about the nature of good, which were echoed in her own life. She was the most serene, generous person, who was kind and good to literally hundreds of people – generous both emotionally and financially. She hardly kept any of the money; she gave most of it away. I think her emotional strength came from her extraordinary marriage to John Bayley. I have never known a married couple with such a truly strong relationship, both as lovers and as friends in a genuine and not cloying way. I last saw her six or seven weeks ago. She was in a dreadful trance-like state. But over the last few years of her illness, although she was occasionally anxious, she kept the sweetness of her nature. She kept smiling.'

The don and critic Dr John Casey said: 'She was the nearest we have in England to Sartre. It is extremely rare for philosophers in the analytical tradition to bring their philosophy into literature. She was a true intellectual. She was remarkable in that she was able to draw the metaphysical into the rest of life. She was a full-time philosopher, thinker, sage, and had a childlike capacity to focus on anything with an extraordinary intensity.'

The critic Frank Kermode called her a 'very serious and brilliant person but not in a heavy way'. He added: 'She was extraordinary as both a novelist and a philosopher. I think her work will endure. She inspired a certain kind of awe; although it was fun to be with her, there was no sense in which triviality was permitted. She had a kind of earnestness that was very charming but you felt how very much more intellectual she was than you. She wasn't just a nice person, you felt she was a good person too.'

Al Alvarez, the poet and critic, who knew her as an Oxford contemporary, said: 'I knew her at Oxford. She was some years senior to me but she was the bright young philosophy lecturer. She lectured on French existentialism and was a marvellous breath of fresh air. I never knew her very well, but I always thought she was terrific and I loved her early novels. She had a real talent. I remember reading her first, *Under the Net*, and thinking it had a real wit and energy to it, which seemed to fit because she was such a lively lady. She was a marvellously clever woman, so her illness seemed doubly terrible.'

Iris Murdoch, writer, born 15 July 1919; died 8 February 1999●

18 January 1999

John Rodda

Blood on the tracks

His body, almost as white as his England singlet, tottering helplessly towards a finishing line he did not reach, is the way the world remembers Jim Peters, who has died at the age of 80. The newsreel pictures of his anguish as he failed by about 200 yards to win the marathon gold medal at the British Empire and Commonwealth Games of 1954 in Vancouver are an indelible memory of a sportsman driving himself to the brink of death.

The day was very hot, 75 degrees at times, and sports science and the sport had not come to terms with combating dehydration. Peters entered the stadium an absurd 17 minutes ahead of the second runner, so the tolerance of his will – rather than thought of his safety – was probably greater than had there been another runner in contention. He staggered from one side of the track to the other, falling half a dozen times in an attempt to complete the final quarter-mile. At the point of another fall, the agony ended when an official grasped him and the battle to save his life began. Peters never raced again, and for the rest of his days was reminded of the experience by bouts of giddiness and headaches.

Like another marathon hero who did not reach the finishing line, Dorando Pietri of Italy in the 1908 Olympic race at the White City, London, Peters was honoured by royalty. He received a gold medal from the Duke of Edinburgh, who was one of the spectators in Vancouver; Edinburgh did not forget the incident, and on his eightieth birthday Peters received a letter of good wishes from him. Yet famous newsreel footage was scant recognition for a man who pushed back a barrier of athletic achievement by moving the event on from one for plodding ex-track runners to racing.

In the space of two years Peters broke the world-best mark three times, lowering it from 2 hours 25 minutes 39 seconds to 2 hours 17 minutes 39.4 seconds, a degree of improvement never since matched. He did so by taking his track-running training regime and increasing the volume, while maintaining the quality to race over the 26-mile course.

Peters was born in Homerton, east London, in the closing days of the First World War. Like many of his age, he was deprived of his best athletic years by the Second World War, when service in the Royal Army Medical Corps led to him qualifying as an optician. However, he brought his club, Essex Beagles, honours by winning the AAA three-miles title in 1946, at the age of 27, and the 10-miles title two years later.

In 1948 he ran the 10,000 metres in the London Olympic Games, finishing ninth, and was depressed that he had been lapped. For a man who accepted the harsh discipline of athletic training, and with such a will to win, this was a humiliation, and for a while he considered retiring. His coach, Johnny Johnston, persuaded him to consider the marathon, and Peters went back into training – this time to work every day, something that few athletes attempted, and certainly not long-distance runners.

It was this workload which brought the phenomenal breakthrough. Peters ran in a few road races and produced times to arouse attention: in his first marathon, from Windsor to Chiswick, he broke the British record with a time of 2 hours 29 minutes 54 seconds. The following spring he showed that he was getting out of reach of the opposition, but few could have expected the sensation in his second Windsor to Chiswick race, where he recorded 2 hours 20 minutes 42 seconds. There was enough cynicism to call for a recount, but the course measured 260 yards more than the marathon distance.

In the Olympic race in Helsinki that year he set off at his usual blistering pace. Leading by 100 yards at 10 miles, one of his opponents sidled up alongside and said: 'Is this the pace to run?', to which Peters nodded. When Peters slowed because of cramp, his opponent forged ahead to win. It was Emil Zatopek in his first marathon.

In 1953 Peters won all four marathons in which he ran, breaking the world record in the Chiswick event, and did so the following year, to make himself firm favourite for the Commonwealth and European titles, which he was not to win.

He was justified in feeling deprived of a prize. A few days earlier he had driven over the course with his coach and the British team manager, and the mileometer registered 27 miles – an error of measurement which would not occur today. Peters is survived by his wife, Frieda, a daughter and son.

James Peters, athlete, born 24 October 1918; died 9 January 1999 ●

....

8 January 1999
Tim Hilton
Life on a broad canvas

Henrietta Moraes, who has died at the age of 67, was one of those people whose life was divided into two periods: the first devoted to drink or drugs (both, in her case), while the second half was clean and sober. Her autobiography *Henrietta*, published in 1994, surveyed her dissipated past and ends with the brave, contrite sentence: 'My grandchildren and my dog have never seen me drunk, and I trust and pray that they never will.'

This dog, Max, who survives her, is a long-haired dachshund of equable temperament who accompanied his volatile mistress in the routines of her later life. Henrietta, infirm and poor, lived in one room in Chelsea. Rising later than many of her neighbours, she and Max would set off for the King's Road in search of the *Daily Mail* (the only paper she liked) and three packets of Camels. Charity shops were monitored for her gorgeous, dowdy clothes, which she sometimes stole, on the grounds that she herself deserved charity. In various chemist's shops, pills were bought, not of the dangerous variety. She simply liked taking pills. In her last illness there was a horrible professionalism in the way she shook open the various packets of painkillers and swallowed them down.

She was born Audrey Wendy Abbott in Simla in 1931. Her father, who was in the Indian Air Force, deserted her mother. Little Audrey was brought up in England by a horrific grandmother who disciplined her with a leather strap. There was an education, of sorts, then a spell at a secretarial college. She thought of becoming an actress, but by 1950 was working as a model in various London art schools.

In this year she met her first husband, the film-maker Michael Law, who gave her the name Henrietta. They set up home in an attic in Dean Street. Now began her career as the queen of Soho's artistic life. Her haunts, besides many others, were the Carlisle (nowadays the Nelly Dean), the Café Torino, the French Pub (which also functioned as her bank), the Gay Hussar and the Gargoyle Club. At the Gargoyle, where she was always the youngest person present, she mixed with such notables as Cyril Connolly, Brian Howard, her best friend Francis Wyndham, Philip Toynbee and Donald Maclean; but was more at home in the company of artists, who included Michael Wishart, 'Johnny Minton and 20 sailors', Francis Bacon and Lucian Freud. She drank all day and her love life was uninhibited.

Henrietta was close to Minton, who financed her in many ways and introduced her to his friend the body-builder Norman Bowler, whom she shortly married. Bowler was the father of Henrietta's children, Joshua and Caroline, who survive her. During their childhood she was intermittently employed running a coffee bar in David Archer's bookshop in Greek Street. It was through Archer, always interested in young writers, that she met the elfin Indian poet Dom Moraes. This was in 1956, when her marriage to Bowler ended. Moraes was 18, and on his way to Oxford.

In 1957, the rich, generous, alcoholic Minton bequeathed Henrietta a house in Chelsea, just off Cheyne Walk. Here she seduced Moraes, to give him a good start to his undergraduate career, and began the short, best years of her life. She was often in Oxford and (Ved Mehta's autobiographical *Up at Oxford* tells us) was an alarming visitor to the university. The bohemia of Soho and Chelsea was her true home, and perhaps she was the muse of that society. Certainly she is commemorated in many paintings, particularly in canvases by Francis Bacon.

Henrietta sat for Lucian Freud in the early 1950s. He painted slowly; there may not be more than three of her portraits from his brush. Bacon worked quickly. Henrietta thought that he painted her 18 times. When she told me this, she could not remember clearly, and in any case the situation is confused.

For Bacon's portraits were derived from pornographic photographs of Henrietta taken by their mutual friend John Deakin. Though he used these photos, Bacon also needed Henrietta's naked presence in the studio, for reasons apparent to anyone who ever met her. Some models inspire painters by their looks, others by their personality. Henrietta was foul-mouthed, amoral, a thief, a violent drunkard and a drug addict. Yet she was witty, wonderfully warm and lovable. Her presence in any room immediately told you that life is more thrilling than we dull folk imagine. She had a good heart. Never was a woman less demure, but other women liked Henrietta and often got her out of scrapes. And her aura of danger must have helped the mood of Bacon's paintings.

Henrietta married Dom Moraes in 1961, and lived with him, on and off, until he left the Chelsea house one day to buy cigarettes and never returned. In the early 1960s she began to take drugs, as though the immense intake of booze was not enough to satisfy the cravings of her addictive personality. Normally forthcoming, she was quiet about the origin of her drug habit. From odd remarks I gathered that it began after the Eichmann trial in Jerusalem in 1961. The *Times of India* had sent her new husband there to report. Every day she sat with him in the courtroom. A more devastating honeymoon can scarcely be imagined. Henrietta, not by nature a political person, was a great hater of prejudice and of people in power. In the next years she moved from the art world to the hippie scene. Every drug, except heroin, was eagerly consumed. The Chelsea house was lost. There were long expeditions in gypsy caravans to New Age shrines in the Celtic West Country. In the late 1960s Henrietta and some companions took four years to travel from London to Wales. She enjoyed life in Ireland, where there were young, upper-class addicts in ramshackle mansions. For a time – she could not remember how long – Henrietta was a general assistant to Marianne Faithfull. Many other things about these times were forgotten.

Back in London, her head buzzing with amphetamines and Carlsberg Special Brew, she had an unsuccessful career as a cat burglar. After her release from Holloway Prison she settled down somewhat. She became sober, with only one or two backslidings, when doctors found cirrhosis of the liver. Alas, she did not write enough in recent times. Short stories remain unpublished. A further volume of memoirs was to be called *Encore Henrietta*. Another putative title was *Fuck Off, Darling*, her famous catch-phrase from the old Soho days. She spent last Christmas Day with her agent and helper, Alexandra Pringle. She was as exciting and as beautiful as ever, also very kind to all the children. Max is safe with Maggi Hambling.

Henrietta Moraes (Audrey Wendy Abbott), bohemian, born 1931; died 6 January 1999 ●

6 May 1999

Frank Keating

Sir Alf departs a land unfit for heroes

ootball is too manic these days to spare time for reflection, remembrance or humanity, even in death. It knows the price of its past, of course – 'Wanna buy a "traditional" replica strip?' – but it knows nothing of the value of its goodness or grandeur.

No wonder Lady Ramsey has in effect told the Football Association, and London in general, to go jump in the Thames. She is organising her beloved Sir Alf's memorial service herself, thank you, and it is going to be on Saturday week at St Mary-le-Tower in their home town of Ipswich.

Football badly uses its heroes when it has done with them. Remember how Bill Shankly 'died of a broken heart' when his Liverpool turned its back on him after retirement? Remember how Ramsey's own princely lieutenant, Bobby Moore, was left to languish? Prophet Ramsey had earlier been allowed to slink away without honour. Not once did the FA seek to use his expertise or unique experience. In his 12 years' stewardship of the England team, in spite of its unparalleled successes, the FA never paid him a salary of more than £10,000.

When the World Cup was won, he shared one twenty-second of the bonus of £22,000 the FA had put up for the squad. When it unceremoniously booted Ramsey out in 1974, it could not even manage a year's salary pay-off – just 10 months' and £8,000.

He asked the FA if it could strike him a replica World Cup winner's medal – easily done – but it held up its hands in horror and refused. It never asked him to seminars, functions or even matches. In 1996, even as his ill-health began to take hold, he could have managed a trip to watch England at Euro '96. Nobody invited him.

Sir Alf's private funeral is in Ipswich tomorrow, but Saturday week will be his show and this time football will have to come to him. The FA had no involvement with the memorial service, a Lancaster Gate spokesman was quoted yesterday, 'other than sending a strong contingent'.

The vicar, Rev. Peter Townley, said Lady Vickie had requested 'a celebration of Alf's life; it is not simply for the people of Ipswich but for whoever wants to come'. There is no league football that day and they might well be flooding into the old town from points further off than Lancaster Gate.

It was just as one of his successors as England manager, Glenn Hoddle, was settling into his notorious 1998 World Cup diary with his FA ghost David Davies that football was alerted – by an earlier Ipswich and England manager,

Bobby Robson — to the sharp decline in Sir Alf's poor health after a stroke.

For three months, with both prostate cancer and Alzheimer's disease taking their grip, Sir Alf lay in the general ward of Ipswich Hospital. Robson said their mutual former secretary at Portman Road, Pat Godbold, had been distressed at visiting her former boss and finding him 'wandering around not knowing where he was and suffering on a public ward with staff too overworked to properly look after him'.

Robson offered to pay for Sir Alf's private treatment but Lady Ramsey sharply retorted that she was perfectly satisfied with her husband's treatment and the outstanding care he was receiving.

Lady Vickie was with him when he died last Wednesday. She registered his death in Ipswich on Friday, entering his occupation simply as 'Knight of the Realm, England football manager (retired)'.

It says it all in a way: the Dagenham boy who became a son of Ipswich and then all England too. All things considered, St Mary-le-Tower is far more fitting than Westminster and London. Though partially rebuilt in the nineteenth century from the foundation that young butcher's son Cardinal Wolsey knew, St Mary's has close connections with other great men of England's culture: the artists Thomas Gainsborough and John Constable, for instance, not to mention Mr Pickwick at the nearby Great White Horse. It is rich in timeless brasses and memorial busts.

Wolsey was hurrying from York to be buried there. He did not quite make it, of course, but Shakespeare's epitaph to the Ipswich cardinal sits perfectly too on Ipswich's football knight. The FA might care to note it on its wreath: 'Lofty and sour to them that loved him not; but to those men that sought him, sweet as summer . . . So may he rest; his faults lie gently on him.'

Alf Ramsay, football manager, born 1920; died 28 April 1999 ●